More 20th century conductors

Jochum : Fricsay
Schuricht : Weingartner : Krips
Klemperer : Kleiber

Discographies compiled by
John Hunt

1993

More 20th Century Conductors
Published by John Hunt.
Designed by Richard Chluparty
© 1993 John Hunt
reprinted 2009
ISBN 978-0-951026-87-8

Sole distributors:
Travis & Emery,
17 Cecil Court,
London, WC2N 4EZ,
United Kingdom.
(+44) 20 7 459 2129.
sales@travis-and-emery.com

Acknowledgement

This publication has been made possible by generous support from the following:

Richard Ames, New Barnet
Yoshihiro Asada, Osaka
Mike Ashman, London
Andrew Barker, Rochester
Wes Burgar, Warren Michigan
David Carroll, London
Edward Chibas, Caracas
David Crighton, Cambridge
John Derry, Newcastle-upon-Tyne
Erik Dervos, London
Robert Donaldson, Edinburgh
Christopher Dowling, London
Henry Fogel, Chicago
Johann Gratz, Vienna
Tadashi Hasegawa, Nagoya
Hiromichi Hatta, Nagoya
John Hughes, Brisbane
Eugene Kaskey, New York
Hisao Kimura, Falls Church Virginia
Bengt Klovorg, Hörsholm
Sylvia Loeb, London
Ernst Lumpe, Soest
Norman MacDougall, St Andrews
Bruce Morrison, Gillingham
Gregory Page-Turner, Bridport
Tully Potter, Billericay
Gordon Reeves, Birmingham
Patrick Russell, Calstock
Robin Scott, Bradford
David Selwyn, Lampeter
Clare Shepherd, Beckenham
Roger Smithson, London
Göran Söderwall, Stockholm
Kazuhiko Soma, Kawasaki
Neville Sumpter, Northolt
Carl Suneson, Stockholm
Yoshihiko Suzuki, Tokyo
Malcolm Walker, Harrow
Urs Weber, St Gallen
Björn Westberg, Saltsjö-Boo

Contents

3   Acknowledgement

5   Introduction

9   Eugen Jochum

55   Ferenc Fricsay

97   Carl Schuricht

125   Felix Weingartner

153   Josef Krips

193   Otto Klemperer

265   Erich Kleiber

300   Credits

Published 1993 by John Hunt

Designed by Richard Chlupaty, London

Copyright 1993   John Hunt

Introduction

This further group of discographies includes some of the great names from the heyday of the conductor as charismatic interpreter. They were men who gained a reputation for their control of the orchestra, and who also realised the value of committing their interpretations to the new medium of the gramophone record. Their careers commenced in the shellac era and, with the exception of Weingartner, carried on into the blossoming of the LP in the 1950s and beyond.

Some of these recording careers were far from systematic, a fact which, at least in the cases of Weingartner and Kleiber, was dictated by the still comparatively primitive state of recording in the first decades of the 20th century. Weingartner's most illustrious disciple, Krips, also left behind fewer recordings than one would have liked from a man whose concert and opera appearances were so well integrated - I undertand that at least part of the cause was the conductor's difficult behaviour when in the recording studio.

In the instances of Jochum and Fricsay, their involvement in the post-war period with Germany's newly-established radio orchestras in Munich and Berlin respectively brought them much recording work with those ensembles. A surprisingly extensive discography was chalked up by Fricsay in the short period before his tragic death at the comparatively early age of 50. I firmly contend that with this, and with the even more appalling passing of Cantelli in 1956, Karajan lost his two most serious rivals.

When Schuricht came to give concerts with the London Symphony Orchestra at the very end of his long career, I for one knew very little about his recorded work but was sufficiently spurred on by those performances to investigate a varied discography stretching back to the early 1930s. That was a time when Polydor, eager to add competitive versions of the standard repertoire to its burgeoning catalogue, frequently entrusted such work to Schuricht. As far as English collectors were concerned, Klemperer was of course much more of a known quantity through his involvement with Columbia during the years of the glorious mono LP and into the stereo age.

Eminent conductors are not always noted for the generosity in assessing the powers of their colleagues, but it is interesting to hear what Wilhelm Furtwängler said about two of the maestri featured in this volume. Of Weingartner he wrote: "Weingartner was, in the days of our youth, above all the conductor of Beethoven symphonies. What he did to maintain the dignity and purity of the classical style will, in the history of conducting, never be forgotten". And his comment "It cannot be performed better than that !" was made after he had attended a performance of the Beethoven Fifth conducted by Schuricht !

Is there a common characteristic, either of style or influence, uniting these conductors ? They were certainly all heavily involved with the standard German and Austrian classics, and are justifiably associated with that repertory. Yet it is interesting to note how frequently Klemperer, Fricsay, Jochum and Kleiber were associated with modern music, or simply with less central repertoire from diverse periods of European music.

With only one exception, our 7 conductors have immersed themselves in the lighter Viennese muse, in the music of the Johann Strauss dynasty and associates. Indeed, the recorded evidence of a master like Kleiber suggests that, had he lived, he would have been a serious contender for the permanent direction of Vienna's New Year concerts after Krauss.

From the oldest to the youngest, from Weingartner to Fricsay, we are concerned with professional all-rounders, masters who can put their hand to almost any musical task regardless of the "labels" attached to them (Jochum as a Bruckner man, Klemperer as a Beethoven specialist), serving the music without failing to give it their personal stamp.

In the case of Weingartner, I have included the piano rolls of his playing made very early this century, although first-hand knowledge of these is in all probability restricted to a few choice collectors of the older generation.

My terms of reference remain as they were for "Italian conductors", "Viennese sopranos", "Mid-century conductors" and "More Viennese singers": to give first issue numbers of each recording, some important re-issues and the most recent or currently available versions. There is no claim to have included all issues in all countries, but I have attempted to include all commercially made records, including unpublished ones, and the ever-growing number of live and unofficial publications. A veritable wealth of live material on tape circulating among collectors still remains unpublished, particulary in the case of Klemperer. The highly reputable German label Archiphon is doing excellent work in bringing out less well-known performances by Klemperer, Schuricht and Kleiber.

A word on how the various catalogue numbers of a particular recording are arranged. In the case of 78s, two sets of numbers are often given side by side to identify the manual and automatic coupling sequences in which works occupying several sides were often made available. For the earliest stereo LPs, separate numbers are given for the mono and stereo (in that order) editions in which such recordings were invariably published. In these days of the CD, where far more recordings are issued both on single discs and as part of multiple sets, the two separate catalogue numbers are similarly placed side by side.

Abbreviations, mainly to describe the orchestras, are kept to a minimum and those which are used (BPO, VPO, LPO, LSO) are of course commonly understood by collectors. I have continued to make certain simplifications such as using "VPO" to include that group's appearances on disc in its other guise of Vienna State Opera Orchestra, where presumably less than first-desk players were sometimes employed. "Berlin RO" is still used to cover the various names given at different times to that city's main broadcasting ensemble (RIAS, RSO).

For those conductors who were Decca artists I have again added the potted biographies taken from the 1956 publication "Decca Book of Opera", but for background information on all of these men I would refer all readers to the invaluable "Conductors on Record" by John L. Holmes, either in its original hardback or shortened paperback versions. However, I must also draw your attention to the amusing personal recollection of Jochum contributed at the end of that discography by my friend Jim Parsons. As illustration material you will find more caricatures taken from the book "Im Konzertsaal karikiert" (Langen-Müller, Munich 1959), and many playbills, concert programmes and record advertisements which help place the recording work of our conductors into the broader perspective of their public appearances.

To conclude, I wish all readers good browsing and success in tracking down copies of those rare and elusive recordings.

John Hunt

Eugen Jochum
1902-1987

with valuable assistance from
Malcolm Walker

Discography compiled by John Hunt

Bach

Christmas Oratorio

Munich 1967	Bavarian Radio Orchestra & Chorus Ameling, Fassbänder, Laubenthal, Prey	LP: Philips 6703 037 CD: Philips 416 4022 Excerpts LP: Philips 6527 070 CD: Philips 422 2522

Mass in B minor

Ottobeuren December 1957	Bavarian Radio Orchestra & Chorus L.Marshall, Töpper, Pears, Borg	LP: Philips 875 003-875 005 CY LP: Philips 6768 214
Munich March and April 1980	Bavarian Radio Orchestra & Chorus Donath, Fassbänder, Ahnsjö, R.Hermann, Holl	LP: EMI SLS 5215

Saint John Passion

Amsterdam June 1967	Concertgebouw Orchestra Netherlands Radio Choir Giebel, Höffgen, Häfliger, Berry, Crass	LP: Philips SC 71 AX 303/ 802 810-802 812 AY LP: Philips SAL 3652-3654 LP: Philips 6747 019 CD: Philips 426 6452

Saint Matthew Passion

Amsterdam November 1965	Concertgebouw Orchestra Netherlands Radio Choir Giebel, Höffgen, Häfliger, Berry, Crass	LP: Philips 835 372-835 375 AY/ SAL 3562-3565 LP: Philips 6747 019/6747 371 CD: Philips 420 9002 Excerpts LP: Philips 802 786 LY LP: Philips 6527 116

Cantata No 51 "Jauchzet Gott in allen Landen"

Munich October 1951	Bavarian RO Schwarzkopf	LP: Melodram MEL 082 CD: Melodram MEL 16501

Beethoven

Symphony No 1

Munich 1958	Bavarian RO	LP: DG LPM 18 519/SLPM 138 037 LP: DG LPEM 19 293-19 299 LP: DG 2538 074/2548 224
Amsterdam March 1967	Concertgebouw Orchestra	LP: Philips 839 777-839 785 LY/ SC 71 AX 900/AXS 9000 LP: Philips 6500 087/6580 148 CD: Philips 422 9662
London October 1978	LSO	LP: EMI SLS 5178

Symphony No 2

Berlin January 1958	BPO	LP: DG LPEM 19 173/SLPEM 136 019 LP: DG LPEM 19 293-19 299 LP: DG 2538 075/2548 214
Amsterdam March 1969	Concertgebouw Orchestra	LP: Philips 839 777-839 785 LY/ SC 71 AX 900/AXS 9000 LP: Philips 6500 088/6580 175 CD: Philips 422 9662
London June and July 1978	LSO	LP: EMI SLS 5178

Symphony No 3 "Eroica"

Berlin June 1937	BPO	78: Telefunken E 2311-2316 CD: Teldec 9031 764442
Berlin February 1954	BPO	LP: **DG LPM 18 179** LP: DG LPEM 19 293-19 299 LP: DG 478 072/89 642
Amsterdam May 1969	Concertgebouw Orchestra	LP: Philips 839 777-839 785 LY/ SC 71 AX 900/839 779 LY/AXS 9000 LP: Philips 6580 137 CD: Philips 426 0662/434 5282
London July and October 1976	LSO	LP: EMI SLS 5178/ASD 3376

Symphony No 4

Berlin November 1956	BPO	LP: DG LPM 18 206 LP: DG LPEM 19 293-19 299
Berlin January 1961	BPO	LP: DG LPM 18 694/SLPM 138 694 LP: DG 2548 225
Amsterdam June 1968	Concertgebouw Orchestra	LP: Philips 839 777-839 785 LY/ 　　SC 71 AX 900/AXS 9000 LP: Philips 6500 089/6580 146 CD: Philips 422 9672/438 8392
London June 1977	LSO	LP: EMI SLS 5178

Symphony No 5

Berlin May 1951	BPO	LP: Philips A 00102 L LP: Epic (USA) LC 3002 LP: Philips NBR 6030/GBL 5556 CD: Philips (Japan) PHC 1295
Munich 1958	Bavarian RO	LP: DG LPEM 19 293-19 299 LP: DG 2538 060 CD: DG 427 1952/429 5332
Amsterdam November and December 1968	Concertgebouw Orchestra	LP: Philips 839 777-785 LY/ 　　SC 71 AX 900/839 781 LY/AXS 9000 LP: Philips 6580 145 CD: Philips 422 4742
London October 1978	LSO	LP: EMI SLS 5178/ASD 3484

Symphony No 6 "Pastoral"

Berlin March 1951	BPO	LP: Movimento musica 08.001
Berlin November 1954	BPO	LP: DG LPM 18 202 LP: DG LPEM 19 293-19 299 LP: DG 478 429/89 503
Amsterdam November and December 1968	Concertgebouw Orchestra	LP: Philips 839 777-839 785 LY/ 　　SC 71 AX 900/839 782 LY/AXS 9000 LP: Philips 6527 045/6580 139 CD: Philips 426 0612/450 0582
London October 1977	LSO	LP: EMI SLS 5178/ASD 3583 CD: EMI CD-EMX 2019

The London Symphony Orchestra

Leader: John Georgiadis

Founded 1904

Patron
HER MAJESTY THE QUEEN

Principal Conductor
ANDRE PREVIN

Principal Guest Conductors
CLAUDIO ABBADO
COLIN DAVIS

Conductor Laureate
EUGEN JOCHUM

BEETHOVEN
Overture: Coriolan, Op. 62

Violin Concerto in D major, Op. 61

Interval

Symphony No. 4 in B flat major, Op. 60

Eugen Jochum
conductor

Gidon Kremer
violin

Tuesday, 21st June at 8.00pm

Greater London Council
Royal Festival Hall
Director: George Mann, OBE

Programme Book 25p

PHILHARMONIE
BERLINER PHILHARMONISCHES ORCHESTER

5. ABONNEMENTSKONZERT DER SERIE A

Sonnabend, den 6., Sonntag, den 7. und Montag, den 8. März 1971, 20 Uhr

Dirigent
EUGEN JOCHUM

Solisten
RUGGIERO RICCI

JAMES GALWAY   GERHARD STEMPNIK

ARTHUR HONEGGER
Concerto da camera für Flöte und Englisch Horn
mit Begleitung des Streichorchesters
Allegretto amabile · Andante · Vivace

GOTTFRIED VON EINEM
Violinkonzert op. 33
Andante · Allegro ma non troppo · Sostenuto ·
Presto · Andante · Presto · Adagio

LUDWIG VAN BEETHOVEN
Symphonie Nr. V in c-moll op. 67
Allegro con brio · Andante con moto · Allegro · Allegro · Presto

Symphony No 7

Berlin 1938	BPO	78: Telefunken SK 2763-2767
Berlin November 1952	BPO	LP: DG LPM 18 069 LP: DG LPEM 19 293-19 299 LP: Decca (USA) DL 9690 LP: DG 478 439
Amsterdam September 1967	Concertgebouw Orchestra	LP: Philips 839 777-839 785 LY/ SC 71 AX 900/AXS 9000 LP: Philips 6500 090/6580 176 CD: Philips 422 9672/438 8392
London September and October 1977	LSO	LP: EMI SLS 5178/ASD 3627

Symphony No 8

Berlin April and May 1958	BPO	LP: DG LPM 18 519/SLPM 138 037 LP: DG LPEM 19 293-19 299 LP: DG 2538 074/2548 224
Amsterdam March 1969	Concertgebouw Orchestra	LP: Philips 839 777-839 785 LY SC 71 AX 900/AXS 9000 LP: Philips 6500 087/6580 148 CD: Philips 422 4742/450 0582
London October 1978	LSO	LP: EMI SLS 5178/EMX 2040

Symphony No 9 "Choral"

Hamburg ca. 1937	Philharmonisches Staatsorchester Philharmonic Choir Fahrni, Hammer, W.Ludwig, Watzke	78: Telefunken SK 2615-2613
Munich 1949	Bavarian Radio Orchestra & Chorus Ebers, Pitzinger, W.Ludwig, Frantz	78: DG LVM 72 306-72 310 LP: DG LP 16 070-LPM 18 070 LP: DG LPEM 19 293-19 299 Last movement only LP: DG LPM 19 074
Amsterdam June 1969	Concertgebouw Orchestra Netherlands Radio Choir Rebmann, Reynolds, Ridder, Feldhoff	LP: 839 777-839 785 LY/ SC 71 AX 900/AXS 9000 LP: Philips 6700 040/6780 033 CD: Philips 422 4642/432 2252
London February and March 1978	LSO LSO Chorus Kanawa, Hamari, Burrows, Holl	LP: EMI SLS 5178/EMX 2040 CD: EMI CDM 764 6332/CDM 769 0302

Piano Concerto No 1

Bamberg 1973	Bamberg SO Jochum von Moltke	LP: Philips 6580 086
Vienna 1981	VPO Pollini	LP: DG 2532 103/2740 284 CD: DG 410 5112/419 7932

Piano Concerto No 2

Vienna 1981	VPO Pollini	LP: DG 2740 284 CD: DG 413 4452/419 7932

Piano Concerto No 4

Munich November 1951	Bavarian RO E.Fischer	CD: Orfeo C 270 921A

Piano Concerto No 5 "Emperor"

Berlin 1937	Städtische Oper Orchestra Hansen	78: Telefunken SK 2303-2307

A Berlin radio recording of the opening of the Emperor Concerto (E.Fischer/ Berlin RO/Jochum) was noted in the catalogue of the Reichsrundfunk, but the recording is now lost. Presumably this is what John Holmes refers to in "Conductors on Record" when he states that Jochum made his first recording for Telefunken in 1932 accompanying Fischer in a (Mozart) concerto. Jochum's own recollection of his first recording, in a conversation with John Hunt, was Bruckner Sixth Symphony, but this again must have been a radio recording

Violin Concerto

Berlin April 1959	BPO Schneiderhan	LP: DG SLPM 138 045 Mono version presumably also issued
Berlin May 1962	BPO Schneiderhan	LP: DG SLPM 138 999/135 081 LP: DG 2535 120 CD: DG 413 1452

This version features the first movement cadenza with timpani part, which was originally intended for the transcription of the concerto's solo part for piano

Missa Solemnis

Amsterdam September 1970	Concertgebouw Orchestra Netherlands Radio Choir Giebel, Höffgen, Häfliger, Ridderbusch	LP: Philips 6799 001 CD: Philips 426 6482

Coriolan, Overture

Amsterdam June 1960	Concertgebouw Orchestra	LP: Philips A 02034L/835 054 AY LP: Philips 6780 033
London October 1977	LSO	LP: EMI SLS 5178
Bamberg 1985	Bamberg SO	CD: RCA/BMG 09026 612122 Issued on LP by Eurodisc

Egmont, Overture

Berlin September 1938	BPO	78: Telefunken E 2683
Amsterdam June 1960	Concertgebouw Orchestra	LP: Philips A 02034L/835 054 AY LP: Philips 6780 033
London March 1977	LSO	LP: EMI SLS 5178
Bamberg 1985	Bamberg SO	CD: RCA/BMG 09026 612122 Issued on LP by Eurodisc

Fidelio: Excerpts (1. Ha welch ein Augenblick!; 2. Abscheulicher!)

Munich 1951	Bavarian State Orchestra & Chorus Braun (2), Frantz (1)	LP: Melodram MEL 091

Fidelio, Overture

Munich 1958	Bavarian RO	LP: DG 2538 060/2548 138/2548 225
Amsterdam November and December 1968	Concertgebouw Orchestra	LP: Philips 839 777-839 785 LY/ SC 71 AX 900/839 781 LY/AXS 9000 LP: Philips 6580 145 CD: Philips 426 0662/434 5282
London October 1977	LSO	LP: EMI SLS 5178 CD: EMI CDM 764 6332
Bamberg 1985	Bamberg SO	CD: RCA/BMG 09026 612122 Isuued on LP by Eurodisc

Die Geschöpfe des Prometheus, Overture

Munich 1958	Bavarian RO	LP: DG LPEM 19 173/SLPEM 136 019 LP: DG 135 041/2538 075/2548 214
Bamberg 1985	Bamberg SO	CD: RCA/BMG 09026 612122 Issued on LP by Eurodisc

Leonore No 1, Overture

Amsterdam March 1969	Concertgebouw Orchestra	LP: Philips SC 71 AX 900/AXS 9000 LP: Philips 6500 089/6580 146 CD: Philips 422 9662
Bamberg 1985	Bamberg SO	CD: RCA/BMG 09026 612122 Issued on LP by Eurodisc

Leonore No 2, Overture

Berlin January 1961	BPO	LP: DG LPM 18 694/SLPM 138 694 LP: DG 135 041/2548 138/2548 225 CD: DG 413 1452
Amsterdam May 1969	Concertgebouw Orchestra	LP: Philips SC 71 AX 900/AXS 9000 LP: Philips 6500 088/6700 040 LP: Philips 6580 146 CD: Philips 426 0612

Leonore No 3, Overture

Berlin September 1937	BPO	78: Telefunken E 2278-2279
Amsterdam June 1960	Concertgebouw Orchestra	LP: Philips A 02034L/835 054 AY
Berlin January 1961	BPO	LP: DG 2548 138
Amsterdam November and December 1968	Concertgebouw Orchestra	LP: Philips 839 777-839 785 LY/ SC 71 AX 900/AXS 9000 LP: Philips 6700 040/6580 175 CD: Philips 426 0662 /434 5282
London June 1977	LSO	LP: EMI SLS 5178
Bamberg 1985	Bamberg SO	CD: RCA/BMG 09026 612122 Issued on LP by Eurodisc

Namensfeier, Overture

Amsterdam June 1960	Concertgebouw Orchestra	LP: Philips A 02034L/835 054 AY LP: Philips 6780 033

Die Ruinen von Athen, Overture

Munich 1958	Bavarian RO	LP: DG LPEM 19 173/SLPEM 136 019 LP: DG 135 041/2538 075 LP: DG 2548 138/2548 214
Bamberg 1985	Bamberg SO	CD: RCA/BMG 09026 612122 Issued on LP by Eurodisc

Die Weihe des Hauses, Overture

Amsterdam June 1960	Concertgebouw Orchestra	LP: Philips A 02034L/835 054 AY

Brahms

Symphony No 1

Berlin 1938	BPO	78: Telefunken E 2703-2707
Berlin December 1953	BPO	LP: DG LPM 18 182 LP: DG LPM 18 451-18 454
London June, July and October 1976	LPO	LP: EMI SLS 5093 CD: EMI CDZ 762 6042

Symphony No 2

Berlin March 1951	BPO	78: DG LVM 72 080-72 082 LP: DG LPM 18 008 LP: DG LPM 18 451-18 454 LP: Decca (USA) DL 9556 LP: DG 478 085
London June, July and October 1976	LPO	LP: EMI SLS 5093

Symphony No 3

Hamburg 1938	Philharmonisches Staatsorchester	78: Telefunken SK 3024-3027 LP: Capitol P 8045
Berlin April 1956	BPO	LP: DG LPM 18 309 LP: DG LPM 18 451-18 454 LP: DG 478 440
London June, July and October 1976	LPO	LP: EMI SLS 5093

Symphony No 4

Berlin 1953	BPO	LP: DG LPM 18 183 LP: DG LPM 18 451-18 454 LP: DG 478 079/2548 110 LP: Longanesi periodici GCL 37 CD: Memories HR 4246 <u>Longanesi and Memories editions</u> <u>incorrectly dated July 1951</u>
London June, July and October 1976	LPO	LP: EMI SLS 5093

Piano Concerto No 1

Berlin November 1954	BPO Solomon	CD: Myto MCD 89005
Berlin June 1972	BPO Gilels	LP: DG 2530 258/2535 390 LP: DG 2707 064/2726 082 CD: DG 419 1582

Piano Concerto No 2

Berlin June 1972	BPO Gilels	LP: DG 2530 259 LP: DG 2707 064/2726 082 CD: DG 419 1582/435 5882

Violin Concerto

Vienna December 1974	VPO Milstein	LP: DG 2530 592

Haydn Variations

London 1977	LSO	LP: DG 2530 586 CD: DG 413 4242

Academic Festival Overture; Tragic Overture

London June, July and October 1976	LPO	LP: EMI SLS 5093 CD: EMI CDZ 762 6042

Bruckner

Symphony No 1

Berlin
October 1965

BPO

LP: DG SKL 929-939/139 131
LP: DG 2720 047/2721 010/2740 136
CD: DG 429 0792

Dresden
December 1978

Dresden
Staatskapelle

LP: EMI SLS 5252/ASD 3825
CD: EMI CZS 762 9352

Symphony No 2

Munich
December 1966

Bavarian RO

LP: DG SKL 929-939/139 132
LP: DG 2720 047/2721 010/2740 136
CD: DG 429 0792

Dresden
December 1975

Dresden
Staatskapelle

LP: EMI SLS 5252/ASD 4081
CD: EMI CZS 762 9352

Symphony No 3

Munich
January 1967

Bavarian RO

LP: DG SKL 929-939/139 133
LP: DG 2720 047/2721 010
LP: DG 2740 136/2535 265
CD: DG 429 0792
Second movement rehearsal and performance
LP: DG 104 808

Dresden
January 1977

Dresden
Staatskapelle

LP: EMI SLS 5252/ASD 4009
CD: EMI CZS 762 9352

Symphony No 4 "Romantic"

Hamburg June 1939	Philharmonisches Staatsorchester	78: Telefunken SK 3032-3039 CD: Dante LYS 007-008
Munich 1954	Bavarian RO	LP: DG LPEM 19 055-19 056/ LPEM 19 057-19 058 LP: Decca (USA) DXE 146
Berlin June 1965	BPO	LP: DG SKL 929-939/139 134-139 135 LP: DG 2720 047/2721 010/2740 136 LP: DG 2707 025/2535 111 CD: DG 429 0792/427 2002
Dresden December 1975	Dresden Staatskapelle	LP: EMI SLS 5252 CD: EMI CZS 762 9352

Symphony No 5

Hamburg 1938	Philharmonisches Staatsorchester	78: Telefunken E 2672-2680 LP: Capitol P 8049-8050
Munich February 1958	Bavarian RO	LP: DG LPM 18 500-18 501/ SLPM 138 004-138 005 LP: DG SKL 929-939/138 967-138 968 LP: DG 2720 047/2721 010/2740 136 LP: DG 2707 020/2726 074 CD: DG 429 0792

Ottobeuren
May 1964
	Concertgebouw
	Orchestra
		LP: Philips A 02347-02348L/
		    835 225-835 226 AY
		LP: Philips AL 3532-3533/
		    SAL 3532-3533
		CD: Philips 426 1072

Paris October 1969	Orchestre National	CD: Disques Montaigne TCE 8770
Dresden February and March 1980	Dresden Staatskapelle	LP: EMI SLS 5252 CD: EMI CZS 762 9352

Symphony No 6

Munich July 1966	Bavarian RO	LP: DG SKL 929-939/139 136 LP: DG 2720 047/2721 010/2740 136 CD: DG 429 0792
Dresden February 1978	Dresden Staatskapelle	LP: EMI SLS 5252/ASD 4080 CD: EMI CZS 762 9352

Symphony No 7

Vienna 1935-1936	VPO	78: Telefunken SK 3000-3007 LP: Capitol P 8067-8068 CD: Dante LYS 007-008
Berlin March and April 1952	BPO	LP: DG LPM 18 033-18 034/ LPM 18 112-18 113 LP: Decca (USA) DXE 146
Berlin October 1964	BPO	LP: DG SKL 929-939/139 137-139 138 LP: DG 2720 047/2721 010/2740 136 LP: DG 2707 026/2726 054 CD: DG 429 0792
Dresden December 1976	Dresden Staatskapelle	LP: EMI SLS 5252/SLS 5194 CD: EMI CZS 762 9352
Paris February 1980	Orchestre National	CD: Disques Montaigne TCE 8770

Symphony No 8

Hamburg
1948
	Philharmonisches
	Staatsorchester
		78: DG LV 68 338-68 348/
		     69 548-69 555 auto
		LP: DG LPM 18 124-18 125/
		    LPM 18 051-18 052
		LP: Decca (USA) DX 109
		LP: DG 478 430

Berlin January 1964	BPO	LP: SKL 929-939/138 918-138 919 LP: DG 2720 047/2721 010/2740 136 LP: DG 2707 017/2726 077 CD: DG 429 0792/431 1632
Dresden November 1976	Dresden Staatskapelle	LP: EMI SLS 5252/SLS 5147 CD: EMI CZS 762 9352

Symphony No 9

Munich 1956	Bavarian RO	LP: DG LPM 18 247-18 248 LP: Decca (USA) DX 139 LP: DG 89 551
Berlin December 1964	BPO	LP: DG SKL 929-939/139 117-139 118 LP: DG 2720 047/2721 010/2740 136 LP: DG 2707 024/2535 173 CD: DG 429 0792/429 5142/422 4642
Dresden January 1978	Dresden Staatskapelle	LP: EMI SLS 5252 LP: EMI ASD 4218/EG 29 04921 CD: EMI CZS 762 9352

Te Deum

Munich 1948	Bavarian Radio Orchestra & Chorus Cunitz, Pitzinger, Fehenberger, Hann	78: DG LVM 72 020-72 021 LP: DG LP 16 002/LPE 17 155 LP: DG LPM 18 247-18 248 LP: Decca (USA) DX 109
Munich May 1954	Bavarian Radio Orchestra & Chorus Kupper, Siewert, Fehenberger, Borg	CD: Orfeo C 195 892H
Berlin July 1965	BPO Deutsche Oper Chorus Stader, Wagner, Häfliger, Lagger	LP: DG 139 117-139 118 LP: DG 136 552.139 999 LP: DG 2707 026/2720 054/2740 136 CD: DG 423 1272

Psalm 150

Berlin June 1966	BPO Deutsche Oper Chorus Stader	LP: DG 139 137-139 138/139 999 LP: DG 2720 054 CD: DG 423 1272

Mass No 1

Munich January 1972	Bavarian Radio Orchestra & Chorus Mathis, Schiml, Ochman, Ridderbusch	LP: DG 2530 314/2720 054 CD: DG 423 1272

Mass No 2

Munich February 1971	Bavarian Radio Wind ensemble and Chorus	LP: DG 2530 139/2720 054 CD: DG 423 1272

Mass No 3

Munich July 1962	Bavarian Radio Orchestra & Chorus Stader, Hellmann, Häfliger, Borg	LP: DG LPM 18 829/SLPM 138 829 LP: DG 2720 054 CD: DG 423 1272 Gloria only LP: DG 139 999

Afferentur regi

Munich June 1966	Bavarian Radio Chorus	LP: DG 2530 139/2720 054 CD: DG 423 1272

Ave Maria

Munich June 1966	Bavarian Radio Chorus	LP: DG 139 134-139 135/136 552 LP: DG 2707 025/2545 055/2720 054 CD: DG 423 1272

Christus factus est

Munich	Bavarian Radio	LP: DG 139 137-139 138
June 1966	Chorus	LP: DG 2707 026/2720 054
		CD: DG 423 1272

Ecce sacerdos

Munich	Bavarian Radio	LP: DG 139 134-139 135/136 552
June 1966	Chorus	LP: DG 2707 025/2720 054
		CD: DG 423 1272

Locus iste

Munich	Bavarian Radio	LP: DG 136 552/2707 025/2720 054
June 1966	Chorus	CD: DG 423 1272
	Holm	

Os justi

Munich	Bavarian Radio	LP: DG 139 137-139 138
June 1966	Chorus	LP: DG 2707 026/2720 054
		CD: DG 423 1272

Pange lingua

Munich	Bavarian Radio	LP: DG 2530 139/2720 054
June 1966	Chorus	CD: DG 423 1272

Tota pulchra es

Munich	Bavarian Radio	LP: DG 139 134-139 135/136 552
June 1966	Chorus	LP: DG 2707 025/2720 054
	Holm	CD: DG 423 1272

Vexilla regis

Munich	Bavarian Radio	LP: DG 139 137-139 138
June 1966	Chorus	LP: DG 2707 026/2720 054
		CD: DG 423 1272

Virga Jesse

Munich	Bavarian Radio	LP: DG 139 134-139 135/136 552
June 1966	Chorus	LP: DG 2707 025/2720 054
		CD: DG 423 1272

Deutsche Grammophon Gesellschaft

EUGEN JOCHUM
conducting the
BERLIN PHILHARMONIC ORCHESTRA

HAYDN
Symphony No. 88, G major
Symphony No. 98, B flat
33 = LPM 18 823 (Mono)
33 = SLPM 138 823 (Stereo)

BEETHOVEN
Symphony No. 1, C major, Op. 21*
Symphony No. 8, F major, Op. 93
*Bavarian Radio Symphony Orchestra
33 = LPM 18 519 (Mono)
33 = SLPM 138 037 (Stereo)

BEETHOVEN
Symphony No. 2, D major, Op. 36
The Ruins of Athens, Overture, Op. 113*
The Creature of Prometheus, Overture, Op. 43*
*Bavarian Radio Symphony Orchestra
33 = LPEM 19 173 (Mono)
33 = SLPEM 136 019 (Stereo)

BEETHOVEN
Symphony No. 4, B flat, Op. 60
Leonore II Overture, Op. 72
33 = LPM 18 694 (Mono)
33 = SLPM 138 694 (Stereo)

BRUCKNER
Symphony No. 7, E major
33 = LPM 18 112/13 (Mono)

Prices (inc. Purchase Tax):
LPM series (Mono) 37/6d.
SLPM series (Stereo) 37/6d.
LPEM series (Mono) 31/9d.
SLPEM series (Stereo) 37/6d.

BEETHOVEN
Symphony No. 3, E flat major, Op. 55 "Eroica"
33 = Heliodor 478 072 (Mono)

BEETHOVEN
Symphony No. 6, F major, Op. 68
"Pastoral"
33 = Heliodor 478 429 (Mono)

BEETHOVEN
Symphony No. 7, A major, Op. 92
Choral Fantasia, C minor, Op. 80*
Andor Foldes, Piano with Berlin Motet Choir
Conductor: Fritz Lehmann*
33 = Heliodor 478 439 (Mono)

BRAHMS
Symphony No. 2, D major, Op. 73
33 = Heliodor 478 085 (Mono)

BRAHMS
Symphony No. 3, F major, Op. 90

GLUCK
Overture: "Iphigenia in Aulis"*
*Munich Philharmonic Orchestra
Conductor: Arthur Rother
33 = Heliodor 478 440 (Mono)

BRAHMS
Symphony No. 4, E minor, Op. 98
33 = Heliodor 478 079 (Mono)

Price (inc. Purchase Tax): 22/-

DEUTSCHE GRAMMOPHON (GREAT BRITAIN) LIMITED
12/13, Rathbone Place, Oxford Street, London, W.1.
Tel: LANgham 8156/7/8/9

The Cathedral Church of St. Michael
Coventry

BERLIN PHILHARMONIC ORCHESTRA

Conductor Eugen Jochum
Leader Michel Schwalbe

TUESDAY 28 JANUARY 1964
7.30 pm

Chopin

Piano Concerto No 2

Berlin	Berlin RO	CD: Hunt CD 511
January 1954	Arrau	

Delden

Concerto per 2 orchestre d'archi

Amsterdam	Concertgebouw	CD: Etcetera KTC 1156
March 1968	Orchestra	

Piccolo concerto

Amsterdam	Concertgebouw	CD: Etcetera KTC 1156
February 1964	Orchestra	

Dvorak

Violin Concerto

Berlin	BPO	78: Telefunken SK 3237-3240
June 1941	Kulenkampff	LP: Capitol P 8052
		LP: Telefunken LGX 66020

Elgar

Enigma Variations

London	LSO	LP: DG 2530 586
1978		CD: DG 413 8522

Francaix

Serenade for 12 instruments

Hamburg	Hamburg	78: Telefunken A 10037-10038
1948	Chamber Orchestra	LP: Capitol L 8051
		LP: Telefunken LGM 65021
		World's Encyclopaedia of Recorded Music states that this recording was conducted by Schmidt-Isserstedt

Haydn

Symphony No 88

Berlin October 1961	BPO	LP: DG LPM 18 823/SLPM 138 823 LP: DG 2548 241

Symphony No 91

Munich 1958	Bavarian RO	LP: DG LPM 18 499/SLPM 138 007 LP: DG 2548 147

Symphony No 93

Dresden 1967	Dresden Staatskapelle	LP: Eterna 826 006
Barking April 1972	LPO	LP: DG 2720 064 CD: DG 437 2012

Symphony No 94 "Surprise"

Dresden 1967	Dresden Staatskapelle	LP: Eterna 826 006
Barking April 1972	LPO	LP: DG 2720 064/2530 628/2545 008 CD: DG 423 8832/437 2012

Symphony No 95

Dresden 1970	Dresden Staatskapelle	LP: Philips 6530 066
Barking April 1972	LPO	LP: DG 2720 064/2530 420 CD: DG 437 2012

Symphony No 96 "Miracle"

Barking October 1972	LPO	LP: DG 2720 064/2530 420 CD: DG 437 2012

Symphony No 97

Barking October 1972	LPO	LP: DG 2720 064 CD: DG 437 2012

Symphony No 98

Berlin May 1962	BPO	LP: DG LPM 18 823/SLPM 138 823 LP: DG 2548 241
Dresden 1970	Dresden Staatskapelle	LP: Philips 6530 066
Barking October 1972	LPO	LP: DG 2720 064 CD: DG 437 2012

Symphony No 99

Barking February 1973	LPO	LP: DG 2530 459 CD: DG 437 2012

Symphony No 100 "Military"

Barking February 1973	LPO	LP: DG 2720 064/2530 459/2535 347 CD: DG 437 2012

Symphony No 101 "Clock"

Barking February 1973	LPO	LP: DG 2720 064/2530 628 CD: DG 423 8832/437 2012

Symphony No 102

Barking October 1971	LPO	LP: DG 2720 064 CD: DG 437 2012

Symphony No 103 "Drum Roll"

Munich 1958	Bavarian RO	LP: DG LPM 18 499/SLPM 138 007 LP: DG 2548 147
Barking October 1971	LPO	LP: DG 2720 064/2530 525/2535 392 CD: DG 437 2012

Symphony No 104 "London"

Barking October 1971	LPO	LP: DG 2720 064/2530 525 LP: DG 2535 347/2543 531 CD: DG 437 2012

Saint Cecilia Mass

Munich 1959	Bavarian Radio Orchestra & Chorus Stader, Höffgen, Holm, Greindl	LP: DG LPM 18 545-18 546/ SLPM 138 028-138 029 Excerpts LP: DG 136 491

Die Schöpfung

Munich 1952	Bavarian Radio Orchestra & Chorus Seefried, W.Ludwig, Hotter	LP: Melodram MEL 208 LP: Movimento musica 02.021
Munich 1966	Bavarian Radio Orchestra & Chorus Giebel, Kmennt, Frick	LP: Philips SC 71 AX 201 LP: Philips AL 3596-3597/ SAL 3596-3597 LP: Philips 6700 002

Heppener

Eglogues

Amsterdam March 1965	Concertgebouw Orchestra	LP: Donemus DAVS 6503 CD: Donemus CVCD 10/BFOA 6 CD: Colophon CVCD 4-7

Hindemith

Cello Concerto

Munich 1957	Bavarian RO Mainardi	CD: Orfeo C 272 921B

Symphonic Dances

Munich 1957	Bavarian RO	CD: Orfeo C 272 921B

Höller

Sweelinck Variations; Symphonic Fantasy

Munich   Bavarian RO   LP: DG LPM 18 407
1957

Landré

Symphony No 3

Amsterdam   Concertgebouw   LP: Donemus DAVS 6403
November 1961   Orchestra

Mahler

Das Lied von der Erde

Amsterdam March and April 1963	Concertgebouw Orchestra Merriman, Häfliger	LP: DG LPM 18 865/SLPM 138 865 LP: DG 2535 184

Rudolf Mengelberg

Magnificat

Amsterdam April 1952	Concertgebouw Orchestra Woud	78: Philips A 11241G

Moniuszko

Halka: Excerpt (Peasants' Chorus)

Hamburg 1935	Philharmonisches Staatsorchester and Chorus Schwer Sung in German	78: Telefunken E 1934

Monteverdi

L'Orfeo, Excerpts

Munich April 1954	Bavarian Radio Orchestra & Chorus Lindermeier, L.Fischer, Böhme, Wächter	LP: Gioielli della lirica GML 79

Mozart Fest 1957

SYMPHONIE-KONZERT

27. JUNI

KAMMERORCHESTER
DES BAYERISCHEN RUNDFUNKS

Leitung:

EUGEN JOCHUM

Symphonie-Konzert

27. JUNI 1957, 20 UHR

FOLGE

Aus dem Divertimento in B-dur   KV 287
("2. Lodronsche Nachtmusik")
    Allegro · Adagio · Menuetto · Andante (Rezitativ)
    — Allegro molto
       Solo-Violine: Rudolf Köckert

Szene und Duett Ilia-Idamantes aus "Idomeneo"
                                        KV 366
    Solisten: Erika Köth
               Léopold Simoneau

Konzertarie für Sopran   KV 368
"Ma, che vi fece, o stelle!"
    Solistin: Erika Köth

PAUSE

Konzertarie für Tenor "Misero, o sogno"   KV 431
    Solist: Léopold Simoneau

Duett Constanze-Belmonte aus der Oper
"Die Entführung aus dem Serail"
    Solisten: Erika Köth
               Léopold Simoneau

Symphonie in D-dur   KV 504
("Prager Symphonie")
    Adagio — Allegro · Andante · Finale (Presto)

PHILHARMONISCHE GESELLSCHAFT
PHILHARMONISCHES STAATSORCHESTER HAMBURG

Montag, 4. März 1935, Conventgarten, Großer Saal

9. Philharmonisches Konzert

Leitung: EUGEN JOCHUM — Solistin: VIORICA URSULEAC

Claude Debussy: Nocturne
Richard Strauß: Lieder mit Orchester*)
Richard Strauß: Till Eulenspiegel*)
Johs. Brahms: 1. Sinfonie

*) anläßlich des 70. Geburtstages des Komponisten

Mozart

Symphony No 33

Munich 1955	Bavarian RO	LP: DG LPM 18 228/478 435/89 621
Munich July 1985	Bamberg SO	LP: Eurodisc 206.715 425

<u>A version of this symphony conducted by Jochum with the Berlin Philharmonic in 1949 may have been published on Urania LP 7.27 but this could not be confirmed</u>

Symphony No 35 "Haffner"

Amsterdam December 1960	Concertgebouw Orchestra	LP: Philips A 02083L/835 079 AY LP: Philips SFM 23013
Bamberg October 1984	Bamberg SO	LP: Eurodisc 206.714 425 CD: Eurodisc 610.277 231

Symphony No 36 "Linz"

Munich 1955	Bavarian RO	LP: DG LPM 18 228/478 435/89 621
Amsterdam November and December 1961	Concertgebouw Orchestra	LP: Philips A 02222L/835 111 AY LP: Philips SAL 3541/6580 023
Munich July 1985	Bamberg SO	LP: Eurodisc 206.715 425

Symphony No 38 "Prague"

Amsterdam November and December 1961	Concertgebouw Orchestra	LP: Philips A 02222L/835 111 AY LP: Philips SAL 3541/6580 023
Bamberg October 1984	Bamberg SO	LP: Eurodisc 206.714 425 CD: Eurodisc 610.277 231

Symphony No 39

Munich 1954	Bavarian RO	LP: DG LP 16 099/LPX 29 251 LP: DG 478 133/89 620
Bamberg March and November 1982	Bamberg SO	LP: Orfeo S 045 832H CD: Orfeo C 045 901A

Symphony No 40

Amsterdam June 1943	Concertgebouw Orchestra	78: Telefunken SK 3752-3754 LP: Capitol L 8016
Munich 1954	Bavarian RO	LP: DG LPEM 19 120 LP: DG 478 445/89 676
Bamberg March and November 1982	Bamberg SO	LP: Orfeo S 045 832H CD: Orfeo C 045 901A

Symphony No 41 "Jupiter"

Berlin ca. 1942	BPO	78: Telefunken E 3333-3336
Amsterdam December 1960	Concertgebouw Orchestra	LP: Philips A 02083L/835 079 AY LP: Philips GBL 5501/SFM 23013
Boston 1972	Boston SO	LP: DG 2530 357/2543 531
Bamberg March and November 1982	Bamberg SO	LP: Orfeo S 045 832H CD: Orfeo C 045 902A

Piano Concerto No 14

Bamberg 1973	Bamberg SO Jochum von Moltke	LP: Philips 6580 086

Piano Concerto No 20

Munich December 1954	Bavarian RO E.Fischer	LP: Discocorp IGI 290 CD: Memories HR 4246

Violin Concerto No 4

Munich 1954	Bavarian RO Martzy	LP: DG LP 16 119/LPX 29 251 LP: DG 478 133/89 620

Flute and Harp Concerto

Rome April 1965	RAI Rome Orchestra Gazzeloni Zabaleta	CD: Memories HR 4125

Serenade No 7 "Haffner"

Munich April 1986	Bamberg SO	CD: Eurodisc 257.674 231

Serenade No 10 for 13 wind instruments

Munich February 1962	Bavarian RO	LP: DG LPM 18 830/SLPM 138 830 LP: DG 2542 001

Serenade No 13 "Eine kleine Nachtmusik"

Munich 1952	Bavarian RO	78: DG LVM 72 057-72 058 78: DG LVM 72 440 45: DG EPL 30053 LP: DG LPE 17 020/89 625
Munich April 1986	Bamberg SO	CD: Eurodisc 257.674 231

Maurerische Trauermusik

Bamberg March and November 1982	Bamberg SO	LP: Orfeo S 045 832H CD: Orfeo C 045 902A

Coronation Mass

Munich July 1976	Bavarian Radio Orchestra & Chorus Moser, Hamari, Gedda, Fischer-Dieskau	LP: EMI ASD 3373 CD: EMI CDM 769 0232

Mass in C minor

Würzburg June 1956	Bavarian Radio Orchestra & Chorus Seefried, Kupper, Fehenberger, Borg	CD: Orfeo C 245 891A

Requiem

Vienna December 1955	VSO Vienna Opera Chorus Seefried, Pitzinger, Holm, Borg	LP: DG LPEM 19 504-19 505/ APM 14 111-14 112 LP: DG LPM 18 284/89 508 19 504-5 and 14 111-2 also include complete liturgy of the service in St Stephen's Cathedral at which the performance was recorded, on the eve of the Mozart bi-centenary celebrations

Vesperae solennes de confessore

Munich July 1976	Bavarian Radio Orchestra & Chorus Moser, Hamari, Gedda, Fischer-Dieskau	LP: EMI ASD 3373

Così fan tutte

Berlin December 1962 and April 1963	BPO RIAS Choir Seefried, Merriman, Köth, Häfliger, Prey, Fischer-Dieskau	LP: DG LPM 18 861-18 863/ SLPM 138 861-138 863 LP: DG 2709 012/2728 010 Excerpts LP: DG LPM 18 792/SLPM 138 792 LP: DG LPEM 19 278/SLPEM 136 278 LP: DG LPEM 19 477/SLPEM 136 477 LP: DG 135 040/135 113/2535 300 LP: DG 2535 476/2537 019 LP: DG 2548 116/410 8471 CD: DG 437 6772

Die Entführung aus dem Serail

Munich December 1965	Bavarian State Orchestra & Chorus Köth, Schädle, Wunderlich, Lenz, Böhme	LP: DG 139 213-139 215 LP: DG 2709 021/2726 051 Excerpts LP: DG 136 429/2535 277/2535 631 LP: DG 2548 277/2563 357 CD: DG 435 1452

Le Nozze di Figaro, March and Fandango

Munich 1952	Bavarian RO	78: DG LVM 72 038 45: DG NL 32 029 LP: DG LPEM 19 066 LP: DG LPM 18 558-18 559

Mussorgsky

Boris Godunov: Excerpt (Revolution scene, abridged)

Hamburg 1935	Philharmonisches Staatsorchester and Chorus Sung in German	78: Telefunken E 1934

Orff

Carmina burana

Munich 1953	Bavarian Radio Orchestra & Chorus Trötschel, Kuen, Braun, Hoppe	LP: DG LP 16 068-16 069/ LP 16 045-16 046 LP: DG LPM 18 483-18 485 LP: DG LPM 18 303 LP: Decca (USA) DL 9706
Berlin October 1967	Deutsche Oper Orchestra & Chorus Janowitz, Stolze, Fischer-Dieskau	LP: DG 139 362/2726 510 CD: DG 423 8862/427 8782 Excerpts LP: DG 2705 001/2721 084/415 0461

Catulli carmina

Munich 1953	Bavarian Radio Chorus Kupper, Hom	LP: DG LPM 18 293/LPM 18 304 LP: DG LPM 18 483-18 485 Excerpt LP: DG LP 16 117
Berlin 1970	Deutsche Oper Chorus Auger, Ochman	LP: DG 2530 074/2726 510 CD: DG 427 8782

Trionfo di Afrodite

Munich 1953	Bavarian Radio Chorus Kupper, Holm	LP: DG LPM 18 305 LP: DG LPM 18 483-18 485

Die Kluge: Excerpts (O hätt' ich meiner Tochter nur geglaubt; Als die Treue ward geboren)

Munich ca. 1950	Bavarian RO Fehenberger, Lobel, Frick, Böhme	45: DG NL 32 219

Pfitzner

Von deutscher Seele

Munich July 1952	Bavarian Radio Orchestra & Chorus Ebers, Pitzinger, W.Ludwig, Hotter	CD: Orfeo C 273 922I

Das dunkle Reich

Munich January 1955	Bavarian Radio Orchestra & Chorus Kupper, Hotter	CD: Orfeo C 273 922I

Reger

Serenade in G

Amsterdam June 1943	Concertgebouw Orchestra	78: Capitol 89.80100-89.80104 LP: Capitol P 8026
Berlin Date uncertain	BPO	LP: Urania 7052

Schubert

Symphony No 4 "Tragic"

Amsterdam September 1960	Concertgebouw Orchestra	LP: Philips A 02072L/835 071 AY

Symphony No 5

Munich 1957	Bavarian RO	LP: DG LPEM 19 120/478 445

Symphony No 8 "Unfinished"

Amsterdam April 1952	Concertgebouw Orchestra	LP: Philips A 00604R/GBL 5501 LP: Epic LC 3006
Boston 1972	Boston SO	LP: DG 2530 357 CD: DG 427 1952/429 5332

Symphony No 9 "Great"

Munich 1956	Bavarian RO	LP: DG LPM 18 497/89 511/2548 108

Schumann

Symphony No 4

Amsterdam December 1960	Concertgebouw Orchestra	LP: Philips A 02072L/835 071 AY

Piano Concerto

Berlin May 1957	BPO Haas	LP: DG LP 16 007/LPE 17 142 LP: Decca (USA) DL 7522 LP: DG 89 521

Sibelius

Night Ride and Sunrise; The Oceanides; The Tempest, Overture

Munich 1955	Bavarian RO	LP: DG LPE 17 075

Richard Strauss

Don Juan

Amsterdam April 1952	Concertgebouw Orchestra	LP: Philips A 00608R LP: Epic LC 3031
Amsterdam June 1960	Concertgebouw Orchestra	LP: Philips A 02060L/835 006 AY LP: Philips 6580 129

Schlagobers, Waltz

Berlin February 1954	BPO	78: DG LV 72 474 45: DG EPL 30 056 LP: DG LPE 17 020

Till Eulenspiegels lustige Streiche

Amsterdam April 1952	Concertgebouw Orchestra	LP: Philips A 00608R LP: Epic LC 3031
Amsterdam June 1960	Concertgebouw Orchestra	LP: Philips A 02060L/835 006 AY LP: Philips 6580 129

Daphne

Munich 1950	Bavarian State Orchestra Kupper, L.Fischer, Hopf, Fehenberger, Hann	LP: Melodram MEL 107

Elektra

Hamburg June 1944	Philharmonisches Staatsorchester Schlüter, Kupper, Hammer, Markwort, Hagen	LP: Acanta DE 23.073/40.23073 CD: Acanta 44.21282 <u>First LP edition incorrectly named</u> <u>conductor as Schmidt-Isserstedt</u>

Der Rosenkavalier, Waltz sequences Acts 2 and 3

Amsterdam September 1960	Concertgebouw Orchestra	LP: Philips A 02060L/835 006 AY LP: Philips 6580 129

Der Rosenkavalier, Waltz sequence Act 3

Berlin December 1953	BPO	78: DG LV 72 474 45: DG EPL 30 056 LP: DG LPE 17 020/LPEM 19 015

Verdi

Messa da Requiem

Munich December 1950	Bavarian Radio Orchestra & Chorus Cunitz, Höngen, W.Ludwig, Greindl	CD: Orfeo C 195 892H

Otello: Excerpt (Già nella notte densa)

Munich 1953	Bavarian State Orchestra Rysanek, Aldenhoff <u>Sung in German</u>	LP: Melodram MEL 085 LP: Rodolphe RP 12433-12434

Philharmonia Orchestra

Patron: HRH The Prince of Wales
KG, KT, PC, GCB

President: Vincent Meyer

Principal Conductor:
Giuseppe Sinopoli

Principal Guest Conductor:
Esa-Pekka Salonen

Composer in Residence:
Oliver Knussen

Leaders:
Christopher Warren-Green & Peter Thomas

Eugen Jochum

Monday
20 January 1986
at 7.30

The Philharmonia Orchestra is most grateful to Eugen Jochum for undertaking this performance at very short notice, in place of Lorin Maazel, who is indisposed.

Eugen Jochum asks for the audience's understanding that, due to the lack of time available for him to prepare tonight's programme, he will conduct Mozart's Symphony No. 41 in place of Brahms's Symphony No. 2.

Furtwängler Centenary Concert

Mozart: Symphony No. 41 (Jupiter)

Beethoven: Symphony No. 7

The Philharmonia Orchestra gratefully acknowledges the sponsorship of this concert by

Burda Publication

Greater London Council
Royal Festival Hall
Programme 80p

Jochum's final London concert

Prinzregenten-Theater

Samstag, 10. Dezember 1949   Preise A

Neuinszenierung

DIE MEISTERSINGER VON NÜRNBERG

In drei Aufzügen von RICHARD WAGNER

Musikalische Leitung: Eugen Jochum   Inszenierung: Heinz Arnold
Bühnenbild: Helmut Jürgens   Chöre: Herbert Erlenwein

Hans Sachs, Schuster		Hans Hotter
Veit Pogner, Goldschmied		Max Proebstl
Kunz Vogelgesang, Kürschner		Franz Klarwein
Konrad Nachtigall, Spengler		Karl Hoppe
Sixtus Beckmesser, Stadtschreiber		Benno Kusche
Fritz Kothner, Bäcker	Meister-	Egmont Koch
Balthasar Zorn, Zinngießer	singer	Karl Mücke
Ulrich Eißlinger, Würzkrämer		Hans Kern
Augustin Moser, Schneider		Karl Mösch
Hermann Ortel, Seifensieder		Fritz Richard Bender
Hans Schwarz, Strumpfwirker		Walter Bracht
Hans Folz, Kupferschmied		Rudolf Wünzer
Walther von Stolzing, ein Ritter aus Franken		Günther Treptow
David, Sachsen's Lehrbube		Paul Kuen
Eva, Pogners Tochter		Annelies Kupper
Magdalena, Eva's Amme		Ruth Michaelis
Ein Nachtwächter		Fritz Richard Bender

Bürger und Frauen aller Zünfte, Gesellen, Lehrbuben, Mädchen, Volk.
Nürnberg - Um die Mitte des 16. Jahrhunderts

Gesamtchor der Bayerischen Staatsoper, verstärkt durch den Aushilfs-Chor
und Mitglieder des Lehrergesangvereins

Beginn **17** Uhr   Pausen nach dem 1. und 2. Aufzug   Ende gegen **22**½ Uhr

Wagner

Der fliegende Holländer, Overture

| Munich | Bavarian RO | LP: Philips 698 005 CL |
| 1956 | | |

Götterdämmerung, Siegfried's Funeral March

| Berlin | Städtische Oper | 78: Telefunken E 3128 |
| ca. 1940 | Orchestra | |

Lohengrin

Munich	Bavarian Radio	LP: DG LPM 18 119-18 123/
1952	Orchestra & Chorus	LPM 18 084-18 088
	Kupper, H.Braun,	LP: Decca (USA) DX 131
	Fehenberger,	LP: DG 2703 001
	Frantz, Rohr	Excerpts
		LP: DG LPEM 19 107
		Act 1 Prelude
		LP: DG LPE 17 080/478 413/89 654
		Act 3 Prelude
		LP: DG 478 413/89 654
Bayreuth	Bayreuth Festival	LP: Cetra LO 77
August 1954	Orchestra & Chorus	LP: Melodram MEL 541
	Nilsson, Varnay,	CD: Laudis LCD 44015
	Windgassen,	Excerpts
	Uhde, Adam	LP: Gioielli della lirica GML 20
		CD: Memories HR 4424-4425

Lohengrin, Act 1 Prelude

Berlin	Städtische Oper	78: Telefunken E 3174
1942	Orchestra	
Berlin	BPO	78: DG LVM 36 007
June 1951		LP: Decca (USA) DL 4030
		LP: DG 478 089

Lohengrin, Act 3 Prelude

Berlin	BPO	78: Telefunken E 1425
June 1933		
Berlin	Städtische Oper	78: Telefunken E 3227
1942	Orchestra	
Berlin	BPO	45: DG EPL 32 213/EPL 30 468
June 1951		LP: Decca (USA) DL 4030

Die Meistersinger von Nürnberg

Munich December 1949	Bavarian State Orchestra & Chorus Kupper, Michaelis, Treptow, Kuen, Hotter, Pröbstl, Kusche	LP: Melodram MEL 428 Excerpts LP: Gioielli della lirica GML 37 Gioielli della lirica incorrectly labelled Bayreuth 1952, listing cast and conductor for that performance
Berlin April 1976	Deutsche Oper Orchestra & Chorus Ligendza, C.Ludwig, Domingo, Laubenthal, Fischer-Dieskau, Lagger, R.Hermann	LP: DG 2713 011/2740 149 CD: DG 415 2782 Excerpts LP: DG 2536 383/2537 041

Die Meistersinger von Nürnberg, Overture

Munich 1956	Bavarian RO	LP: Philips 698 005 CL

Die Meistersinger von Nürnberg, Act 3 Prelude

Berlin June 1933	BPO	78: Telefunken A 1658
Munich 1956	Bavarian RO	LP: Philips 698 005 CL

Parsifal: Excerpts (1. Titurel, der fromme Held; 2. Ich sah das Kind; 3. Wehe! Was tat ich...to end Act 2)

Munich November 1957	Bavarian State Orchestra Schech, Aldenhoff, Frantz	LP: Melodram MEL 091 (1) LP: Melodram MEL 086 (2) LP: Melodram MEL 418 (3)

Parsifal, Prelude

Berlin 1942	Städtische Oper Orchestra	78: Telefunken E 3226-3227
Munich December 1957	Bavarian RO	LP: DG LPE 17 140 LP: DG LPM 18 500-18 501/ SLPM 138 004-138 005 LP: DG 136 479/2726 054/2548 221

Prelude, Good Friday Music

Amsterdam June 1943	Concertgebouw Orchestra	78: Telefunken SK 3712-3713
Munich December 1957	Bavarian RO	LP: DG LPE 17 140 LP: DG LPM 18 500-18 501/ SLPM 138 004-138 005 LP: DG 136 479/2726 054/2548 221

Tannhäuser, Overture

Berlin June 1933	BPO	78: Telefunken E 1424-1425 CD: Teldec 9031 764442
Munich 1956	Bavarian RO	LP: Philips 698 005 CL

Tristan und Isolde

Bayreuth July 1953	Bayreuth Festival Orchestra & Chorus Varnay, Malaniuk, Vinay, Weber, Neidlinger	LP: Melodram MEL 535 CD: Hunt CDLSMH 34030 Also issued on LP by Documents

Tristan und Isolde, Prelude and Liebestod

Berlin 1938	BPO	78: Telefunken E 2715-2716
Munich 1956	Bavarian RO	LP: Philips 698 005 CL

Weber

Abu Hassan, Overture

Berlin 1942	Städtische Oper Orchestra	78: Telefunken E 3153

Euryanthe, Overture

Berlin 1942	Städtische Oper Orchestra	78: Telefunken E 3152-3153

Der Freischütz

Munich December 1959	Bavarian Radio Orchestra & Chorus Seefried, Streich, Holm, Böhme, Wächter, Kreppel	LP: DG 18 639-18 640/ SLPM 138 639-138 640 LP: DG 2707 009/2726 061 Excerpts LP: DG LPEM 19 221/SLPM 136 221 LP: DG LPEM 19 477/136 477 LP: DG 2535 280/2535 746/2536 486 LP: DG 2548 212/410 8471 CD: DG 423 8692/437 6772

Der Freischütz, Overture

Berlin June 1933	BPO	78: Telefunken E 1493

Oberon, Overture

Berlin 1942	Städtische Oper Orchestra	78: Telefunken E 3142
Berlin June 1951	BPO	78: DG LV 36 002 LP: Decca (USA) DL 4006 LP: DG LPEM 19 037/478 120

Miscellaneous

Erzähltes Leben

Eugen Jochum talks about his life and career, with musical examples	LP: DG LPM 18 734

A personal reminiscence of Eugen Jochum: Jim Parsons

Although Eugen Jochum had introduced me to the symphonies of Bruckner at the Edinburgh Festival in 1957 when he performed the Seventh with his Bavarian Radio Symphony Orchestra, our friendship really took off following a rehearsal and concert (Bruckner Fifth with the Swiss Festival Orchestra) on 23 August 1969, which we attended with Elisabeth Furtwängler and were introduced to Maria, Eugen's wife.

As a result of this meeting, Vera Harrey and I were invited to spend a week in the autumn of the following year in the Rhineland area, travelling from Wuppertal to Ludwigshafen and on most evenings listening to Jochum and the Vienna Symphony Orchestra performing Bruckner's Fourth after either Schubert's Eighth or Beethoven's Second. The conviviality and joint celebrations on the last Sunday, 1 November, when Vera and Eugen revealed that it was their birthday, was tempered by the news that his brother, Georg Ludwig Jochum, the conductor on the Saga set of Bruckner's Second in the early days of LP, had died. The final concert included a deeply-moving interpretation of the Fourth Symphony.

That year also saw Jochum's only appearance at the London Proms, when he performed Beethoven's "Missa Solemnis". It was on that occasion, in an Italian restaurant in Knightsbridge, that Jochum spoke of his association with Furtwängler and how the latter had taught him to ski in return for his teaching Furtwängler to drive a car ! On the way back to the hotel, we walked through Hyde Park and he revealed his own "Desert Island Discs", headed by his personal favourite, the Bach Mass in B minor, a work he hoped one day he might record (he achieved his wish when EMI released the album in 1982).

Further invitations followed, to Bayreuth in 1971 for "Parsifal", but our personal highlight was Jochum's visit to Birmingham in September 1974 with the LSO, after which Vera and I took Maria and Eugen to the Midland Hotel for what proved to be a really first-class meal. It was after 11pm and we were the only ones left in the restaurant apart from a pianist, who was playing classical selections. Eugen turned to me and whispered "How much do we have to pay the pianist to get him to go home ?"

The next day we took them to Oxford, where they were to stay before returning to London for further concerts. As we went through Wootten Wawen, Eugen expressed a desire to visit the church and for over 20 minutes extemporised on the organ to the delight of the vicar, who persuaded him to sign the visitors' book, and to the delight of the ladies who had volunteered to decorate the church for the harvest festival to be held on the morrow. On we went to the Shakespeare Hotel in Stratford for coffee. The head porter, who recognised Jochum as he had been at the Birmingham concert, showed us round the hotel, and Eugen caused amusement when he enquired why there were three beds in the Romeo and Juliet room..... "presumably for the nurse to act as chaperon !" he commented. A visit to the parish church and a short tour backstage at the Memorial Theatre were followed by lunch in Burford (more Musak... this time Tchaikovsky's "Pathétique" !) and eventually Oxford.

Ferenc Fricsay
1914-1963

Discography compiled by John Hunt

Bartok

Concerto for orchestra

Berlin April 1957	Berlin RO	LP: DG LPM 18 377/2535 701 CD: DG 427 4102

Music for strings, percussion and celesta

Berlin June 1953	Berlin RO	LP: DG LP 16 074/LPM 18 493 LP: DG 2535 702 CD: DG 437 6752

Dance Suite

Berlin June 1953	Berlin RO	LP: DG LPM 18 153 LP: DG 2535 705

Divertimento

Berlin April 1953	Berlin RO	LP: DG LP 18 153/2535 702 CD: DG 437 6752

2 Portraits

Berlin June 1952	Berlin RO	LP: DG LP 16 054/LPM 18 493 LP: DG 2535 705 CD: DG 437 6752

Piano Concerto No 1

Berlin October 1960	Berlin RO Anda	LP: DG LPM 18 708/SLPM 138 708 LP: DG 2726 005 CD: DG 427 4102

Piano Concerto No 2

Vienna May 1955	VSO Sandor	CD: Orfeo C 276 921B
Lucerne August 1956	Swiss Festival Orchestra Anda	CD: Relief CR 1883
Berlin September 1959	Berlin RO Anda	LP: DG LPM 18 611/SLPM 136 111 LP: DG 2726 005 CD: DG 427 4102

Piano Concerto No 3

Berlin January 1950	Berlin RO Kentner	LP: Longanesi periodici GCL 59
Berlin April 1954	Berlin RO Haas	LP: DG LPM 18 223/89 738
Berlin September 1959	Berlin RO Anda	LP: DG LPM 18 611/SLPM 138 111 LP: DG 2726 005 CD: DG 427 4102
Munich November 1960	Bavarian RO A.Fischer	CD: Orfeo C 200 891A

Rhapsody for piano and orchestra

Berlin October 1960	Berlin RO Anda	LP: DG LPM 18 708/SLPM 138 708 LP: DG 2726 005 CD: DG 427 4102

Violin Concerto No 2

Berlin January 1951	BPO Varga	78: DG LVM 72075-72077 LP: DG LPM 18 006 LP: DG 2535 704
Berlin September 1951	Berlin RO Varga	LP: Longanesi periodici GCL 59

Bluebeard's Castle

Stockholm February 1953	Stockholm RO Nilsson, Sönnerstedt Sung in German	LP: Swedish Radio SRLP 1377
Berlin October 1958	Berlin RO Töpper, Fischer-Dieskau Sung in German	LP: DG LPM 18 565/SLPM 138 030 LP: DG 2535 703

Beethoven

Symphony No 1

Berlin January 1953	BPO	LP: DG LPM 18 100/89 613 LP: DG 2548 143/2730 015 2nd movement 45: DG EPL 30 306

Symphony No 3 "Eroica"

Berlin October 1958	BPO	LP: DG LPM 18 576/SLPM 138 038 LP: DG 2548 088/2730 015

Symphony No 5

Berlin September 1961	BPO	LP: DG LPM 18 813/SLPM 138 813 LP: DG 2548 028/2730 015

Symphony No 7

Berlin October 1960	BPO	LP: DG LPM 18 757/SLPM 138 757 LP: DG 89864/2548 107/2730 015

Symphony No 8

Berlin April 1953	BPO	LP: DG LPM 18 100/89 613 LP: DG 2548 143/2730 015

Symphony No 9 "Choral"

Berlin December 1957 and January 1958	BPO St Hedwig's Choir Seefried, Forrester, Häfliger, Fischer-Dieskau	LP: DG LPM 18 512-18 513/ SLPM 138 002-138 003 LP: DG 2700 108/89 727-89 728 LP: DG 2730 015/2535 203

Piano Concerto No 3

Munich December 1957	Bavarian State Orchestra A.Fischer	LP: DG LPM 18 607/SLPM 138 087 LP: DG 89 513/2548 238

Triple Concerto

Berlin May and June 1960	Berlin RO Anda, Schneiderhan, Fournier	LP: DG LPEM 19 236/SLPEM 136 236 LP: DG 2535 153/2721 128/2726 008 CD: DG 429 9342

Egmont, Overture

Berlin September 1958	BPO	LP: DG LPM 18 512-18 513/ SLPM 138 002-138 003 LP: DG LPEM 19 226/SLPEM 136 226 LP: DG LPE 17 168/89 727-89 728 LP: DG 2700 108/135 003

Fidelio

Munich May, June and July 1957	Bavarian State Orchestra & Chorus Rysanek, Seefried, Häfliger, Lenz, Frick, Engen, Fischer-Dieskau	LP: DG LPM 18 390-18 391/ SLPM 138 390-138 391 LP: DG 2726 088/2727 006 CD: DG 437 3452 Excerpts 45: DG EPL 30 408/SEPL 30 408 LP: DG LPEM 19 215/SLPEM 136 215 LP: DG LPE 17 168/135 018/135 113 LP: DG LPEM 19 477-SLPEM 136 477 LP: DG 2535 298/2535 631 LP: DG 2535 746/2548 118 CD: IMP IMPX 9021 CD: DG 437 6772 DG's first stereo recording

Leonore No 3, Overture

Berlin September 1958	BPO	LP: DG LPM 18 512-18 513/ SLPM 138 002-138 003 LP: DG 2700 108/89 727-89 728 CD: DG 437 3452

Berlioz

Le Carnaval romain, Overture

Paris	Lamoureux	45: DG NL 32 038
March 1952	Orchestra	LP: DG LPEM 19 061/2535 738

La Damnation de Faust: Excerpt (Danse des sylphes)

Berlin	Berlin RO	78: DG LVM 72 297
March 1952		LP: DG LPEM 19 061/2535 738

La Damnation de Faust: Excerpt (Marche hongroise)

Berlin	BPO	78: DG LVM 72 297
July 1950		45: DG EPL 30 005/NL 32 305
		LP: DG LPEM 19 061
		LP: DG 2548 064/2535 738
Berlin	Berlin RO	LP: DG 135 015/135 017/2535 631
October 1961		Fricsay's final recording

Bizet

Carmen: Excerpts

Munich	Bavarian State	LP: DG LPEM 19153/LPEM 19191
January 1958	Orchestra & Chorus	LP: DG SLPEM 136 032/2535 297
	Dominguez, Stader,	
	Simandi, Metternich	
	Sung in German	

Carmen: Excerpt (Votre toast)

Berlin	Berlin RO	LP: DG LPE 17 095
January 1957	Metternich	CD: Preiser 90125
	Sung in German	
Berlin	Berlin RO	LP: DG LPM 18 700/SLPM 138 700
January 1961	Fischer-Dieskau	

Carmen, Suite and Ballet music

Berlin	Berlin RO	LP: DG LPE 17 092/2535 738
September 1956		

Les Pêcheurs de perles: Excerpt (L'orage s'est calmé...O Nadir)

Berlin	Berlin RO	LP: DG LPM 28 700/SLPM 138 700
January 1961	Fischer-Dieskau	

Blacher

Paganini Variations

Berlin	Berlin RO	45: DG NH 56 001
October 1950		LP: DG LP 16 054/LPM 18 494

Borodin

Polovtsian Dances

Berlin	Berlin RO	78: DG LVM 72 056
April 1950		45: DG EPL 30 440
		LP: DG LP 16 006/LPE 17 071
		LP: DG 2535 727

In the Steppes of Central Asia

Berlin	Berlin RO	78: DG LVM 72 297
March 1952		LP: DG LPEM 19 061
		LP: DG 2535 727/2548 064

Brahms

Piano Concerto No 1

Berlin
April 1953

Berlin RO
Hansen

LP: Longanesi periodici GCL 50

Piano Concerto No 2

Berlin
May 1960

BPO
Anda

LP: DG LPM 18 683/SLPM 138 683

Double Concerto

Berlin
June 1961

Berlin RO
Schneiderhan,
Starker

LP: DG LPE 17 237/SLPE 133 237
LP: DG SLPEM 139 126
LP: DG 2535 140/2726 008
CD: DG 429 9342

Haydn Variations

Berlin
September 1957

Berlin RO

LP: DG LPM 18 458

Alto Rhapsody

Berlin
September 1957

Berlin RO
RIAS Choir
Forrester

LP: DG LPE 17 199

Bruch

Violin Concerto No 1

Berlin
October 1958

Berlin RO
Morini

LP: DG 2548 170

Debussy

Prélude à l'après-midi d'un faune

| Berlin
January 1953 | Berlin RO | LP: DG 2535 725 |

Danse sacré et danse profane

| Berlin
January 1957 | Berlin RO
Zabaleta | LP: DG LPE 17 115
LP: DG 2535 725 |

Dukas

L'apprenti sorcier

| Paris
March 1952 | Lamoureux
Orchestra | 78: DG LV 36 027
45: DG EPL 30 281
LP: DG LPEM 19 061/2535 738 |

Dvorak

Symphony No 9 "New World"

| Berlin
September 1953 | Berlin RO | LP: DG LPM 18 142
2nd movement
LP: DG LPE 17 087 |

| Berlin
October 1959 | BPO | LP: DG LPM 18 627/SLPM 138 127
LP: DG 135 053/2535 141/2721 172
CD: DG 423 3842
CD: Belart/Karussel 450 0332 |

Violin Concerto

| Berlin
June 1953 | Berlin RO
Martzy | LP: DG LPM 18 152
LP: DG 478 428/2535 729 |

Egk

Französische Suite

Berlin September 1955	Berlin RO	LP: DG LPM 18 401

Kleine Abraxas Suite

Berlin September 1949	Berlin RO	78: DG LVM 72 050 45: DG EPL 30 228

Einem

Dantons Tod

Salzburg August 1947	VPO Vienna Opera Chorus Cebotari, Patzak, Weber, Hann, Schöffler	LP: Ed Smith ANNA 1056 CD: Stradivarius STR 10067 World premiere performance

Piano Concerto

Berlin February 1961	Berlin RO Herzog	LP: DG LPM 18 759/SLPM 138 759

Ballade for orchestra

Berlin September 1961	Berlin RO	LP: DG LPM 18 828/SLPM 138 828

Capriccio

Berlin March 1952	Berlin RO	45: DG NL 32 041 LP: DG LPM 18 494

Falla

Nights in the Gardens of Spain

Berlin April 1957	Berlin RO M.Weber	LP: DG LPEM 19 098 LP: DG 2535 722

Fortner

Finale (Symphony 1947)

Berlin December 1949	Berlin RO	78: DG LM 68 418 45: DG NL 32 140

Francaix

Concertino for piano and orchestra

Berlin September 1956	Berlin RO M.Weber	LP: DG LPM 18 338

Franck

Variations symphoniques

Berlin June 1957	Berlin RO M.Weber	LP: DG LPEM 19 098 LP: DG 2535 722

Fricsay

Merei March

Budapest ca. 1937	Instrumental ensemble	78: details uncertain Other marches not composed by Fricsay may also have been recorded at this time

Giordano

Andrea Chenier: Excerpt (Nemico della patria)

Berlin April 1961	Berlin RO Fischer-Dieskau	LP: DG LPM 19 700/SLPM 138 700

Glazunov

Violin Concerto

Berlin October 1958	Berlin RO Morini	LP: DG 2548 170

Glière

Symphony No 3 "Ilya Mourumetz"

Berlin September 1955	Berlin RO	LP: DG LPM 18 311 LP: DG 2535 726

Gluck

Orfeo ed Euridice

Berlin September 1956	Berlin RO RIAS Choir Stader, Streich, Fischer-Dieskau Sung in German	LP: DG LPM 18 343-18 344/ LPM 18 345-18 346 LP: DG 2700 103 Excerpts 45: DG EPL 30405/EPL 30444 45: DG EPL 30650 LP: DG LPEM 19 411

Gounod

Faust, Ballet music and Waltz

Berlin February 1961	Berlin RO	LP: DG LPEM 19 211/SLPEM 136 211 LP: DG 2535 603/2535 638/2563 482 Waltz only LP: DG 135 009/135 015 LP: DG 136 375/2705 006

Faust: Excerpt (Avant de quitter ces lieux)

Berlin April 1961	Berlin RO Fischer-Dieskau	LP: DG LPM 18 700/SLPM 138 700

Handel

Harp Concerto in B flat op 4 no 6

Berlin	Berlin RO	45: DG EPA 37 188
January 1957	Zabaleta	LP: DG LPE 17 115

Hartmann

Symphony No 6

Berlin	Berlin RO	LP: DG LPE 17 246
September 1955		

Adagio appassionato (Symphony for strings)

Berlin	Berlin RO	78: DG LM 68 417
December 1949		45: DG NL 32 140

Haydn

Symphony No 44 "Trauer"

Berlin June 1953	Berlin RO	LP: DG LPM 18 180 LP: DG 89 516/2535 714

Symphony No 48 "Maria Theresa"

Berlin August and September 1951	Berlin RO	LP: DG 2535 714

Symphony No 95

Berlin September 1953	Berlin RO	LP: DG LPM 18 180 LP: DG 2535 715

Symphony No 98

Berlin September 1954	Berlin RO	LP: DG LP 16 124/LPM 18 339 LP: DG 2548 111/2535 715

Symphony No 100 "Military"

Berlin May 1954	Berlin RO	LP: DG 2535 716 LP: Movimento musica 01.048

Symphony No 101 "Clock"

Berlin September 1951	Berlin RO	LP: DG LP 16 013.LPM 28 339 LP: DG 89 516/2548 111/2535 716 LP: Movimento musica 01.048

Die Jahreszeiten

Berlin January 1952	Berlin RO RIAS Choir St Hedwig's Choir Trötschel, W.Ludwig, Greindl	LP: DG LPM 18 486-18 488/ LPM 18 025/18 028
Berlin November 1961	Berlin RO St Hedwig's Choir Stader, Häfliger, Greindl	LP: DG 2721 170

Te Deum

Berlin September and October 1961	Berlin RO RIAS & NDR Choirs	LP: DG LPEM 19 398/ SLPEM 136 398 LP: DG 135 030/2535 712

Hindemith

Symphonic Dances

Berlin   Berlin RO   DG unpublished
October 1950

Honegger

Concertino for piano and orchestra

Berlin   Berlin RO   LP: DG LPM 18 338
June 1955   M.Weber

Hubay

Csardas Scene for violin and orchestra

Berlin   Berlin RO   78: DG LVM 72 489
1954   Zacharias   45: DG EPL 30 089
                                        LP: DG LPE 17 071

A 1942 Budapest Radio recording of Fricsay conducting this piece also exists

Kodaly

Dances of Galanta

Berlin	Berlin RO	45: DG EPL 30 443
September 1953		LP: DG LPE 17 060/2535 706

Dances of Marossek

Berlin	Berlin RO	LP: DG 17 060
September 1954		LP: DG 2535 706

Hary Janos, Suite

Berlin	Berlin RO	LP: DG LPM 18 223
September 1954		LP: DG 2535 706
Berlin	Berlin RO	LP: DG LPM 18 828/SLPM 138 828
November 1961		

Psalmus Hungaricus

Berlin	Berlin RO	LP: DG LPM 18 203/18 204
October 1954	RIAS Choir	LP: DG LPEM 19 073/2535 707
	Häfliger	

Leoncavallo

I Pagliacci: Excerpt (Prologue)

Berlin	Berlin RO	LP: DG LPM 17 700/
April 1961	Fischer-Dieskau	SLPM 138 700

ROYAL FESTIVAL HALL
General Manager: T. E. Bean, C.B.E.

HAROLD HOLT LTD.
Managing Director: Ian Hunter

announce

YEHUDI MENUHIN

with

BERLIN RADIO SYMPHONY ORCHESTRA

conductor
FERENC FRICSAY

Dances of Galanta	Kodaly
Violin Concerto	Tchaikovsky
Symphony No. 3 (Eroica)	Beethoven

Wednesday, 10th May, 1961 at 8 p.m.

TICKETS: (now available): 30/-, 21/-, 15/- 12/6, 10/-, 7/6

From: Royal Festival Hall, WAT 3191
Ibbs and Tillett Ltd., 124 Wigmore Street, W.1.
WEL 8418 and usual agents

Liebermann

Furioso for orchestra

Berlin May 1954	Berlin RO	45: DG EPL 30 113

Suite on Swiss folksongs

Berlin June 1955	Berlin RO	45: DG EPL 30 113

Liszt

Les Préludes

Berlin
September 1959
	Berlin RO	LP: DG LPE 17 219/SLPE 133 219
		LP: DG LPEM 19 226/
		    SLPEM 136 226
		LP: DG LPM 18 647-18 648/
		    SLPM 138 647-138 648
		LP: DG 135 138/2535 628
		CD: DG 423 3842

Hungarian Rhapsodies Nos 1 and 2

Berlin September 1954	Berlin RO	LP: DG LPE 17 055

Mahler

Rückert-Lieder

Berlin September 1958	Berlin RO Forrester	LP: DG LPE 17199

Martin

Petite symphonie concertante

Berlin April 1950	Berlin RO Herzog, Kind, Helmis	78: DG LVM 72 064-72 065 LP: DG LPM 18 035/LPM 18 494

Mendelssohn

Violin Concerto

Berlin	Berlin RO	LP: DG LPE 17 085
September 1956	Schneiderhan	LP: DG LPEM 19 124/2548 170
		CD: Amadeo 423 3452/431 3432

Ein Sommernachtstraum, Incidental music

Berlin	Berlin RO	78: DG LVM 72 013-72 016
June and	RIAS Choir	LP: DG LPM 18 001/89 629/478 032
July 1950	Streich, Eustrati	LP: DG 2548 201/2535 736
		Excerpts
		45: DG EPL 30 001

Mozart

Symphony No 29

Berlin September and October 1955	Berlin RO	LP: DG LPE 17 187/LPM 18 296 LP: DG LPM 18 554-18 555/2535 708
Vienna March 1961	VSO	LP: DG LPM 18 709/SLPM 138 709 LP: DG 2535 130/2726 003

Symphony No 35 "Haffner"

Berlin September 1952	Berlin RO	LP: DG LPM 18 066/89 677 LP: DG 478 415/2535 709 CD: Theorema TH 121.138 2nd movement 45: DG EPL 30 306

Symphony No 39

Vienna November and December 1959	VSO	LP: DG LPM 18 625/SLPM 138 125 LP: DG 2535 130/2726 003

Symphony No 40

Vienna November and December 1959	VSO	LP: DG LPM 18 625/SLPM 138 125 LP: DG 135 143/2726 003 LP: DG 2535 114/2535 710 CD: Belart/Karussel 450 0342 CD: Theorema TH 121.138 Theorema issue incorrectly labelled VPO

Symphony No 41 "Jupiter"

Berlin September 1953	Berlin RO	LP: DG LP 16 038/LPM 18 296 LP: DG LPM 18 554-18 555 LP: DG 89 677/2535 709 CD: Theorema TH 121.138
Vienna March 1961	VSO	LP: DG LPM 18 709/SLPM 138 709 LP: DG 135 143/2535 114/2726 003 CD: Belart/Karussel 450 0342

Piano Concerto No 19

Berlin January 1953	Berlin RO Haskil	LP: Rococo 2086 LP: Longanesi periodici GCL 36
Berlin September 1955	BPO Haskil	LP: DG LPM 18 383 LP: DG LPM 18 554-18 555 LP: DG 2548 209 CD: DG 431 8722

Piano Concerto No 20

Berlin January 1954	Berlin RO Haskil	LP: DG 2535 708 CD: Myto MCD 92361 CD: DG 437 6762

Piano Concerto No 27

Munich September 1957	Bavarian State Orchestra Haskil	LP: DG LPM 18 383/2548 209 CD: DG 431 8722

Concert Rondos K382 and K386

Munich September 1959	Bavarian State Orchestra A.Fischer	LP: DG LPM 18 607/SLPM 138 087 LP: DG 89 513/135 059/2548 238

Clarinet Concerto

Berlin September 1957	Berlin RO Geuser	LP: DG LPEM 19 130/89 593 LP: DG 2535 711

Flute and Harp Concerto

Berlin March 1952	Berlin RO Schmitz, Helmis	LP: Longanesi periodici GCL 53

Adagio and Fugue in C minor

Berlin January 1960	Berlin RO	45: DG EPL 30 552 LP: DG LPEM 19 398/SLPEM 136 398 LP: DG 135 135/2535 712

Maurerische Trauermusik

Berlin January 1960	Berlin RO	45: DG EPL 30 552 LP: DG LPEM 19 398/SLPEM 136 398 LP: DG 2535 712 CD: DG 429 1612

Eine kleine Nachtmusik

Berlin April 1958	BPO	45: DG EPL 30 430 LP: DG LPEM 19 226/SLPEM 136 226 LP: DG 135 042/121 027 LP: DG 2535 710/2705 004 CD: Belart/Karussel 450 0632

Serenata notturna

Berlin February 1951	Berlin RO	CD: Myto MCD 92361

Wind Serenade K375

Berlin September 1952	Berlin RSO members	LP: Longanesi periodici GCL 63

Mass in C minor

Berlin September and October 1959	Berlin RO St Hedwig's Choir Stader, Töpper, Häfliger, Sardi	LP: DG LPM 18 624/SLPM 138 124 LP: DG LPEM 19 291/SLPEM 136 291 CD: DG 429 1612 Excerpts LP: DG 2535 158/2535 654/2563 632

Requiem

Berlin March 1951	Berlin RO RIAS Choir St Hedwig's Choir Grümmer, Pitzinger, Krebs, Hotter	LP: DG 2535 713

Vesperae solennes de confessore: Excerpt (Laudate dominum)

Berlin April 1960	Berlin RO Stader	LP: DG LPEM 19 291/SLPEM 136 291 LP: DG 2535 712

Exsultate jubilate

Berlin January 1954	Berlin RO Stader	78: DG LVM 72 473 45: DG EPL 30 082 LP: DG LPE 17 027 LP: DG LPM 18 554-18 555/89 539
Berlin June 1960	Berlin RO Stader	45: DG EPL 30 595 LP: DG LPEM 19 291/SLPEM 136 291 LP: DG 136 511/2705 005/2535 712 CD: DG 435 1422

Don Giovanni

Berlin September 1958	Berlin RO RIAS Choir Jurinac, Stader, Seefried, Häfliger, Fischer-Dieskau, Kohn, Kreppel	LP: DG LPM 18 580-18 502/ SLPM 138 050-138 052 LP: DG 2728 003/2730 014 CD: DG 437 3412 Excerpts LP: DG LPEM 19 224/SLPEM 136 204 LP: DG LPEM 19 477/SLPEM 136 477 LP: DG 135 040/2535 746/410 8471 CD: DG 437 6772

Don Giovanni: Excerpts (Don Ottavio, son morta...Or sai che l'onore; Calmatevi idol mio....Non mir dir)

Berlin August 1961	Deutsche Oper Orchestra Grümmer, Grobe Sung in German	LP: Melodram MEL 083

Don Giovanni: Excerpts (Batti batti; Vedrai carino)

Berlin January 1957	Berlin RO Stader Sung in German	45: DG EPL 30266 LP: DG 89 539

Die Entführung aus dem Serail

Berlin December 1949	Berlin RO RIAS Choir Barabas, Streich, Dermota, Krebs, Greindl	LP: Movimento musica 02.007 CD: Myto MCD 92361 Excerpts LP: Gioielli della lirica GML 62
Berlin May 1954	Berlin RO RIAS Choir Stader, Streich, Häfliger, Vantin, Greindl	LP: DG LPM 18 197-18 198/ LPM 18 184-18 185 LP: DG 2700 010/2730 014 LP: DG 89 756-89 757 Excerpts LP: DG LPE 17 027/LPE 17 113/89 539 LP: DG LPEM 19 409/413 8241 CD: DG 431 8752

Die Entführung aus dem Serail: Excerpt (Ich baue ganz)

Berlin May 1954	Berlin RO Häfliger	DG unpublished Recorded as part of the above complete recording of the opera, but omitted from published editions

Idomeneo

Salzburg July 1961	VPO Vienna Opera Chorus Lorengar, Grümmer, Kmennt, Häfliger, Capecchi, Wächter	LP: Melodram MEL 701

Le Nozze di Figaro

Berlin Berlin RO LP: DG LPM 18 697-18 699/
September 1960 RIAS Choir SLPM 138 697-138 699
 Stader, Seefried, LP: DG 2728 004/2730 014
 Töpper, Capecchi, CD: DG 437 6712
 Fischer-Dieskau Excerpts
  LP: DG LPEM 19 272/SLPEM 136 272
  LP: DG LPEM 19 477/SLPEM 136 477
  LP: DG 135 040/2535 710
  LP: DG 2535 746/410 8471
  CD: DG 437 6772

Le Nozze di Figaro: Excerpts (1. Che soave zeffiretti; 2. Crudel perchè finora ?)

Cologne WDR Orchestra LP: Melodram MEL 083 (1)
May 1951 Güden (1,2), LP: Melodram MEL 084 (2)
 Grümmer (1),
 Schöffler (2)
 Sung in German

Le Nozze di Figaro: Excerpt (Deh vieni non tardar)

Berlin Berlin RO 45: DG EPL 30 266
January 1957 Stader LP: DG 89 539
 Sung in German

Die Zauberflöte

Berlin Berlin RO LP: DG LPM 18 264-18 266/
June 1955 RIAS Choir LPM 18 267-18 269
 Stader, Streich, LP: 2701 003/2728 009
 Otto, Häfliger, LP: DG 2730 014/89 662-89 664
 Fischer-Dieskau, CD: DG 435 7412
 Greindl, Borg Excerpts
  LP: DG LPM 18 554-18 555
  LP: DG LPE 17 074/LPEM 19 194
  LP: DG 89 539/89 653/413 8241
  CD: DG 431 8752

Mussorgsky

Night on Bare Mountain

Berlin March 1952	Berlin RO	LP: DG LPEM 19 061 LP: DG 2548 064/2535 727

Orff

Antigonae

Salzburg August 1949	VPO Vienna Opera Chorus Zadek, R.Fischer, Ilosvay, Krebs, Fehenberger, Häfliger, Uhde, Kusche, Greindl	CD: Stradivarius STR 10060

Ponchielli

La Gioconda, Dance of the Hours

Berlin January and February 1960	Berlin RO	LP: DG LPEM 19 211/SLPEM 136 211 LP: DG LPEM 19 399/SLPEM 136 399 LP: DG 135 008/2535 638/2705 006 Part only LP: DG 2563 649/2721 073

Prokofiev

Symphony No 1 "Classical"

Berlin January 1954	Berlin RO	78: DG LVM 72 457 45: DG EPL 30 212 LP: DG LPE 17 042/LPM 18 336 LP: DG 89 624/2548 033

Puccini

La Bohème: Excerpt (Che gelida manina)

Berlin January 1957	Berlin RO Kozub	45: DG EPL 30 269

Tosca: Excerpt (Recondita armonia)

Berlin January 1957	Berlin RO Kozub	45: DG EPL 30 269

Rachmaninov

Variations on a theme of Paganini

Berlin	Berlin RO	LP: DG LPM 18 710/SLPM 138 710
June 1960	M.Weber	LP: DG 2535 728

Ravel

Bolero

Berlin	Berlin RO	45: DG EPL 30 448
April 1953		LP: DG LPE 17 042/LPM 18 336
		LP: DG 2548 003/2548 064
		LP: DG 89 624/2535 725

Introduction and Allegro

Berlin	Berlin RO	LP: DG LPE 17 135/2535 704
January 1957	Zabaleta	

La valse

Berlin	Berlin RO	LP: DG 2535 725

Rimsky-Korsakov

Scheherazade

Berlin	Berlin RO	LP: DG LPEM 19 075/89 618
September 1956		LP: DG 2535 730

Rosenberg

Marionetter, Overture

Stockholm	Stockholm	LP: Orfeus 1-73
November 1955	Philharmonic	LP: Bis BISLP 331-333

Rossini

La Boutique fantasque (arr. Respighi)

Berlin February 1955	Berlin RO	LP: DG LPE 17 054

Il Barbiere di Siviglia, Overture

Berlin Berlin RO 78: DG LVM 72 490
January 1954   45: DG EPL 30 090
                LP: DG 2535 717

Il Barbiere di Siviglia: Excerpt (Largo al factotum)

Berlin   Berlin RO   LP: DG LPE 17 095/88 025
January 1957 Metternich   CD: Preiser 90125
             Sung in German

La Gazza ladra, Overture

Berlin   Berlin RO   78: DG LV 36 080
January 1953   45: DG EPL 32 226
                         LP: DG LPEM 19 041/LPE 17 076
                         LP: DG 2548 127/2535 717

L'Italiana in Algeri, Overture

Berlin   BPO   78: DG LVM 72 061
September 1949   45: DG EPL 30 064
                        LP: DG LPEM 19 041
                        LP: DG 2548 127/2535 717

La Scala di seta, Overture

Berlin   BPO   78: DG LVM 72 061
January 1950   45: DG EPL 30 064
                    LP: DG LPEM 19 041
                    LP: DG 2548 127/2535 717

Semiramide, Overture

Berlin September 1951	Berlin RO	LP: DG LPE 17 076/LPEM 19 041 LP: DG 2548 127/2535 717

Semiramide: Excerpt (Bell raggio lusinghier)

Berlin September 1952	Berlin RO Streich	45: DG EPL 30 225

Il Signor bruschino, Overture

Berlin September 1951	Berlin RO	78: DG LV 36 049 45: DG EPL 30 270 LP: DG LPEM 19 041 LP: DG 2548 127/2535 717

Tancredi, Overture

Berlin September 1952	Berlin RO	78: DG LV 36 049 45: DG EPL 30 270 LP: DG LPEM 19 041 LP: DG 2548 127/2535 717

Il Viaggio a Reims, Overture

Berlin October 1954	Berlin RO	78: DG LVM 72 490 45: DG EPL 20 090 LP: DG 2535 717

William Tell: Excerpt (Reste immobile)

Berlin April 1961	Berlin RO Fischer-Dieskau Sung in Italian	LP: DG LPM 18 700/SLPM 138 700

Stabat mater

Cologne March 1953	WDR Orchestra and Chorus Grümmer, Ilosvay, W.Ludwig, Fehn	CD: Melodram CDM 16523
Berlin September 1954	Berlin RO RIAS Choir Stader, Radev, Häfliger, Borg	LP: DG LPM 18 203-18 204 LP: DG LPM 18 340/89 610 LP: DG 2548 126/2535 718

ROYAL FESTIVAL HALL

General Manager: T. E. Bean, C.B.E.

PHILHARMONIA CONCERT SOCIETY

Artistic Director: WALTER LEGGE

PHILHARMONIA ORCHESTRA

LEADER: HUGH BEAN

FERENC FRICSAY

ANNIE FISCHER

KODÁLY:	Suite, Háry János
BARTÓK:	Piano Concerto No. 3
	Interval
DVOŘÁK:	Symphony No. 5 in E minor ('From the New World')

Friday, June 9, at 8 p.m.

Sarasate

Zigeunerweisen for violin and orchestra

Berlin	Berlin RO	78: DG LVM 72 489
1954	Zacharias	45: DG EPL 30 089

Schubert

Symphony No 8 "Unfinished"

Berlin	Berlin RO	LP: DG LPE 17 158/LPM 18 458
September 1957		LP: DG 2535 735

Schumann

Symphony No 1 "Spring"

Berlin	Berlin RO	LP: DG LPM 18 235/LPEM 19 186
February 1955		LP: DG 478 141/2535 735

Piano Concerto

Berlin	Berlin RO	LP: Replica RPL 2749
May 1951	Cortot	

Smetana

The Moldau (Ma Vlast)

Berlin January 1953	BPO	78: DG LVM 72 320 45: DG EPL 30 049 LP: DG LPE 17 018/478 428/2535 728
Berlin January 1960	BPO	45: DG EPL 30 556 LP: DG LPE 17 219/SLPE 133 219 LP: DG LPEM 19 226/SLPEM 136 226 LP: DG 121 556 CD: DG 423 3842
Stuttgart June 1960	SDR Orchestra	Rehearsal and performance LP: DG LPEM 19 471 LP: DG 2721 172/004 170 Also exists in a filmed version

From Bohemia's Woods and Fields (Ma Vlast)

Berlin July 1953	BPO	45: DG 30 511 LP: DG LPE 17 018/LPEM 19 186 LP: DG 478 141/2535 729

Johann Strauss father

Radetzky March

Berlin June 1952	Berlin RO	45: DG EPL 30 005
Berlin February 1961	Berlin RO	LP: DG LPEM 19 238/SLPEM 136 238 LP: DG 135 017/2538 141 LP: DG 2535 134/2535 631 CD: DG 427 2172

Johann & Josef Strauss

Pizzicato Polka

Berlin July 1950	BPO	78: DG L 62870 45: DG NL 32 123
Berlin February 1951	Berlin RO	LP: Melodram MEL 226

Johann Strauss

An der schönen blauen Donau, Waltz

Berlin September 1949	BPO	78: DG LVM 72 052 45: DG EPL 30 073
Berlin May 1950	Berlin RO	CD: Curcio-Hunt CON 17
Berlin February 1961	Berlin RO	LP: DG LPEM 19 238/SLPEM 136 238 LP: DG 135 009/2535 134/2538 141 CD: DG 427 2172

Annen Polka

Berlin February 1951	Berlin RO	LP: Melodram MEL 226
Berlin June 1952	Berlin RO	78: DG LVM 72 335 LP: DG LPM 18 050/LPEM 19 035 LP: DG 89 562
Berlin February 1961	Berlin RO	LP: DG LPEM 19 238/SLPEM 136 238 LP: DG 2535 134/2538 141 CD: DG 427 2172

Eljen a Magyar

Berlin February 1961	Berlin RO	LP: DG LPEM 19 238/SLPEM 136 238 LP: DG 2535 134/2538 141 CD: DG 427 2172

Die Fledermaus

Berlin November 1949	Berlin RO RIAS Choir Schlemm, Streich, Anders, Krebs, Brauer	CD: Melodram MEL 29001 Excerpts LP: Melodram MEL 226

Die Fledermaus, Overture

Berlin June 1952	Berlin RO	78: DG LV 36 111 45: DG EPL 30 095 LP: DG LPM 18 050/LPEM 19 035 LP: DG 89 562
Berlin February 1961	Berlin RO	LP: DG LPEM 19 238/SLPEM 136 238 LP: DG 2535 134/2538 141 CD: DG 427 2172

Frühlingsstimmen, Waltz

Berlin June 1952	Berlin RO	78: DG LVM 72 247 45: DG EPL 30 039 LP: DG LPM 18 050/LPEM 19 035 LP: DG 89 562

Gschichten aus dem Wienerwald, Waltz

Berlin February 1951	Berlin RO RIAS Choir	LP: Melodram MEL 226
Berlin February 1961	Berlin RO	LP: DG LPEM 19 238/SLPEM 138 238 LP: DG 2535 134/2538 141/2721 073 CD: DG 427 2172

Kaiswerwalzer

Berlin February 1961	Berlin RO	LP: DG LPEM 19 238/SLPEM 136 238 LP: DG 2535 134/2535 649 LP: DG 2538 141/2653 414 CD: DG 427 2172

Morgenblätter, Waltz

Berlin September 1952	Berlin RO	78: DG LV 36 062 LP: DG LPM 18 050/LPEM 19 035 LP: DG 89 562

Eine Nacht in Venedig: Excerpt (Komm' in die Gondel)

Berlin February 1951	Berlin RO Anders	LP: Melodram MEL 226

Perpetuum mobile

Berlin September 1949	BPO	78: DG L 62 870 45: DG NL 32 123

Rosen aus dem Süden, Waltz

Berlin February 1951	Berlin RO	LP: Melodram MEL 226
Berlin June 1952	Berlin RO	78: DG LVM 72 247 45: DG 30 039 LP: DG LPM 18 050/LPEM 19 035 LP: DG 89 562

Tritsch-Tratsch Polka

Berlin June 1952	Berlin RO	78: DG LVM 72 335 45: DG EPL 30 005 LP: DG LPM 18 050/LPEM 19 035 LP: DG 89 562
Berlin February 1961	Berlin RO	LP: DG LPEM 19 238/SLPEM 136 239 LP: DG 2535 134/2538 141 CD: DG 427 2172

Wein, Weib und Gesang, Waltz

Berlin February 1951	Berlin RO RIAS Choir	LP: Melodram MEL 226

Wiener Blut, Waltz

Berlin January 1951	BPO	78: DG LVM 72 052 45: DG EPL 30 073
Berlin February 1951	Berlin RO	LP: Melodram MEL 226

Der Zigeunerbaron, Overture

Berlin February 1951	Berlin RO	LP: Melodram MEL 226
Berlin September 1952	Berlin RO	78: DG LVM 72 335 45: DG EPL 30 095

Der Zigeunerbaron: Excerpts (Als flotter Geist; So elend und treu; Wer uns getraut)

Berlin February 1951	Berlin RO Musial, Anders	LP: Melodram MEL 226

Richard Strauss

Don Juan

Berlin   Berlin RO   LP: DG 2535 724
October 1952

Till Eulenspiegels lustige Streiche

Berlin   Berlin RO   78: DG LVM 72 024
June 1950   45: DG EPL 30 067
                                             LP: DG LP 16 006/LPEM 29 078
                                             LP: DG LPEM 19 111/89 803
                                             LP: DG 2535 724

Burleske for piano and orchestra

Berlin   Berlin RO   LP: DG LPM 18 338/2535 724
September 1955   M.Weber

Stravinsky

Symphony of Psalms

Berlin	Berlin RO	LP: DG LPM 18 035/LPEM 19 073
January 1951	RIAS Choir	LP: DG 2535 707

Capriccio for piano and orchestra

Berlin	Berlin RO	78: DG LM 68 452-68 453
September 1950	Haas	LP: DG LPM 18 004/2535 722

Movements for piano and orchestra

Berlin	Berlin RO	LP: DG LPM 18 828/SLPM 138 828
September 1960	M.Weber	

Le baiser de la fée

Berlin	Berlin RO	LP: DG LPE 17 135/2535 702
September 1954		

Oedipus Rex

Berlin	Berlin RO	LP: DG 2535 723
September 1960	RIAS & NDR Choirs	
	Töpper, Häfliger,	
	Engen, Sardi	

Petrushka

Berlin	Berlin RO	LP: DG LP 16 112/LPE 17 003
April 1954		LP: DG LPEM 19111/89 803
		LP: DG 2535 720

Le sacre du printemps

Berlin	Berlin RO	LP: DG LPM 18 189/89 718
March 1954		LP: DG 2548 112/2535 721

Tchaikovsky

Symphony No 4

Berlin September 1952	Berlin RO	LP: DG LPM 18 039/89 619 LP: DG 2535 732

Symphony No 5

Berlin September 1949	BPO	78: DG LVM 72 001-72 004 LP: DG LPM 18 012/89 627 LP: DG 2535 733 <u>2nd movement</u> LP: DG LPE 17 087
Vienna May 1955	VSO	CD: Orfeo C 276 921B

Symphony No 5: rehearsal extract

Stockholm Date uncertain	Stockholm Philharmonic	CD: Bis BISCD 424A

Symphony No 6 "Pathétique"

Berlin July 1953	BPO	LP: DG LPM 18 104/89 568 LP: DG 2535 734
Munich November 1960	Bavarian RO	CD: Orfeo C 200 891A

Violin Concerto

Berlin September 1949	Berlin RO Menuhin	LP: Longanesi periodici GCL 29 CD: Movimento musica 011.007 <u>Incorrectly dated August 1949</u>

Serenade for strings

Berlin October 1952	Berlin RO	LP: DG LPE 17 036/LPM 18 336 LP: DG 89 624/89 822/2535 731 <u>Waltz only</u> LP: DG LPEM 19 116

1812 Overture

Berlin January 1953	Berlin RO RIAS Choir	78: DG LVM 72 412 45: DG EPL 30 438 LP: DG LPE 17 022/89 615/2535 727

The Nutcracker, Waltz

Berlin September 1957	Berlin RO	LP: DG LPEM 19 116/89 615

Eugene Onegin, Waltz

Berlin September 1957	Berlin RO	45: DG EPL 30 494 LP: DG LPEM 19 116
Berlin January and February 1960	Berlin RO	LP: DG LPEM 19 211/SLPEM 136 211 LP: DG 135 009/136 375 LP: DG 2535 603/2535 653

Eugene Onegin, Polonaise

Berlin January and February 1960	Berlin RO	LP: DG LPEM 19 211/SLPEM 136 211 LP: DG 2721 084

The Sleeping Beauty, Waltz

Berlin September 1957	Berlin RO	45: DG EPL 30 407 LP: DG LPEM 19 116/2535 731

Swan Lake, Suite

Berlin September 1957	Berlin RO	LP: DG LPEM 19 116/2535 731 <u>Waltz only</u> 45: DG EPL 30 407

Tcherepnin

10 Bagatelles for piano and orchestra

Berlin June 1960	Berlin RO M.Weber	LP: DG LPM 18 710/SLPM 138 710 LP: DG 89 738

Verdi

Messa da Requiem

Berlin September 1953	Berlin RO RIAS Choir St Hedwig's Choir Stader, Radev, Krebs, Borg	LP: DG LPM 18 157-18 158/ LPM 18 155-18 156
Berlin October 1960	Berlin RO St Hedwig's Choir Stader, Dominguez, Carelli, Sardi	LP: DG 2721 171 CD: DG 429 0762

4 pezzi sacri

Berlin January 1952	Berlin RO RIAS Choir St Hedwig's Choir	LP: Movimento musica 01.043 CD: DG 429 0762

Aida, Prelude

Berlin April 1953	Berlin RO	LP: DG 2535 719

Aida, Ballet music (Dance of Priestesses; Dance of Moorish Slaves; Ballabile)

Berlin January 1954	Berlin RO	LP: DG 2535 719
Berlin January and February 1960	Berlin RO	LP: DG LPEM 19 211/SLPEM 136 211 LP: DG 2535 638

Don Carlo: Excerpt (O don fatale)

Berlin January 1957	Berlin RO Töpper Sung in German	45: DG NL 32 231

Falstaff: Excerpt (Va, vecchio John)

Berlin January 1951	Berlin RO Metternich, Fischer-Dieskau Sung in German	LP: DG LPEM 19 029 CD: Preiser 90125

La Forza del destino, Overture

Berlin	Berlin RO	45: DG EPL 30 081
June 1953		LP: DG LPE 17 015/2535 719

La Forza del destino: Excerpt (Morir, fremenda cosa urna fatale)

Berlin	Berlin RO	LP: DG LPM 18 700/SLPM 138 700
April 1961	Fischer-Dieskau	

Nabucco, Overture

Berlin	Berlin RO	45: DG EPL 30 081
October 1952		LP: DG LPE 17 015/2535 719

Otello, Ballet music

Berlin	Berlin RO	LP: DG LPEM 19 211/SLPEM 136 211
January and		LP: DG 2535 638
February 1960		

La Traviata, Preludes Acts 1 and 3

Berlin	Berlin RO	78: DG LV 36 207/L 62 923
June 1953		45: DG EPL 30 494/NL 32 007
		LP: DG LPE 17 015/2535 719

La Traviata: Excerpt (Di provenza il mar)

Berlin	Berlin RO	LP: DG LPM 18 700/SLPM 138 700
April 1961	Fischer-Dieskau	

Il Trovatore: Excerpt (Stride la vampa)

Berlin	Berlin RO	45: DG NL 32 231
January 1957	Töpper	
	Sung in German	

I Vespri siciliani, Overture

Berlin	Berlin RO	78: DG LV 36 031
March 1952		LP: DG LPE 17 015/2535 719

Wagner

Der fliegende Holländer

Berlin October 1952	Berlin RO RIAS Choir Kupper, Wagner, Windgassen, Metternich, Greindl	Lp: DG LPM 18 116-18 118/ LP: LPM 18 063-18 065 LP: DG 2701 009 Excerpts 45: DG EPL 30 446 LP: DG LPE 17 022/LPEM 19 122 LP: DG LPX 29 260/478 089/89 652

Die Walküre

Berlin June 1951	Städtische Oper Orchestra Buchner, Müller, Klose, Suthaus, J.Herrmann, Greindl	CD: Myto MCD 93381

Weber

Aufforderung zum Tanz

Berlin February 1961	Berlin RO	LP: DG 136 375/199 029

Clarinet Concerto

Berlin September 1957	Berlin RO Geuser	LP: DG LPEM 19 130/2535 711

Konzertstück

Berlin October 1960	Berlin RO M.Weber	LP: DG LPM 18 710/SLPM 138 710 LP: DG 135 050

Miscellaneous

Erzähltes Leben

Ferenc Fricsay talks about his life and career, with musical examples	LP: DG LPM 18 741

Carl Schuricht
1880-1967

Discography compiled by John Hunt

Bach

Cantata choruses: No 50 "Nun ist das Heil"; No 104 "Die Hirten Israel höre"

Berlin ca. 1935	BPO Philharmonic Choir	78: Telefunken E 1709 78: Capitol ECL 8077 LP: Capitol L 8077

The 6 Brandenburg Concerti

Zürich May 1966	Zürich Baroque Ensemble	LP: Concert Hall AM 2378/SMS 2378 LP: Columbia (Japan) OW 7876-7877 CD: Denon (Japan) 30CO 1343-1344

Orchestral Suites Nos 2 and 3

Frankfurt 1961	Hessischer Rundfunkorchester	LP: Columbia (Japan) OW 7881 Probably also published by Concert Hall

Beethoven

Symphony No 1

Berlin 1941	Städtische Oper Orchestra	78: Polydor 67884-67887 CD: Philips (Japan) SGR 6001-6005
Vienna May 1952	VPO	LP: Decca LXT 2824/LXT 5362 LP: Decca LX 3084/ACL 147 CD: London (Japan) KICC 2192/2323
Paris September 1958	Paris Conservatoire Orchestra	LP: EMI XLP 20016 LP: Pathé TRI 33333-33339 LP: Electrola F669.895-669.899 CD: EMI CZS 762 9102
Paris June 1965	Orchestre National	CD: Disques Montaigne TCE 8841

Symphony No 2

Geneva February 1947	Suisse Romande Orchestra	78: Decca AK 1610-1613
Vienna May 1952	VPO	LP: Decca LXT 2724/ACL 116 CD: London (Japan) KICC 2192/2323
Berlin November 1953	Berlin RO	LP: Movimento musica 08.001
Paris September 1958	Paris Conservatoire Orchestra	LP: Pathé TRI 33333-33339 LP: Electrola F669.895-669.899 CD: EMI CZS 762 9102

Symphony No 3 "Eroica"

Berlin 1941	BPO	78: Polydor 67793-67798 LP: American Columbia ML 4503 CD: Philips (Japan) SGR 6001-6005
Paris December 1957	Paris Conservatoire Orchestra	LP: HMV ALP 1685/EMI MFP 2029 LP: Pathé TRI 33333-33339 LP: Electrola F669.895-669.899 CD: EMI CZS 762 9102
Paris May 1965	Orchestre National	CD: Disques Montaigne TCE 8841

Symphony No 4

Berlin 1942	Städtische Oper Orchestra	78: Polydor 68139-68143 CD: Philips (Japan) SGR 6001-6005
Paris September 1958	Paris Conservatoire Orchestra	LP: EMI XLP 20016 LP: Pathé TRI 33333-33339 LP: Electrola F669.895-669.899 CD: EMI CZS 762 9102

Symphony No 5

Paris June 1949	Paris Conservatoire Orchestra	78: Decca AK 2253-2256 LP: Decca LXT 2513/ACL 1 CD: London (Japan) KICC 2193/2324
Paris April 1957	Paris Conservatoire Orchestra	LP: EMI XLP 20001-20002 LP: Pathé TRI 33333-33339 LP: Electrola F669.895-669.899 CD: EMI CZS 762 9102

Symphony No 6 "Pastoral"

Berlin 1943	BPO	78: Polydor 68194-68199 CD: Philips (Japan) SGR 6001-6005
Paris June 1957	Paris Conservatoire Orchestra	LP: EMI XLP 20012 LP: Pathé TRI 33333-33339 LP: Electrola F669.895-669.895 CD: EMI CZS 762 9102

Symphony No 7

Berlin 1937	BPO	78: Polydor 67162-67166 78: Decca X 206-210 CD: Philips (Japan) SGR 6001-6005
Paris June 1957	Paris Conservatoire Orchestra	LP: HMV ALP 1707 LP: Pathé TRI 33333-33339/6145 LP: Electrola CZS 762 9103 CD: EMI CZS 762 9102
Vienna June 1957	VPO	CD: Refrain (Japan) DR 920028

Symphony No 8

Paris May 1957	Paris Conservatoire Orchestra	LP: EMI XLP 20022 LP: Pathé TRI 33333-33339 LP: Electrola F669.895-669.899 CD: EMI CZS 762 9102

Symphony No 9 "Choral"

Paris May 1958	Paris Conservatoire Orchestra Brasseur Choir Lipp, Höngen, Dickie, Frick	LP: EMI XLP 20001-20002 LP: Pathé TRI 33333-33339 LP: Electrola F669.895-669.899 CD: EMI CZS 762 9102

In "Conductors on Record" John Holmes refers to a Schuricht recording of the Ninth Symphony recorded before 1945 with Städtische Oper forces in Berlin; at time of going to press, this has been announced for issue on CD by Philips (Japan) on SGR 6006-6007/further details awaited

Missa Solemnis

Montreux September 1957	NDR Orchestra St Hedwig's Choir Stader, Cavelti, Häfliger, Rehfuss	CD: Archiphon ARCH 2.1

Piano Concerto No 3

Paris March 1959	Orchestre National Arrau	CD: Melodram MEL 27504

Coriolan, Overture

Berlin 1942	Städtische Oper Orchestra	78: Polydor 67937
London July 1948	LPO	78: Decca K 2079
Paris March 1959	Orchestre National	CD: Melodram CDM 18049
Stuttgart Date uncertain	SDR Orchestra	CD: Refrain (Japan) DR 920024

Egmont, Overture

Berlin 1942	Städtische Oper Orchestra	78: Polydor 67938

THEATRE DES CHAMPS ELYSEES
SOCIÉTÉ DES CONCERTS DU CONSERVATOIRE
2 bis, RUE DU CONSERVATOIRE
123ᵉ Année — Saison d'Automne 1951
Président : Claude DELVINCOURT
Vice-Président Chef d'Orchestre : André CLUYTENS
Secrétaire Général : André HUOT

LISA DELLA CASA - HÉLÈNE BOUVIER
PETER ANDERS - HEINZ REHFUSS
CHORALE ELISABETH BRASSEUR

Beethoven

CORIOLAN (*ouverture*)

IXᵉ SYMPHONIE

Direction :

CARL SCHURICHT

SAMEDI 8 DÉCEMBRE 1951, à 10 heures
DIMANCHE 9 DÉCEMBRE 1951, à 17 h. 45

Bizet

L'Arlésienne, Suite No 1

Berlin   BPO   78: Telefunken E 1850-1851
ca. 1935

Blacher

Concertante Musik

Stuttgart   SDR Orchestra   CD: Refrain (Japan) DR 920024
October 1951

Brahms

Symphony No 1

Geneva
December 1953
Suisse Romande Orchestra
CD: Archiphon ARCH 2.1

Frankfurt
1965
Hessisches Rundfunkorchester
CD: Melodram CDM 18045

Symphony No 2

Vienna
June 1953
VPO
LP: Decca LXT 2859/ACL 256
CD: London (Japan) KICC 2194 /2326

Stuttgart
March 1966
SDR Orchestra
Cassette: Symposium 1019
CD: Archiphon ARCH 2.5
Also issued on CD by Melodram

Symphony No 2, 2nd and 3rd movements

Lucerne
September 1962
VPO
CD: Relief CR 1883

Symphony No 3

Baden-Baden
September 1962
Südwestfunk-Orchester
LP: Musidisc FC 469
CD: Denon (Japan) 30CO 1338
Also published by Concert Hall

Munich
May 1963
Munich Philharmonic
CD: Melodram CDM 18047

Symphony No 4

Paris March 1959	Orchestre National	CD: Melodram CDM 18048
Munich September 1961	Bavarian RO	LP: Concert Hall AM 2249/SMS 2249 LP: Musidisc FC 405 LP: Columbia (Japan) OW 7314 CD: Denon (Japan) 30CO 1337 CD: Adès 13.2782

Piano Concerto No 2

Vienna May 1952	VPO Backhaus	LP: Decca LXT 2723/LXT 5365 LP: Decca (France) 592.135
Montreux September 1956	Orchestre National Casadesus	CD: Melodram CDM 18049
Lugano May 1958	Swiss Italian Radio Orchestra Backhaus	LP: Melodram MEL 202 CD: Musica classica

Violin Concerto

Vienna April 1954	VPO Ferras	LP: Decca LXT 2949/ACL 17 LP: Decca (France) 411 6721

Double Concerto

Geneva July 1947	Suisse Romande Orchestra Kulenkampff, Mainardi	78: Decca AK 2025-2028

Haydn Variations

Baden-Baden September 1962	Südwestfunk- Orchester	LP: Musidisc FC 469 CD: Denon (Japan) 30CO 1338 Also published by Concert Hall

Academic Festival Overture

Dresden 1943	Dresden Philharmonic	Issue details uncertain

Tragic Overture

Munich September 1961	Bavarian RO	LP: Concert Hall AM 2249/SMS 2249 LP: Musidisc FC 405 LP: Columbia (Japan) OW 7314 CD: Denon (Japan) 30CO 1337 CD: Adès 13.2782
London January 1965	LSO	CD: Refrain (Japan) DR 910001

Ein deutsches Requiem

Vienna April 1954	VPO Singakademie Della Casa, Rehfuss	Decca unpublished Recording incomplete
Stuttgart November 1959	SDR Orchestra and Chorus Hessischer Rundfunk Choir Stader, Prey	CD: Archiphon ARCH 2.2

Bruch

Violin Concerto No 1

Berlin 1942	Städtische Oper Orchestra Stanske	78: Polydor 67864-67866 Adagio only 78: Polydor 68065
Zürich January 1947	Tonhalle-Orchester Kulenkampff	78: Decca AK 1603-1605 LP: Artisco C44G 0016-0017

Odysseus, Overture

Turin ca. 1942	EIAR Orchestra	78: Cetra BB 25091

Bruckner

Symphony No 3

Vienna December 1965	VPO	LP: EMI ALP 2284/ASD 2284 CD: EMI CDZ 252 9242 CD: Toshiba TOCE 6841-6843

Symphony No 4 "Romantic"

Stuttgart April 1955	SDR Orchestra	CD: Archiphon ARCH 2.4

Symphony No 5

Vienna February 1963	VPO	CD: DG 435 3322/435 3212 CD: Musica classica

Symphony No 7

Berlin 1938	BPO	78: Polydor 67195-67202
Stuttgart March 1953	SDR Orchestra	CD: Refrain (Japan) DR 910017
Den Haag September 1964	Residentie Orchestra	LP: Concert Hall AM 2394/SMS 2394 CD: Denon (Japan) 30CO 1339

Symphony No 8

Vienna December 1963	VPO	LP: HMV ALP 2053-2054/ ASD 602-603 CD: EMI CDZ 252 9252/CZS 767 2792 CD: Toshiba TOCE 6841-6843

Symphony No 9

Berlin ca. 1941	Städtische Oper Orchestra	78: Polydor 68109-68116
Stuttgart November 1951	SDR Orchestra	CD: Refrain (Japan) DR 910015
Vienna November 1961	VPO	LP: HMV ALP 1929/ASD 493 CD: EMI CDZ 252 2242/CZS 767 2792 CD: Toshiba TOCE 6841-6843

Chabrier

Espana

Dresden 1943	Dresden Philharmonic	Issue details uncertain

Debussy

Prélude à l'après-midi d'un faune

Dresden 1943	Dresden Philharmonic	Issue details uncertain

Franck

Le chasseur maudit

Berlin ca. 1941	Städtische Oper Orchestra	78: Polydor 68086-68087

Grieg

Peer Gynt, Suite No 1

Berlin ca. 1929	Staatskapelle	78: Telefunken A 161-162 78: Clangor M 1557/1569/D 69-70

Handel

Concert grossi: Op 3 no 4; Op 6 nos 4 and 10; C major "Alexander's Feast"

Munich September 1961	Bavarian RO	LP: Concert Hall AM 2266/SMS 2266 LP: Columbia (Japan) OW 7882

Preis 20 Pfg.
Konzertdirektion Hermann Wolff (vorm. Konzertdirektion H. Wolff u. J. Sachs), G. m. b. H., № 9

Philharmonie   Montag, 11. Dezember 1933, abends 8 Uhr

Philharmonischer Chor
Gegründet 1882 von Siegfried Ochs

1. Abonnements-Konzert   Leitung:

Carl Schuricht

REGER: Der Einsiedler
für Bariton-Solo, Chor und Orchester op. 144
(Zum 1. Mal in diesen Konzerten)

BRAHMS:
Ein Deutsches Requiem

Mitwirkende:

Adelheid Armhold - Rudolf Bockelmann

Orgel: Hans Heintze

Das Philharmonische Orchester

Zwischen beiden Werken findet eine kurze Pause statt!

---

2. KONZERT: Montag, den 5. Februar 1934, 8 Uhr · Alte Garnisonkirche:
                   Kantaten von Joh. Seb. Bach, u. a.: Ihr werdet weinen und
                   heulen; Jesu, der Du meine Seele; Du Hirte Israel, höre;
                   Jauchzet Gott; Nun ist das Heil und die Kraft.
                   Karten zu Mk. 1.50 bis 4.50. Verkauf beginnt morgen.

3. KONZERT: Montag, den 19. März 1934, 8 Uhr   Philharmonie:
                   Bruckner: Grosse Messe in f-moll

Haydn

Symphony No 86

Stuttgart May 1954	SDR Orchestra	CD: Melodram CDM 18047 CD: Refrain (Japan) DR 920027

Symphony No 95

Stuttgart April 1955	SDR Orchestra	CD: Refrain (Japan) DR 920027

Symphony No 104 "London"

Stuttgart September 1952	SDR Orchestra	CD: Refrain (Japan) DR 920027
Montreux September 1955	Orchestre National	LP: Erato ERH 16010 CD: Refrain (Japan) DR 910008

Lothar

Schneider Wibbel, Overture

Berlin ca. 1941	Städtische Oper Orchestra	78: Polydor 68269

Mahler

Symphony No 2 "Resurrection"

Paris February 1958	Orchestre National and Chorus Selig, Zareska	CD: Melodram MEL 27504

Symphony No 3

Stuttgart April 1960	SDR Orchestra and Chorus Siewert	CD: Stradivarius STR 10051 CD: Archiphon ARCH 2/6/7

Das Lied von der Erde

Amsterdam October 1939	Concertgebouw Orchestra Thorborg, Ohmann	CD: Archiphon awaiting publication

Lieder eines fahrenden Gesellen

Paris February 1962	Orchestre National Zareska	CD: Melodram CDM 18048 CD: Stradivarius STR 10010

Mendelssohn

Symphony No 4 "Italian"

Stuttgart January 1954	SDR Orchestra	CD: Refrain (Japan) DR 910011

The Hebrides, Overture

Vienna April 1954	VPO	LP: Decca LXT 2921/LW 5193/ACL 33 CD: London (Japan) KICC 2194/2326
Stuttgart January 1955	SDR Orchestra	CD: Refrain (Japan) DR 920024
Stuttgart 1960	SDR Orchestra	LP: Columbia (Japan) OW 7878 CD: Denon (Japan) 30CO 1342 Also issued by Concert Hall

Meeresstille glückliche Fahrt, Overture

Vienna April 1954	VPO	LP: Decca LXT 2921/ACL 33 CD: London (Japan) KICC 2194/2326

A Midsummer Night's Dream, Incidental music

Munich 1960	Bavarian RO	LP: Columbia (Japan) OW 7878 CD: Denon (Japan) 30CO 1342 Also issued by Concert Hall

A Midsummer Night's Dream, Overture

Stuttgart January 1954	SDR Orchestra	CD: Refrain (Japan) DR 920024

Ruy Blas, Overture

Vienna April 1954	VPO	LP: Decca LXT 2921/LW 5193/ACL 33 CD: London (Japan) KICC 2194/2326
Baden-Baden September 1962	Südwestfunk- Orchester	LP: Concert Hall AM 2293/SMS 2293 LP: Columbia (Japan) OW 7884

Die schöne Melusine, Overture

Vienna April 1954	VPO	LP: Decca LXT 2921/ACL 33
Baden-Baden September 1962	Südwestfunk- Orchester	LP: Concert Hall AM 2293/SMS 2293 LP: Columbia (Japan) OW 7884

Mozart

Symphony No 23

Dresden 1943	Dresden Philharmonic	Issue details uncertain

Symphony No 31 "Paris"

Den Haag 1960	Residentie Orchestra	CD: Refrain (Japan) DR 910001

Symphony No 34

Berlin ca. 1940	BPO	78: Polydor 68215-68217

Symphony No 35 "Haffner"

Vienna June 1956	VPO	LP: Decca LXT 5257
Vienna December 1956	VPO	CD: Refrain (Japan) DR 920028
Vienna February 1963	VPO	CD: Refrain (Japan) DR 920020
London 1964	LSO	CD: Refrain (Japan) DR 910001

Symphony No 36 "Linz"

Paris November 1964	Paris Opera Orchestra	LP: Concert Hall AM 2258/SMS 2258 LP: Musidisc FC 420 CD: Denon (Japan) 30CO 1336 CD: Adès 13.2292

Symphony No 38 "Prague"

Salzburg August 1960	VPO	CD: EMI CDH 764 9042
Paris June 1963	Paris Opera Orchestra	LP: Concert Hall AM 2326/SMS 2326 CD: Denon (Japan) 30CO 1336

Symphony No 40

Paris November 1964	Paris Opera Orchestra	LP: Concert Hall AM 2258/SMS 2258 LP: Musidisc FC 420 CD: Denon (Japan) 30CO 1335 CD: Adès 13.2292

Symphony No 41 "Jupiter"

Salzburg August 1960	VPO	CD: EMI CDH 764 9042
Paris June 1963	Paris Opera Orchestra	LP: Concert Hall AM 2326/SMS 2326 CD: Denon (Japan) 30CO 1335

Piano Concerto No 9

Stuttgart May 1952	SDR Orchestra Haskil	CD: Preludio PHC 2140 Previously published on LP

Piano Concerto No 17

Stuttgart September 1954	SDR Orchestra Askenase	CD: Refrain (Japan) DR 920020

Piano Concerto No 19

Ludwigsburg July 1956	SDR Orchestra Haskil	CD: Preludio PHC 2140 Previously published on LP

Violin Concerto No 3

Salzburg August 1960	VPO Boskovsky	CD: EMI CDH 764 9042

Violin Concerto No 5

Lugano Date uncertain	Swiss Italian Radio Orchestra Milstein	CD: Refrain (Japan) DR 910011

Haffner Serenade

Stuttgart December 1962	SDR Orchestra	LP: Movimento musica 01.067 CD: Refrain (Japan) DR 910011 Incorrectly dated 1954

Nicolai

Die lustigen Weiber von Windsor, Overture

| Baden-Baden | Südwestfunk- | LP: Concert Hall AM 2293/SMS 2293 |
| September 1962 | Orchester | LP: Columbia (Japan) OW 7884 |

Poot

Allegro symphonique

| Berlin | Städtische Oper | 78: Polydor 57272 |
| 1942 | Orchestra | 78: DG EM 15 519 |

Reger

Hiller Variations

| London | LSO | CD: Refrain (Japan) DR 910001 |
| 1964 | | |

Reznicek

Donna Diana, Overture

| Milan | La Scala | 78: HMV DB 5402 |
| 1940 | Orchestra | |

Schubert

Symphony No 8 "Unfinished"

| Vienna | VPO | LP: Decca LXT 5257/SPA 225 |
| June 1956 | | |

Besancon	Orchestre	LP: Erato ERH 16010
September 1963	National	CD: Refrain (Japan) DR 910008
		CD: Stradivarius STR 10051

Symphony No 9 "Great"

| Stuttgart | SDR Orchestra | LP: Concert Hall AM 2215/SMS 2215 |
| Date uncertain | | LP: Musidisc FC 427 |

Schumann

Symphony No 2

Paris July 1952	Paris Conservatoire Orchestra	LP: Decca LXT 2745/ACL 236 CD: London (Japan) KICC 2325
Montreux September 1955	Orchestre National	LP: Erato ERH 16009 CD: Refrain (Japan) DR 910008

Symphony No 3 "Rhenish"

Paris June 1953	Paris Conservatoire Orchestra	LP: Decca LXT 2985/LW 5303/ACL 231 LP: Decca (France) 411 6791 CD: London (Japan) KICC 2325
Stuttgart September 1960	SDR Orchestra	Cassette: Symposium 1019 CD: Refrain (Japan) DR 910001
Stuttgart December 1960	SDR Orchestra	LP: Concert Hall AM 2217/SMS 2217 LP: Columbia (Japan) OW 7879

Overture, Scherzo and Finale

Paris June 1954	Paris Conservatoire Orchestra	LP: Decca LXT 2985/ACL 231 LP: Decca (France) 411 6791

Manfred, Incidental music

Stuttgart March 1952	SDR Orchestra and Chorus Various soloists and speakers	CD: Archiphon ARCH 2.3

Manfred, Overture

London March 1948	LPO	Decca unpublished
Stuttgart December 1960	SDR Orchestra	LP: Concert Hall AM 2217/SMS 2217 LP: Columbia (Japan) OW 7879
Paris May 1963	Orchestre National	LP: Erato ERH 16009 CD: Melodram CDM 18045

PHILHARMONIE

Montag, den 3. Oktober 1927, abends 7½ Uhr

KONZERT

mit dem Philharmonischen Orchester

Dirigent:

CARL SCHURICHT

SOLISTEN:

Lotte Leonard / Nevada van der Veer
George Meader / Heinrich Rehkemper

Frederick Delius:

„EINE MESSE DES LEBENS"

für 4 Solostimmen, gemischten Chor und großes Orchester.

Worte aus Friedrich Nietzsche:

„Also sprach Zarathustra"

Es wird dringend empfohlen, den Führer durch das Werk zu benutzen, erschienen im Verlag der Universal-Edition.

Stephan

Musik für Orchester

Berlin 1942	Städtische Oper Orchestra	78: DG EM 15 543-15 545

Johann Strauss

Champagner-Polka

Vienna April 1963	VPO	LP: Concert Hall AM 2321/SMS 2321 LP: Columbia (Japan) OW 7880 CD: Denon (Japan) 30CO 1341

Die Fledermaus, Overture

Berlin ca. 1929	Staatskapelle	78: Telefunken E 145 78: Clangor MD 535 78: Decca K 638 Decca labels the orchestra as New State Symphony Orchestra

Gschichten aus dem Wienerwald, Waltz

Vienna April 1963	VPO	LP: Concert Hall AM 2321/SMS 2321 LP: Columbia (Japan) OW 7880 CD: Denon (Japan) 30CO 1341

Perpetuum mobile

Vienna April 1963	VPO	LP: Concert Hall AM 2321/SMS 2321 LP: Columbia (Japan) OW 7880 CD: Denon (Japan) 30CO 1341

Rosen aus dem Süden, Waltz

Vienna April 1963	VPO	LP: Concert Hall AM 2321/SMS 2321 LP: Columbia (Japan) OW 7880 CD: Denon (Japan) 30CO 1341

Schatz-Walzer

Vienna April 1963	VPO	LP: Concert Hall AM 2321/SMS 2321 LP: Columbia (Japan) OW 7880 CD: Denon (Japan) 30CO·1341

Tritsch-Tratsch Polka

Vienna April 1963	VPO	LP: Concert Hall AM 2321/SMS 2321 LP: Columbia (Japan) OW 7880 CD: Denon (Japan) 30CO 1341

Wein, Weib und Gesang, Waltz

Vienna April 1963	VPO	LP: Concert Hall AM 2321/SMS 2321 LP: Columbia (Japan) OW 7880 CD: Denon (Japan) 30CO 1341

Wiener Blut, Waltz

Vienna April 1963	VPO	LP: Concert Hall AM 2321/SMS 2321 LP: Columbia (Japan) OW 7880 CD: Denon (Japan) 30CO 1341

Richard Strauss

Eine Alpensinfonie

Stuttgart January 1955	SDR Orchestra	CD: Archiphon ARCH 2.6/7

Ein Heldenleben

Stuttgart April 1959	SDR Orchestra	CD: Refrain (Japan) DR 910014

Sinfonia domestica

Milan 1940	La Scala Orchestra	78: HMV DB 5418-5422

Tod und Verklärung

Berlin 1928	Berlin SO	78: Homochord 4.8828-8829 Presumably this was an abridged version of the work

Stravinsky

L'oiseau de feu, Suite

Stuttgart December 1957	SDR Orchestra	CD: Refrain (Japan) DR 910011

Tchaikovsky

Symphony No 4, 2nd movement

Berlin ca. 1940	BPO	78: Telefunken E 1791

Suite No 3, Theme and variations

Berlin ca. 1940	BPO	78: Telefunken E 1752 Abridged version
Paris July 1952	Paris Conservatoire Orchestra	LP: Decca LXT 2761/LW 5274 LP: Decca ACL 89

Capriccio italien

Berlin 1929	BPO	78: Telefunken E 264 78: Ultraphon EP 101 78: Clangor MD 1573 Abridged version
Paris July 1952	Paris Conservatoire Orchestra	LP: LXT 2761/ACL 11

Verdi

Messa da Requiem

Amsterdam November 1939	Concertgebouw Orchestra Toonkunstkoor Souez, L.Fischer, Von Tulder, Schey	CD: Archiphon awaiting publication

Wagner

Der fliegende Holländer, Overture

Berlin	BPO	78: Telefunken E 331/E 23319
1929		78: Clangor MD 59

Götterdämmerung, Siegfried's Rhine Journey and Funeral March (arr. Schuricht)

Paris	Paris	LP: Decca LXT 5026/ACL 117
June 1954	Conservatoire	LP: Decca (France) 411 6731
	Orchestra	CD: London (Japan) KICC 2193/2324

Lohengrin, Prelude

Munich	Bavarian RO	LP: Concert Hall AM 2246/SMS 2246
September 1961		CD: Denon (Japan) 30CO 1340

Die Meistersinger von Nürnberg, Preludes Acts 1 & 3 and Dance of the Apprentices

Munich	Bavarian RO	LP: Concert Hall AM 2246/SMS 2246
September 1961		CD: Denon (Japan) 30CO 1340

Parsifal, Prelude Act 1 and Finale Act 3

Stuttgart	SDR Orchestra	CD: Archiphon ARCH 2.5
March 1966		

Rienzi, Overture

Munich	Bavarian RO	LP: Concert Hall AM 2246/SMS 2246
September 1961		CD: Denon (Japan) 30CO 1340

Siegfried Idyll

Munich	Bavarian RO	LP: Concert Hall AM 2246/SMS 2246
September 1961		CD: Denon (Japan) 30CO 1340

Tristan und Isolde, Prelude and Liebestod

Paris	Paris	LP: Decca LXT 5026/ACL 117
June 1954	Conservatoire	LP: Decca (France) 411 6731
	Orchestra	CD: London (Japan) KICC 2193/2324
Paris	Orchestre	CD: Refrain (Japan) DR 920024
September 1957	National	

Weber

Abu Hassan, Overture

London March 1948	LPO	Decca unpublished

Euryanthe, Overture

Stuttgart December 1957	SDR Orchestra	CD: Refrain (Japan) DR 920024
Baden-Baden September 1962	Südwestfunk- Orchester	LP: Concert Hall AM 2293/SMS 2293 LP: Columbia (Japan) OW 7884

Der Freischütz, Overture

Berlin 1929	Staatskapelle	78: Telefunken E 265 78: Clangor D 69-70 78: Decca K K 460 Decca labels the orchestra as New State Symphony Orchestra
Geneva 1954	Suisse Romande Orchestra	CD: Refrain (Japan) DR 910001

Oberon, Overture

Berlin ca. 1931	BPO	78: Telefunken E 656
Baden-Baden September 1962	Südwestfunk- Orchester	LP: Concert Hall AM 2293/SMS 2293 LP: Columbia (Japan) OW 7884
London September 1963	LSO	CD: Refrain (Japan) DR 910001

Zandonai

Serenata medioevale for violin and orchestra

Milan 1940	La Scala Orchestra Martinenghi	78: HMV DB 5401-5402

Tuscan Dance (La via della finestra)

Turin ca. 1942	EIAR Orchestra	78: Cetra BB 25091

Felix Weingartner
1863-1942

Discography compiled by John Hunt

Bach

Orchestral Suite No 3

Paris	Paris	78: Columbia LX 874-876/
May 1939	Conservatoire	LX 8480-8482 auto
	Orchestra	LP: American Columbia ML 4783

Beethoven

Symphony No 1

Vienna	VPO	78: Columbia LX 677-679/
October 1937		LX 8358-8360 auto
		LP: American Columbia ML 4501
		LP: Toshiba EAC 60079-60084
		LP: Artisco (Japan) YZ 3001-3009

Symphony No 2

London	LSO	78: Columbia LX 725-728/
March 1938		LX 8388-8391 auto
		LP: American Columbia ML 4502
		LP: Toshiba EAC 60079-60084
		LP: Artisco (Japan) YZ 3001-3009

Symphony No 3 "Eroica"

Vienna	VPO	78: Columbia LX 532-537/
May 1936		LX 8273-8278 auto
		LP: American Columbia ML 4503
		LP: EMI 1C 053 01481
		LP: EMI RLS 717
		LP: Toshiba EAC 60079-60084
		LP: Artisco (Japan) YZ 3001-3009
		CD: Preiser 90113

A recording made by Weingartner with VPO at the Salzburg Festival in July 1935 has also been preserved

Symphony No 4

London	LPO	78: Columbia LX 274-277/
November 1933		LX 8075-8078 auto
		LP: American Columbia ML 4504
		LP: Toshiba EAC 60079-60084
		LP: Artisco (Japan) YZ 3001-3009
		CD: Memories (France) 30378

Symphony No 5

London November 1924	LSO	78: Columbia L 1640-1643
London January 1927	Orchestra of the Royal Philharmonic Society	78: Columbia L 1880-1883
London March 1932	British Symphony Orchestra	78: American Columbia M 178 Issued in USA only
London January and February 1933	LPO	78: Columbia DX 516-519/ LX 8072-8075 auto LP: American Columbia ML 4505 LP: Toshiba EAC 60079-60084 LP: Artisco (Japan) YZ 3001-3009 CD: Memories (France) 30378

Symphony No 6 "Pastoral"

London November 1924	LSO	Columbia unpublished Recording incomplete
London January 1927	Orchestra of the Royal Philharmonic Society	78: Columbia L 1893-1897 LP: American Columbia ML 4506 LP: Toshiba EAC 60079-60084 LP: Artisco (Japan) YZ 3001-3009

Symphony No 7

London June 1923 and November 1924	LSO	78: Columbia L 1480-1484
London January 1927	Orchestra of the Royal Philharmonic Society	78: Columbia L 1898-1902
Vienna February 1936	VPO	78: Columbia LX 484-488/ LX 8235-8239 auto LP: American Columbia ML 4507 LP: Toshiba EAC 60079-60084 LP: Artisco (Japan) YZ 3001-3009

COLUMBIA MASTERWORKS ALBUM

BEETHOVEN
Symphony No. 1
in C major
(Op. 21)
(THREE RECORDS)
Played by
FELIX WEINGARTNER
Conducting the
VIENNA PHILHARMONIC ORCHESTRA

Presented with the
Masterworks Album (N
Beethoven Symphony

COLUMBIA MASTERWORKS ALBUM

BEETHOVEN
Symphony No. 6
(Pastoral)
in F major (Op. 68)
(FIVE RECORDS)
Played by FELIX WEINGARTNER and
ROYAL PHILHARMONIC ORCHESTRA

Presented with the Columbia Masterworks Album (No. 6) of Beethoven Symphony No. 6 (Pastoral) in F major.

Symphony No 8

London November 1923 and November 1924	LSO	78: Columbia L 1538-1541
London January 1927	Orchestra of the Royal Philharmonic Society	78: Columbia L 1903-1905 LP: Parnassus 6
Vienna February 1936	VPO	78: Columbia LX 563-565/ LX 8295-8297 auto LP: American Columbia ML165 LP: Columbia COLC 28 LP: Toshiba AB 9096/GR 2150 LP: Toshiba EAC 60079-60084 LP: Artisco (Japan) YZ 3001-3009 CD: Preiser 90113

Symphony No 9 "Choral"

London March 1926	LSO Chorus Licette, Brunskill, Eisdell, Williams Sung in English	78: Columbia L 1775-1782 CD: Trax Classique TRXCD 125
Vienna February 1935	VPO Vienna Opera Chorus Helletsgruber, Anday, Maikl, Mayr	78: Columbia LX 413-420/ LX 8175-8182 auto LP: America Columbia ML 165 LP: Columbia COLC 27-28 LP: Toshiba AB 9095-9096 LP: Toshiba GR 2149-2150 LP: Toshiba EAC 60079-60084 LP: Artisco (Japan) YZ 3001-3009 CD: Memories (France) 30270 CD: Pearl GEMMCD 9407

Piano Concerto No 3

Paris June 1939	Paris Conservatoire Orchestra Long	78: French Columbia LFX 581-584 LP: French Columbia FHX 5007 LP: Toshiba GR 2196 CD: Koch Legacy 3-7128-2

Triple Concerto

Vienna October 1937	VPO Odonoposoff, Auber, Morales	78: Columbia LX 671-675/ LX 8353-8357 auto LP: American Columbia ML 2218 CD: Pearl GEMMCD 9358

Hammerklavier Sonata (orch. Weingartner)

London March 1930	Orchestra of the Royal Philharmonic Society	78: Columbia LX 43-47 LP: American Columbia ML 4675 LP: Toshiba EAC 60079-60084 LP: Artisco (Japan) YZ 3001-3009 CD: Pearl GEMMCD 9358

11 Viennese Dances

London October 1938	LPO	78: Columbia LX 770-771 LP: Toshiba EAC 60079-60084 LP: Artisco (Japan) YZ 3001-3009 CD: Dutton Laboratories CDAX 8005 CD: Pearl GEMMCD 9407

Egmont, Overture

Vienna October 1937	VPO	78: Columbia LX 690 LP: American Columbia ML 4647 LP: Artisco (Japan) YZ 3001-3009

Egmont, Klärchens Tod

London October 1938	LPO	78: Columbia LX 812 LP: Artisco (Japan) YZ 3001-3009 <u>78 issue coupled with Weihe des Hauses Overture</u>

Egmont, Larghetto

London October 1938	LPO	78: Columbia LX 771 LP: Artisco (Japan) YZ 3001-3009 <u>78 issue coupled with 11 Viennese Dances</u>

Fidelio, Overture

London October 1938	LPO	78: Columbia LX 784 LP: American Columbia ML 4647 LP: Artisco (Japan) YZ 3001-3009

Die Geschöpfe des Prometheus, Overture

London November 1933	LPO	78: Columbia LX 277/LX 8075 CD: Memories (France) 30378 <u>78 issues coupled with</u> <u>Symphony No 4</u>
Vienna February 1936	VPO	78: Columbia LX 488/LX 8235 LP: American Columbia ML 4647 LP: Artisco (Japan) YZ 3001-3009 <u>78 issues coupled with</u> <u>Symphony No 7</u>

Leonore No 2, Overture

London February 1938	LSO	78: Columbia LX 712-713 LP: American Columbia ML 4647 LP: EMI RLS 717 LP: Artisco (Japan) YZ 3001-3009

Die Ruinen von Athen, Overture

London February 1940	LSO	78: Columbia LX 898 LP: EMI RLS 717 LP: Artisco (Japan) YZ 3001-3009 <u>78 issue coupled with</u> <u>Liszt Mephisto Waltz</u>

Die Weihe des Hauses, Overture

London October 1938	LPO	78: Columbia LX 811-812 LP: American Columbia ML 4647 LP: Artisco (Japan) YZ 3001-3009

Berlioz

Symphonie fantastique

London March 1925	LSO	Columbia unpublished
London October and November 1925	LSO	78: Columbia L 1708-1713

Marche troyenne (Les Troyens)

Paris July 1939	Paris Conservatoire Orchestra	78: Columbia LX 861 LP: EMI RLS 717 78 issue coupled with Wagner Rienzi Overture

A record of Danse des Sylphes (La Damnation de Faust) issued on German Columbia 78 LWX 236 and labelled Symphony Orchestra/Weingartner is in fact the version by LPO/Beecham

Bizet

L'Arlésienne, Prelude and Adagietto

New York March 1914	Columbia Symphony Orchestra	Columbia Graphophone A 5559

Carmen, Preludes Acts 1 and 4

New York March 1914	Columbia Symphony Orchestra	Columbia Graphophone A 5559

Records of Carmen Suite issued on German Columbia 78s LWX 305-306 and labelled Symphony Orchestra/Weingartner are in fact the version by LPO/Beecham

Boccherini

Minuet (Quartet op 13 no 5)

Paris May 1939	Paris Conservatoire Orchestra	78: Columbia LX 876 Coupled with Bach Suite No 3

Brahms

Symphony No 1

London November 1923 and March 1924	LSO	78: Columbia L 1596-1600
London April 1928	Orchestra of the Royal Philharmonic Society	78: Columbia L 2145-2149 LP: Pearl OPAL 828 CD: Koch Legacy 3-7128-2
London February 1939	LSO	78: Columbia LX 833-837/ LX 8452-8456 auto LP: American Columbia ML 4510 CD: EMI CHS 764 2562 Also published in LP on the Japanese Artisco label

Symphony No 2

London February 1940	LPO	78: Columbia LX 899-903/ LX 8492-8496 auto LP: American Columbia ML 4511 LP: EMI RLS 717 CD: EMI CHS 764 2562 Also published in LP on the Japanese Artisco label

Symphony No 3

London October 1938	LPO	78: Columbia LX 748-751/ LX 8402-8405 auto LP: American Columbia ML 4512 CD: EMI CHS 764 2562 CD: Centaur CRC 2128 Also published in LP on the Japanese Artisco label

Symphony No 4

London February 1938	LSO	78: Columbia LX 705-709/ 　　LX 8377-8381 auto LP: American Columbia ML 4513 CD: EMI CHS 764 2562 CD: Centaur CRC 2128 Also published in LP on the Japanese Artisco label

Haydn Variations

London October 1938	LPO	78: Columbia LX 744-745 LP: American Columbia ML 4783

Academic Festival Overture

London February 1940	LSO	78: Columbia LX 886 CD: EMI CHS 764 2562

Fontanaille

Obstination, Song with orchestra

Vienna June 1910	Hofoper Orchestra Marcel	Columbia Graphophone 3304

Handel

Alcina, Ballet music and Dream music

Paris July 1939	Paris Conservatoire Orchestra	78: Columbia LX 918-919 Dream music only LP: EMI RLS 717

Concerto grosso op 6 no 5

London February 1939	LSO	78: Columbia LX 803-804 LP: American Columbia ML 4676

Concerto grosso op 6 no 6

London February 1939	LSO	78: Columbia LX 831-832 LP: American Columbia ML 4676

✳ CONCERTHAUS — CONVENTGARTEN. ✳

Freitag den 25. October 1895, Abends <u>7</u> Uhr pünktlich

I. ABONNEMENT-CONCERT

Dirigent:

Hofkapellmeister Felix Weingartner.

Orchester:

Das Berliner Philharmonische Orchester.

PROGRAMM.

1. Symphonie No. 2, D-dur (1877) . . . *J. Brahms.*
    Allegro non troppo. — Adagio non troppo. — Allegretto grazioso, quasi Andantino. Presto ma non assai. — Allegro con spirito.

2. Ouverture „Le Carneval Romain" . . *H. Berlioz.*

3. Ouverture zu: „Leonore", No. 3, C-dur *L. v. Beethoven.*

4. Symphonie F-dur, No. 8, op. 93, (1812) *L. v. Beethoven.*
    Allegro vivace e con brio. — Allegretto scherzando. — Tempo di Menuetto. — Allegro vivace.

Liszt

Piano Concerto No 1

Paris December 1938	Paris Conservatoire Orchestra Sauer	78: Columbia LX 789-791/ LX 8432-8434 auto LP: Columbia COLC 81 LP: EMI 1C 053 01458 LP: Toshiba GR 2086 CD: Pearl GEMMCD 9403 Also issued on LP by Turnabout

Piano Concerto No 2

Paris December 1938	Paris Conservatoire Orchestra Sauer	78: Columbia LX 862-864/ LX 8472-8474 auto LP: Columbia COLC 81 LP: EMI 1C 053 01458 LP: Toshiba GR 2086 CD: Pearl GEMMCD 9403 Also issued on LP by Turnabout

Mephisto Waltz

London February 1940	LSO	78: Columbia LX 897-898 LP: EMI RLS 717

Les Préludes

London February 1940	LSO	78: Columbia LX 877-878 LP: EMI RLS 717

Mendelssohn

Symphony No 3 "Scotch"

London March 1929	Orchestra of the Royal Philharmonic Society	78: Columbia 9887-9890 LP: Parnassus 6 LP: Discocorp IGI 336

Leopold Mozart

Toy Symphony

London April 1931	British Symphony Orchestra	78: Columbia DX 311 LP: American Columbia ML 4776

Mozart

Symphony No 39

London November 1923, November 1924 and March 1925	LSO	78: Columbia L 1563-1565
London April 1928	Orchestra of the Royal Philharmonic Society	78: Columbia 9450-9452 LP: Pearl OPAL 828
Paris May 1939	Paris Conservatoire Orchestra	Columbia unpublished
London February 1940	LPO	78: Columbia LX 881-883/ LX 8483-8485 auto LP: American Columbia ML 4776

Eine kleine Nachtmusik

London February 1939	LSO	78: Columbia LX 854-855 LP: American Columbia ML 4776

Nicolai

Excerpts from a Vienna 1935 performance of Die lustigen Weiber von Windsor
have been preserved

| Konzertbüro der | Konzertdirektion |
| Konzerthausgesellschaft | HUGO HELLER |

Samstag, den 14. Juni 1919, abends 7 Uhr
im GROSSEN MUSIKVEREINSSAALE

BEETHOVEN-FEST

III. ABEND

Ausführende:

Das Sinfonieorchester
(Tonkünstler — Konzertverein)

Carl Friedberg (Klavier)

Dirigent:

FELIX WEINGARTNER

PROGRAMM:

1. **Ouvertüre zu „Coriolan".**

2. **Klavierkonzert Es-dur op. 73.**
   Dem Erzherzog Rudolf gewidmet.
   Allegro.
   Adagio un poco mosso —
   Rondo (Allegro ma non troppo).

3. **Sinfonie A-dur op. 92.**
   Dem Reichsgrafen von Fries gewidmet.
   Poco sostenuto — Vivace.
   Allegretto.
   Presto — Presto non assai — Tempo I.
   Allegro con brio.

Klavier: **Bösendorfer.**

Schubert

Rosamunde, Entr'acte No 3

Basle May 1928	Basler Orchester- Gesellschaft	78: Columbia 9645 Coupled with Weber Freischütz Overture

Records of Schubert Symphony No 8 "Unfinished" issued on German Columbia LWX 241-243 and labelled Symphony Orchestra/Weingartner are in fact the version by LPO/Beecham

Schumann

Frisches Grün; Die Lotosblume, Songs with orchestra

New York February 1913	Columbia Symphony Orchestra Marcel	Columbia Graphophone unpublished

Johann Strauss

An der schönen blauen Donau, Waltz

London January 1927	Orchestra of the Royal Philharmonic Society	78: Columbia L 2086 LP: American Columbia ML 4777 78 version also transferred as an experimental 33 1/3 rpm disc but not published in that form

Fragment of a filmed version of this waltz with Weingartner conducting (Vienna ca. 1935-1936) also exists

Frühlingsstimmen, Waltz

London April 1931	British Symphony Orchestra	78: Columbia DX 266 LP: American Columbia ML 4777 LP: EMI RLS 717

Perpetuum mobile

Basle May 1929	Basler Orchester- Gesellschaft	78: Columbia 8861

1001 Nacht, Waltz

Basle May 1929	Basler Orchester- Gesellschaft	Columbia unpublished Existence of this version has not been confirmed
London April 1931	British Symphony Orchestra	78: Columbia LX 133 LP: American Columbia ML 4777 CD: Preiser 90090

Wein, Weib und Gesang, Waltz

Basle May 1929	Basler Orchester- Gesellschaft	78: Columbia 8860 CD: Wing (Japan) WCD 7
Paris July 1939	Paris Conservatoire Orchestra	78: Columbia LX 909 LP: American Columbia ML 4777 LP: EMI RLS 717 CD: Wing (Japan) WCD 7

A recording of fragments from a Vienna 1937 performance of Die Fledermaus has been preserved

Operntheater

Im Abonnement Mittwoch den 4. September 1935 II. Gruppe

Der Ring des Nibelungen
Ein Bühnenfestspiel für drei Tage und einen Vorabend von **Richard Wagner**

Vorabend:

Das Rheingold

Spielleitung: Hr. Dr. Wallerstein   Dirigent: Hr. Dr. Felix Weingartner*

Wotan		. . . * * *	Fricka	. . . Frl. Konetzni
Donner	Götter	. Hr. Madin	Freia } Göttinen	. Fr. Hadrabova
Froh		. Hr. Gallos	Erda	. Fr. Szantho
Loge		. Hr. Graarud	Woglinde	. Fr. Gerhart
Alberich	Nibelungen	. Hr. Wiedemann	Wellgunde } Rheintöchter	. Fr. With
Mime		. Hr. Wernigk	Floßhilde	. Fr. Szantho
Fasolt	Riesen	. Hr. Markhoff		Nibelungen
Fafner		. Hr. Zec		

* Ehrenmitglied

Schauplätze der Handlung:
1. In der Tiefe des Rheines. (1. Szene.)
2. Freie Gegend auf Bergeshöhen, am Rhein gelegen. (2. und 4. Szene.)
3. Die unterirdischen Klüfte Nibelheims. (3. Szene.)

Inszenierung: Dr. Lothar Wallerstein

* * * „Wotan" Hr. Kammersänger **Friedrich Schorr** von der Metropolitan Opera in New York a. G.

Das offizielle Programm nur bei den Billetteuren erhältlich. Preis 50 Groschen — Garderobe frei

Kassen-Eröffnung vor **7 Uhr**   Anfang **7½ Uhr**   Ende nach **10 Uhr**

Während der Vorspiele und der Akte bleiben die Saaltüren zum Parkett, Parterre und den Galerien geschlossen. Zuspätkommende können daher nur während der Pausen Einlaß finden

Der Kartenverkauf findet heute statt für obige Vorstellung und für

Donnerstag den 5. Festvorstellung anläßlich des Bausparkassen-Weltkongresses: Cavalleria rusticana — Österreichische Bauernhochzeit (Anfang 7½ Uhr)
Freitag   den 6. Der Ring des Nibelungen. Erster Tag: Die Walküre. „Wotan" Hr. Kammersänger **Friedrich Schorr** von der Metropolitan Opera in New York a. G. Im Abonnement II. Gruppe (Anfang 7 Uhr)

Weiterer Spielplan:
Samstag den 7. Die Entführung aus dem Serail. Im Abonnement II. Gruppe (Anfang 7½ Uhr)
Sonntag den 8. Tosca. „Tosca" Fr. **Dusolina Giannini** vom Scalatheater in Mailand a. G. (Anfang 7½ Uhr)

Kartenverkauf für alle Bundestheater an den Tageskassen: I., Bräunerstraße 14, an Werktagen von 9—18.30 Uhr (am Vorstellungstage selbst nur bis 16.30 Uhr und an der Abendkassa), an Sonn- u. Feiertagen von 9—17 Uhr. Telephonische Bestellungen von Sitzen (mit Ausnahme der Säulensitze) ausschließlich unter der Telephon-Nummer R-28-5-20

Operntheater

Im Abonnement   Freitag den 6. September 1935   II. Gruppe

Der Ring des Nibelungen
Ein Bühnenfestspiel für drei Tage und einen Vorabend von **Richard Wagner**

Erster Tag:
Die Walküre
In drei Aufzügen

Spielleitung: Hr. Dr. Wallerstein   Dirigent: Hr. Dr. Felix Weingartner*

Personen der Handlung:

Siegmund	Hr. Kalenberg	Gerhilde		Fr. Achsel
Hunding	Hr. Markhoff	Ortlinde		Fr. Bokor
Wotan	**	Waltraute		Fr. With
Sieglinde	Fr. Lehmann*	Siegrune	Walküren	Frl. Michalsky
Brünnhilde	Frl. Konetzni	Roßweiße		Fr. Stroinigg
Fricka	Fr. Thorborg	Grimgerde		Frl. Paalen
Helmwige, Walküre	Fr. Helletsgruber	Schwertleite		Fr. Szantho

* Ehrenmitglied

Schauplatz der Handlung:
Erster Aufzug: Das Innere der Wohnung Hundings
Zweiter Aufzug: Wildes Felsengebirge
Dritter Aufzug: Auf dem Gipfel eines Felsenberges (des „Brünnhildensteines")

Inszenierung: Dr. Lothar Wallerstein
Technische Einrichtung: Bühneninspektor Ferdinand Jaschke — Dekorationen gemalt von Robert Kautsky

** „Wotan" Hr. Kammersänger **Friedrich Schorr** von der Metropolitan Opera in New York a. G.

Nach jedem Aufzug eine größere Pause

Das offizielle Programm nur bei den Billetteuren erhältlich. Preis 50 Groschen — Garderobe frei

Kassen-Eröffnung vor 6½ Uhr   Anfang 7 Uhr   Ende 11½ Uhr

Während der Vorspiele und der Akte bleiben die Saaltüren zum Parkett, Parterre und den Galerien geschlossen. Zuspätkommende können daher nur während der Pausen Einlaß finden.

Der Kartenverkauf findet heute statt für obige Vorstellung und für

Samstag   den 7. Die Entführung aus dem Serail. Im Abonnement II. Gruppe (Anfang 7½ Uhr)
Sonntag   den 8. Tosca. „Tosca" Fr. **Dusolina Giannini** vom Scalatheater in Mailand a. G. (Anfang 7½ Uhr)

Weiterer Spielplan:

Montag   den 9. Der Ring des Nibelungen. Zweiter Tag: Siegfried. „Wanderer" Hr. Kammersänger **Friedrich Schorr** von der Metropolitan Opera in New York als Gast. Theatergemeinde Serie E, gelbe Mitgliedskarten (Anfang 6½ Uhr)
Dienstag   den 10. Manon (Massenet). Im Abonnement I. Gruppe (Anfang 7 Uhr)

Kartenverkauf für alle Bundestheater an den Tageskassen: I., Bräunerstraße 14, an Werktagen von 9—18.30 Uhr (am Vorstellungstage selbst nur bis 16.30 Uhr und an der Abendkassa), an Sonn- u. Feiertagen von 9—17 Uhr. Telephonische Bestellungen von Sitzen (mit Ausnahme der Säulensitze) ausschließlich unter der Telephon-Nummer R-28-5-20

Johann & Josef Strauss

Pizzicato Polka

Basle May 1929	Basler Orchester- Gesellschaft	78: Columbia 8861

Josef Strauss

Sphärenklänge, Waltz

London April 1930	Orchestra of the Royal Philharmonic Society	78: Columbia LX 40

Tchaikovsky

Symphony No 6 "Pathétique": Excerpt (1st movement, 89-160)

New York March 1914	Columbia Symphony Orchestra	Columbia Graphophone A 5594

Verdi

Otello: Excerpt (Ave Maria)

New York February 1913	Columbia Symphony Orchestra Marcel	Columbia Graphophone A 5482 LP: American Columbia ML 6099 LP: CBS BRG 72329

Wagner

Götterdämmerung: Excerpts (Mehr gabst du, Wunderfrau; Schweig ich der Klage)

Vienna	VPO	LP: Teletheater 120.841
September 1934	A.Konetzni,	
	Melchior, Manowarda	

Götterdämmerung: Excerpt (Brünnhilde's Immolation)

Vienna	VPO	LP: Teletheater 762.3589
September 1936	Flagstad	

Götterdämmerung: Excerpt (Siegfried's Rhine Journey)

Paris	Paris	78: Columbia LX 925
July 1939	Conservatoire	LP: American Columbia ML 4680

A live recording of the Rhine Journey (Vienna September 1936) has also been preserved

Fragments from a live recording of Lohengrin (Vienna December 1934) have been preserved

Götterdämmerung: Excerpt (Siegfried's Funeral March)

Paris	Paris	78: American Columbia X 224
July 1939	Conservatoire	LP: American Columbia ML 4680
	Orchestra	

Die Meistersinger von Nürnberg, Prelude

Vienna	VPO	LP: Teletheater 643.333
February 1935		

Act 3 Prelude from this 1935 performance of Meistersinger has also been preserved

Die Meistersinger von Nürnberg: Excerpts (Jerum! Jerum!; Selig wie die Sonne)

Vienna	VPO	LP: Teletheater 643.333
September 1935	Lehmann, Thorborg,	
	Laholm, Wernigk,	
	L.Hofmann, Wiedemann	

Parsifal: Various fragments

Vienna April 1936	VPO Thorborg, Graarud, Kipnis	LP: Ed Smith EJS 460 EJS 460 also contains fragments from an April 1933 performance incorrectly attributed to Weingartner; it is actually conducted by Krauss, with Mayr as Gurnemanz

Excerpts from a 1939 Covent Garden performance of Parsifal conducted by Weingartner have also been preserved

Rienzi, Overture

Paris July 1939	Paris Conservatoire Orchestra	78: Columbia LX 860-861 LP: EMI RLS 717

Siegfried Idyll

London October 1938	LPO	78: Columbia LX 801-802 LP: American Columbia ML 4680 LP: Discocorp IGI 336

Tannhäuser, Venusberg Music

London February 1939	LSO	Columbia unpublished

Tannhäuser, Act 3 Prelude

Paris May 1939	Paris Conservatoire Orchestra	78: Columbia LX 868 LP: American Columbia ML 4680 LP: EMI RLS 717

Excerpts from a Covent Garden performance of Tannhäuser conducted by Weingartner have also been preserved

Tristan und Isolde, Act 3 Prelude

Paris May 1939	Paris Conservatoire Orchestra	78: Columbia LX 866 LP: American Columbia ML 4680 LP: EMI RLS 717

Tristan und Isolde, Isolde's Liebestod

New York February 1913	Columbia Symphony Orchestra Marcel	Columbia Graphophone A 5464 78: Columbia L 1086

Die Walküre, Feuerzauber

New York March 1914	Columbia Symphony Orchestra	Columbia Graphophone A 5594 78: Columbia L 1097 LP: American Columbia GB 14

Opernteater

Montag den 9. September 1935
Theatergemeinde Serie E, gelbe Mitgliedskarten

Der Ring des Nibelungen
Ein Bühnenfestspiel für drei Tage und einen Vorabend von **Richard Wagner**

Zweiter Tag:

Siegfried
In drei Aufzügen

Spielleitung: Hr. Dr. Wallerstein   Dirigent: Hr. Dr. Felix Weingartner*

Siegfried	Hr. Kalenberg
Brünnhilde	Frl. Konetzni
Der Wanderer	* *
Alberich	Hr. Wiedemann
Erda	Fr. Thorborg
Mime	Hr. Wernigk
Fafner	Hr. Zec
Stimme des Waldvogels	Fr. Helletsgruber

Schauplatz der Handlung:
Erster Aufzug: **Eine Felsenhöhle im Walde**
Zweiter Aufzug: **Tiefer Wald**
Dritter Aufzug: **Wilde Gegend am Fuße eines Felsenberges**, dann: **Auf dem Gipfel des „Brünnhildensteines"**

* Ehrenmitglied   In Szene gesetzt von Dr. Lothar Wallerstein
Entwürfe: Alfred Roller

* * „Wanderer" Hr. Kammersänger **Friedrich Schorr** von der Metropolitan Opera in New York a. G.

Nach jedem Aufzuge eine größere Pause

Das offizielle Programm nur bei den Billetteuren erhältlich. Preis 50 Groschen — Garderobe frei

Kassen-Eröffnung vor 6 Uhr   **Anfang 6½ Uhr**   **Ende vor 11½ Uhr**

Während der Vorspiele und der Akte bleiben die Saaltüren zum Parkett, Parterre und den Galerien geschlossen. Zuspätkommende können daher nur während der Pausen Einlaß finden

Der Kartenverkauf findet heute statt für obige Vorstellung und für
Dienstag den 10. Manon (Massenet). „De Grieux" Hr. **Norbert Ardelli** a. G. Im Abonnement I. Gruppe (Anfang 7 Uhr)
Mittwoch den 11. La Traviata. Im Abonnement I. Gruppe (Anfang 7½ Uhr)

Weiterer Spielplan:
Donnerstag den 12. Der Ring des Nibelungen. Dritter Tag: Götterdämmerung. „Gunther" Hr. Kammersänger **Friedrich Schorr** von der Metropolitan Opera in New York a. G. (Anfang 6¼ Uhr)
Freitag den 13. Die Bohème. Bei aufgehobenem Jahres-Abonnement (Anfang 7½ Uhr)
Samstag den 14. Neu einstudiert und inszeniert: Zar und Zimmermann. Im Abonnement I. Gruppe (Anfang 7½ Uhr)
Sonntag den 15. Der Rosenkavalier. „Baron Ochs" Hr. **Emanuel Lift** als Gast. Im Abonnement (Anfang 7 Uhr)

Kartenverkauf für alle Bundestheater an den Tageskassen: I., Bräunerstraße 14, an Werktagen von 9—18·30 Uhr (am Vorstellungstage selbst nur bis 16·30 Uhr und an der Abendkassa), an Sonn- u. Feiertagen von 9—17 Uhr. Telephonische Bestellungen von Sitzen (mit Ausnahme der Säulensitze) ausschließlich unter der Telephon-Nummer R-28-5-20

„Elbemühl", Wien IX.

Operntheater

Donnerstag den 12. September 1935

Der Ring des Nibelungen
Ein Bühnenfestspiel für drei Tage und einen Vorabend von **Richard Wagner**

Dritter Tag:

Götterdämmerung

In drei Aufzügen und einem Vorspiel

Spielleitung: Hr. Dr. Wallerstein Dirigent: Hr. Dr. Felix Weingartner*

Personen der Handlung:

Siegfried	Hr. Kalenberg		Fr. Szantho
Brünnhilde	Frl. Konetzni	Die Nornen	Fr. Anday
Gutrune	Fr. Angerer		Fr. Achsel
Hagen	Hr. Hofmann		Fr. Schumann
Gunther	***	Die Rheintöchter	Fr. Hadrabova
Alberich	Hr. Wiedemann		Fr. Szantho
Waltraute	Fr. Anday		

In Szene gesetzt von Dr. Lothar Wallerstein

* Ehrenmitglied   Entwürfe: Alfred Roller

*** „Gunther" Hr. Kammersänger **Friedrich Schorr** von der Metropolitan Opera in New York a. G.

Nach jedem Aufzug eine größere Pause

Das offizielle Programm nur bei den Billetteuren erhältlich. Preis 50 Groschen — Garderobe frei

Kassen-Eröffnung **vor 6 Uhr**   Anfang 6½ Uhr   Ende **vor 11½ Uhr**

Während der Vorspiele und der Akte bleiben die Saaltüren zum Parkett, Parterre und den Galerien geschlossen. Zuspätkommende können daher nur während der Pausen Einlaß finden.

Der Kartenverkauf findet heute statt für obige Vorstellung und für

Freitag den 13. Die Bohème. Bei aufgehobenem Jahres-Abonnement (Anfang 7½ Uhr)
Samstag den 14. Neu einstudiert: Zar und Zimmermann. Im Abonnement I. Gruppe (Anfang 7½ Uhr)

Weiterer Spielplan:

Sonntag den 15. Der Rosenkavalier. „Baron Ochs" Hr. **Emanuel List** von der Metropolitan Opera in New York a. G. Im Abonnement (Anfang 7 Uhr)
Montag den 16. Margarethe (Faust). „Mephistopheles" Hr. **Ezio Pinza** a. G. (Anfang 7 Uhr)

Kartenverkauf für alle Bundestheater an den Tageskassen: I., Bräunerstraße 14, an Werktagen von 9—18·30 Uhr (am Vorstellungstage selbst nur bis 16·30 Uhr und an der Abendkassa), an Sonn- u. Feiertagen von 9—17 Uhr. Telephonische Bestellungen von Sitzen (mit Ausnahme der Säulensitze) ausschließlich unter der Telephon-Nummer R-28-3-20

Weber

Aufforderung zum Tanz (orch. Weingartner)

New York February 1913	Columbia Symphony Orchestra	Columbia Graphophone A 5464 78: Columbia L 1086 CD: Wing (Japan) WCD 7 This recording is a cut version of Weingartner's orchestration
Basle May 1928	Basler Orchester- Gesellschaft	78: Columbia 9691 CD: Wing (Japan) WCD 7 This is the only complete version of Weingartner's orchestration; it was also transferred as an experimental 33 1/3 rpm disc but not published in that form
London October 1938	LPO	78: Columbia LX 890 CD: Wing (Japan) WCD 7 Further changes were made to the orchestration for the purposes of this recording

Der Freischütz, Overture

Basle May 1928	Basler Orchester- Gesellschaft	78: Columbia 9644-9645

Film of a Paris performance of Freischütz Overture (ca. 1932) also exists

Weingartner

Der Sturm, Entr'acte from the incidental music

London November 1923	LSO	78: Columbia L 1541 <u>Coupled with Beethoven Symphony No 8</u>

Der Sturm, Scherzettino from the incidental music

London June 1923	LSO	78: Columbia L 1484 <u>Coupled with Beethoven Symphony No 7</u>
Basle May 1928	Basler Orchester- Gesellschaft	78: Columbia 8852/DWX 1253

<u>Various excerpts from this incidental music also existed in a private recording which Weingartner made with the VPO in November 1930</u>

Aus vergangener Zeit, Song with orchestra

New York February 1913	Columbia Symphony Orchestra Marcel <u>Sung in English</u>	Columbia Graphophone unpublished

Du bist ein Kind, Song with orchestra

New York February 1913	Columbia Symphony Orchestra Marcel <u>Sung in English</u>	Columbia Graphophone A 5482 LP: Rococo 5370

Frühlingsgespenster, Song with orchestra

Vienna June 1910	Hofoper Orchestra Marcel	Grammophon 2-43385

Schäfers Sonntagslied, Song with orchestra

Vienna June 1910	Hofoper Orchestra Marcel	Grammophon 2-43384 LP: Rococo 5370

Welke Rose, Song with orchestra

New York February 1913	Columbia Symphony Orchestra Marcel <u>Sung in English</u>	Columbia Graphophone unpublished

<u>Rococo LP 5370 also contains other recordings made by the soprano Lucille Weingartner-Marcel which were not conducted by Weingartner</u>

Piano rolls

Bach	Prelude and Fugue in C (Book 2 no 1)	Welte 12301
Beethoven	Hammerklavier Sonata First and third movements	Welte 12302-12303 Blüthner 50031-52791
Chopin	Nocturne op 62 no 2	Welte 12304 Blüthner 53593
Schubert	Sonata No 21 Second and fourth movements	Welte 12305-12306 Blüthner 52102-50389
Schumann	Waldszenen: Eintritt and Vogel als Prophet	Welte 12307-12308 Blüthner 51227-51228
Weingartner	4 Tonbilder zu Stifters "Studien"	Welte 12309-12310
Weingartner	Lose Blätter	Welte 655-656
Weingartner	Aus vergangener Zeit	Welte 657

All rolls originally produced in 1905

Josef Krips
1902-1974

with valuable assistance from
Michael Gray and Malcolm Walker

Discography compiled by John Hunt

Beethoven

Symphony No 1

Walthamstow January, May and June 1960	LSO	LP: Everest 3065 LP: World Records T 162-163/ ST 162-163 Also issued on other LP labels

Symphony No 2

Walthamstow January, May and June 1960	LSO	LP: Everest 3065 LP: World Records T 193/ST 193 Also issued on other LP labels

Symphony No 3 "Eroica"

Walthamstow January, May and June 1960	LSO	LP: Everest 3065 LP: World Records TP 74/STP 74 Also issued on other LP labels

Symphony No 4

Amsterdam September 1953	Concertgebouw Orchestra	LP: Decca LXT 2874 LP: Decca ECS 556
Walthamstow January, May and June 1960	LSO	LP: Everest 3065 LP: World Records T 107/ST 107 Also issued on other LP labels

Symphony No 5

Walthamstow January, May and June 1960	LSO	LP: Everest 3065 Also issued on other LP labels

Symphony No 6 "Pastoral"

Walthamstow January, May and June 1960	LSO	LP: Everest 3065 Also issued on other LP labels

Symphony No 7

Walthamstow January, May and June 1960	LSO	LP: Everest 3065 Also issued on other LP labels

Symphony No 8

Walthamstow January, May and June 1960	LSO	LP: Everest 3065 Also issued on other LP labels

Symphony No 9 "Choral"

Walthamstow January, May and June 1960	LSO BBC Chorus Vyvyan, Verrett, Petrak, Bell	LP: Everest 3065 LP: Joker SM 1284 LP: World Records T 162-163/ ST 162-163 Also issued on other LP labels

Ah perfido!, concert aria

Vienna June 1956	VPO Borkh	LP: Decca LXT 5250 LP: Decca (France) 411 6691

Piano Concerto No 1

New York	Symphony of the Air	LP: RCA RB 16041/SB 2046
December 1956	Rubinstein	LP: RCA GL 42746
		CD: RCA/BMG 09026 612602

Piano Concerto No 2

New York	Symphony of the Air	LP: RCA RB 16042
December 1956	Rubinstein	LP: RCA GL 42746
		CD: RCA/BMG 09026 612602

Piano Concerto No 3

New York	Symphony of the Air	LP: RCA RB 16043/SB 2008
December 1956	Rubinstein	LP: RCA GL 42746
		CD: RCA/BMG 09026 612602

Piano Concerto No 4

New York	Symphony of the Air	LP: RCA RB 16044/SB 2017
December 1956	Rubinstein	LP: RCA GL 42746
		CD: RCA/BMG 09026 612602

Piano Concerto No 5 "Emperor"

New York	Symphony of the Air	LP: RCA RB 16045/SB 2015
December 1956	Rubinstein	LP: RCA GL 42746
		CD: RCA/BMG 09026 612602

Violin Concerto

London	LSO	LP: Decca LXT 2674
December 1951 and	Campoli	LP: Decca ECS 521
January 1952		

Coriolan, Overture

| Vienna | VPO | LP: Concert Hall CM 2274/SMS 2274 |
| 1962 | | Orchestra described on label as Vienna Festival Orchestra |

Egmont, Overture

Walthamstow January, May and and June 1960	LSO	LP: Everest 3065 LP: Vedette (France) VDS 285 Also issued on other LP labels
Vienna 1962	VPO	LP: Concert Hall CM 2274/SMS 2274 Orchestra described on label as Vienna Festival Orchestra

Fidelio, Overture

Vienna 1962	VPO	LP: Concert Hall CM 2274/SMS 2274 Orchestra described on label as Vienna Festival Orchestra

Leonore No 3, Overture

Walthamstow January, May and June 1960	LSO	LP: Everest 3065 LP: Vedette (France) VDS 285 LP: World Records T 107/ST 107
Vienna 1962	VPO	LP: Concert Hall CM 2274/SMS 2274 Orchestra described on label as Vienna Festival Orchestra

Die Weihe des Hauses, Overture

Vienna 1962	VPO	LP: Concert Hall CM 2274/SMS 2274 Orchestra described on label as Vienna Festival Orchestra

Bellini

La Sonnambula: Excerpt (Vi ravviso)

London April 1949	LSO Arié	78: Decca K 2328 LP: Decca LX 3041 CD: EMI CHS 769 7412

Bizet

Les Pêcheurs de perles: Excerpt (Je crois entendre encore)

London April 1949	LSO Lewis	78: Decca K 2291

Brahms

Symphony No 1

Vienna October 1958	VPO	LP: Decca LXT 5292 LP: Decca ECS 643
Vienna June 1962	VPO	LP: Concert Hall CM 2268/SMS 2268 Orchestra described on label as Vienna Festival Orchestra

Symphony No 2

Zürich June 1960	Tonhalle- Orchester	LP: Musidisc FC 450 CD: Adés 13.2742 Originally issued on LP by Concert Hall

Symphony No 4

London April 1950	LSO	78: Decca X 482-486 LP: Decca LXT 2517/LXT 5368 LP: Decca ACL 132
Paris October 1954	Orchestre National	CD: Disques Montaigne TCE 8821

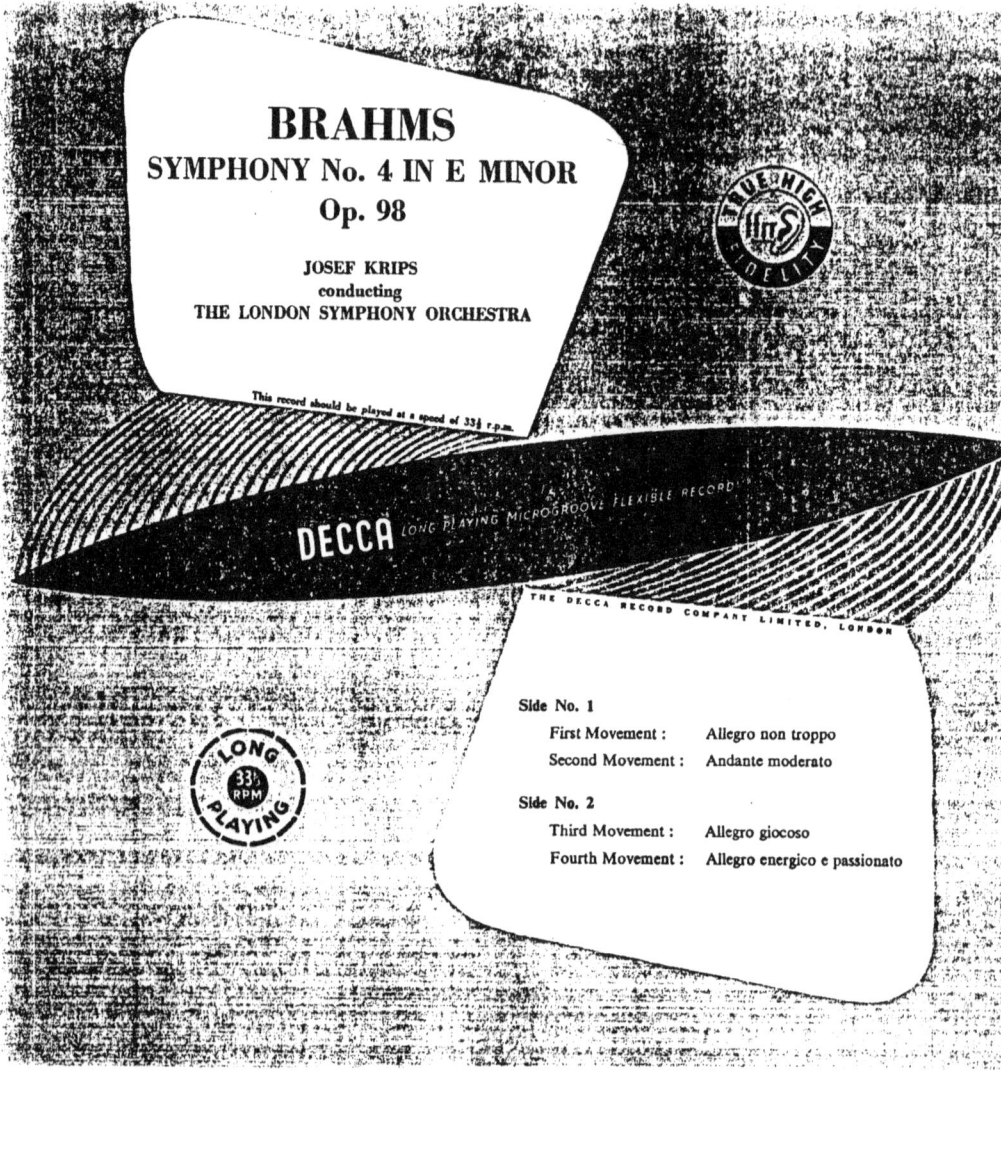

Piano Concerto No 2

New York April 1958	RCA Victor Orchestra Rubinstein	LP: RCA RB 16185/SB 2069 CD: RCA RD 85671 CD: RCA/BMG 09026 614422

Haydn Variations

London June 1963	Philharmonia	LP: EMI ALP 2023./ASD 573

Academic Festival Overture

Zürich June 1960	Tonhalle- Orchester	LP: Musidisc FC 450 CD: Adès 13.2742 Originally issued on LP by Concert Hall
London June 1963	Philharmonia	LP: EMI ALP 2023/ASD 573

Tragic Overture

London June 1963	Philharmonia	LP: EMI ALP 2023/ASD 573

Dvorak

Symphony No 9 "New World"

Zürich October 1960	Tonhalle- Orchester	LP: Musidisc FC 409 Originally issued on LP by Concert Hall

Cello Concerto

London November 1951	LSO Nelsova	LP: Decca LXT 2727 LP: Decca ACL 92

Serenade for strings

Amsterdam September 1953	Concertgebouw Orchestra	Decca unpublished

Gounod

Faust: Excerpts (1. Vains échos de la joie humaine; 2. Je puis contenter ton caprice: 3. Le veau d'or; 4. Il se fait tard; 5. Avant de quitter ces lieux; 6. Salut demeure; 7. Quel trouble dans ma coeur)

Vienna November 1936	VPO Vienna Opera Chorus Helletsgruber, Rosvaenge, Berglund, Sved Sved sings in Hungarian, the others in German	LP: UORC Records UORC 242 (1,2,3,4,6,7) LP: Teletheater 762.3589 (2,5,6)

Faust: Excerpts (1. Avant de quitter ces lieux; 2. Le veau d'or; 3. Ne permettez-vous pas?; 4. Salut demeure; 5. Il se fait tard; 6. Quittons ce lieu sombre; 7. Final trio)

Vienna March and/or July 1937	VPO Vienna Opera Chorus Rethy, Kullmann/Björling, Pinza/Kipnis/Sved Björling sings in Swedish, Pinza in Italian, Sved in Hungarian, the others in German	LP: UORC Records UORC 242 (2,4,5) LP: HRE Records HRE 376 (1,2,3,4,5,6,7)

Handel

L'Allegro, il pensieroso ed il moderato: Excerpt (Sweet bird)

Vienna November 1946	VPO Schwarzkopf	78: Columbia LX 1010 LP: EMI ALP 143 5501 LP: EMI RLS 154 6133 CD: EMI CDH 763 2012

Giulio Cesare: Excerpt (V'adoro pupille)

Vienna November 1946	VPO Seefried	Columbia unpublished

Haydn

Symphony No 92 "Oxford"

London	LSO	LP: Decca LXT 2819/LW 5293
March 1953		LP: Decca ACL 135/ECS 717

Symphony No 94 "Surprise"

Vienna	VPO	LP: Decca LXT 5418/SXL 2098
September 1957		LP: Decca ECS 828
		LP: London (Japan) K18C 8222

Symphony No 99

Vienna	VPO	LP: Decca LXT 5418/SXL 2098
September 1957		LP: Decca ECS 828

Symphony No 100 "Military"

London	LPO	LP: Decca LXT 2683
April 1949		

Symphony No 104 "London"

London	LPO	78: Decca X 53091-53093
April 1949		LP: LXT 2683
		LP: Decca ACL 90
Walthamstow	RPO	LP: Pickwick PMC 7105
September 1961		LP: RCA GL 42292
		CD: Chesky CD 16
		Originally recorded by Decca for Reader's Digest

Die Schöpfung: Excerpts (1. Nun beut die Flur; 2. Auf starkem Fittiche)

Vienna	VPO	78: Columbia LX 1011 (1)
November 1946	Seefried	78: Columbia LX 1245 (2)
		LP: EMI EX 29 10563/EX 29 12363

Humperdinck

Hänsel und Gretel: Excerpts (1. Abends will ich schlafen gehn: 2. Der kleine Sandmann bin ich; 3. Suse, liebe Suse)

London September 1947	Philharmonia Schwarzkopf (1,2,3) Seefried (1,3)	78: Columbia LX 1036-1037 (1,2,3) LP: EMI RLS 763 (1,2,3) CD: EMI CDH 769 7932 (3)

Mahler

Das Lied von der Erde

Vienna June 1972	VSO Reynolds J.Thomas	CD: Orfeo C 278 921

Massenet

Manon: Excerpt (En fermant les yeux)

London April 1949	LSO Lewis	78: Decca K 2291

Mendelssohn

Symphony No 4 "Italian"

London October 1953	LSO	LP: Decca LXT 2887/LXT 5361 LP: Decca LW 5258 LP: Decca ACL 90/ECS 527

Elijah

London September 1954	LPO LPO Chorus Delman, Procter, Maran, Boyce	LP: Decca LXT 5000-5002 LP: Decca ACL 220-222 LP: Decca ECS 650-652 Excerpts 45: Decca 45-71082 LP: Decca ECS 532

Mozart

Symphony No 21

Amsterdam September 1973	Concertgebouw Orchestra	LP: Philips 6500 525 LP: Philips 6747 130/6747 374 LP: Philips 6725 032 CD: Philips 426 9732

Symphony No 22

Amsterdam June and July 1973	Concertgebouw Orchestra	LP: Philips 6500 528 LP: Philips 6747 130/6747 374 CD: Philips 426 9732

Symphony No 23

Amsterdam June 1973	Concertgebouw Orchestra	LP: Philips 6500 527 LP: Philips 6747 130/6747 374 CD: Philips 426 9732

Symphony No 24

Amsterdam September 1973	Concertgebouw Orchestra	LP: Philips 6500 529 LP: Philips 6747 130/6747 374 CD: Philips 426 9732

Symphony No 25

Amsterdam June and July 1973	Concertgebouw Orchestra	LP: Philips 6500 529 LP: Philips 6747 130/6747 374 CD: Philips 426 9732

Symphony No 26

Amsterdam June and July 1973	Concertgebouw Orchestra	LP: Philips 6500 529 LP: Philips 6747 130/6747 374 CD: Philips 426 9742

Symphony No 27

Amsterdam September 1973	Concertgebouw Orchestra	LP: Philips 6500 528 LP: Philips 6747 130/6747 374 CD: Philips 426 9742

Symphony No 28

Amsterdam September 1973	Concertgebouw Orchestra	LP: Philips 6500 527 LP: Philips 6747 130/6747 374 CD: Philips 426 9742

Symphony No 29

Amsterdam June 1973	Concertgebouw Orchestra	LP: Philips 6500 528 LP: Philips 6747 130/6747 374 CD: Philips 426 9742

Symphony No 30

Amsterdam June and July 1973	Concertgebouw Orchestra	LP: Philips 6500 527 LP: Philips 6747 130/6747 374 CD: Philips 422 9782

Symphony No 31 "Paris"

London December 1951	LSO	LP: Decca LXT 2689/LW 5327 LP: Decca ACL 128 LP: Decca (France) 411 6981
Amsterdam November 1972	Concertgebouw Orchestra	LP: Philips 6500 466/6747 130 LP: Philips 6747 374/6599 704 LP: Philips 6725 032 CD: Philips 426 0632

Symphony No 31 "Paris": alternative Andante movement

Amsterdam June 1973	Concertgebouw Orchestra	LP: Philips 6500 466/6747 130 LP: Philips 6747 374/6599 704 CD: Philips 426 0632

Symphony No 32

Amsterdam June 1973	Concertgebouw Orchestra	LP: Philips 6500 526 LP: Philips 6747 130/6747 374 CD: Philips 422 4762

Symphony No 33

Amsterdam June and July 1973	Concertgebouw Orchestra	LP: Philips 6500 526/6747 130 LP: Philips 6747 374/6725 032 CD: Philips 426 9782 Rehearsal extracts LP: Philips 6529 144/6725 032

Symphony No 34

Amsterdam September 1973	Concertgebouw Orchestra	LP: Philips 6500 526 LP: Philips 6747 130/6747 374 CD: Philips 426 9782

Symphony No 35 "Haffner"

Tel Aviv March and April 1957	Israel Philharmonic	LP: Decca LXT 5414/SXL 2220 LP: Decca SPA 336
Walthamstow September 1961	RPO	LP: RCA GL 32520 CD: Chesky CD 16 Originally recorded by Decca for Reader's Digest
Amsterdam June 1972	Concertgebouw Orchestra	LP: Philips 6500 429 LP: Philips 6747 130/6747 374 LP: Philips 6725 032/6998 010 CD: Philips 426 0632

Symphony No 36 "Linz"

Amsterdam June 1973	Concertgebouw Orchestra	LP: Philips 6500 525 LP: Philips 6747 130/6747 374 LP: Philips 6725 032/6998 010 CD: Philips 426 0632

Symphony No 38 "Prague"

Amsterdam September 1972	Concertgebouw Orchestra	LP: Philips 6500 466/6747 130 LP: Philips 6747 374/6725 032 LP: Philips 6770 009/6998 010 CD: Philips 422 4762

Symphony No 39

London October 1947	LSO	78: Decca AK 1829-1831 LP: Decca LXT 2689/LXT 5356 LP: Decca LW 5289/ACL 135 LP: Decca (France) 411 6984
Amsterdam June 1972	Concertgebouw Orchestra	LP: Philips 6500 430/6747 130 LP: Philips 6747 374/6725 032 LP: Philips 6770 009/6998 010 CD: Philips 422 9742

Symphony No 40

London March 1953	LSO	LP: Decca LXT 2819/LXT 5356 LP: Decca LW 5265 LP: Decca ACL 128/ECS 716
Paris November 1965	Orchestre National	CD: Disques Montaigne TCE 8821
Amsterdam June 1972	Concertgebouw Orchestra	LP: Philips 6500 430 LP: Philips 6747 130/6747 374 LP: Philips 6527 188/6725 032 LP: Philips 6770 009/6998 010 CD: Philips 422 4762/432 2202

Symphony No 41 "Jupiter"

London April 1949	LSO	78: Decca AX 492-495 LP: Decca LX 3010
Tel Aviv March and April 1957	Israel Philharmonic	LP: Decca LXT 5414/SXL 2220 LP: Decca BR 3050/SWL 8006 LP: Decca SPA 336
Amsterdam June 1972	Concertgebouw Orchestra	LP: Philips 6500 429 LP: Philips 6747 130/6747 374 LP: Philips 6527 188/6725 032 LP: Philips 6770 009/6998 010 CD: Philips 422 9742/432 2202

Piano Concerto No 17

London	LSO	RCA unpublished
July 1959	Rubinstein	Recording incomplete

Piano Concerto No 20

London	LSO	RCA unpublished
July 1959	Rubinstein	Recording incomplete

Piano Concerto No 23

London	LSO	LP: Decca LXT 2867
October 1953	Curzon	LP: Decca (France) 411 6781
London	LSO	RCA unpublished
July 1959	Rubinstein	Recording incomplete

Piano Concerto No 24

London	LSO	LP: Decca LXT 2867
October 1953	Curzon	LP: Decca (France) 411 6781
New York	RCA Victor	LP: RCA RB 16248/SB 2177
December 1958 and	Orchestra	CD: RCA/BMG GD 87968
December 1959	Rubinstein	

Piano Concerto No 25

London	Philharmonia	78: HMV DB 6604-6607/
October 1947	E.Fischer	DB 9827-9830
		LP: Victor LHMV 1004
		LP: Turnabout THS 65094
		LP: EMI 2C 051 43326/2C 061 01408
		CD: EMI CHS 763 7192

Violin Concerto No 4

London	New Symphony	LP: **Decca** LXT 5078
May 1955	Orchestra	LP: Decca (France) 411 8841
	Elman	

Violin Concerto No 5

London	New Symphony	LP: Decca LXT 5078
May 1955	Orchestra	LP: Decca (France) 411 8841
	Elman	

Andante (Cassation K63)

London April 1949	LSO	Decca unpublished

Turkish March from Piano Sonata No 11 (arr. Herbeck)

Vienna June 1950	VPO	78: Decca (Switzerland) KX 28353 Fill-up to 78 issue of complete Entführung aus dem Serail; some doubt exists as to whether this was conducted by Krips

Requiem Mass

Vienna June 1950	Hofmusik- kapelle & Chorus Pech, Breitschopf, W.Ludwig, Pröglhöf	78: Decca AX 366-372 LP: Decca LX 3030-3031 LP: Decca ACL 39 LP: Decca (France) 411 6821

Et incarnatus est (Mass in C minor)

London October 1947	Philharmonia Berger	78: HMV DB 6536 LP: Victor LM 6130 LP: EMI EX 29 05983 CD: EMI CMS 763 7502

Exsultate jubilate

Vienna November 1946	VPO Schwarzkopf	Columbia unpublished

Mia speranza adorata; No, no, che non sei capace, Concert arias

London January 1951	LSO I.Hollweg	LP: Decca LX 3054

ROYAL ALBERT HALL

(Manager: C. S. Taylor)

VICTOR HOCHHAUSER presents
TWO EXTRA CONCERTS
WITH THE
VIENNA PHILHARMONIC ORCHESTRA

Conductor: **JOSEPH KRIPS**

Principal Conductor of the Vienna State Opera

TUESDAY EVENING, OCTOBER 5th, at 8.0
MOZART - MAHLER - SCHUBERT CONCERT

Soloist: **ELISABETH HÖNGEN**

(Vienna State Opera)

PROGRAMME

Eine Kleine Nachtmusik	MOZART
Lieder Eines Fahrenden Gesellen	MAHLER
Symphony No. 7 in C major (The Great)	SCHUBERT

THURSDAY EVENING, OCTOBER 7th, at 8.0
GRAND JOHANN STRAUSS CONCERT

PROGRAMME

Ouvertüre Zigeunerbaron	Tritsch-Tratsch Polka	G'schichten aus dem Wiener Wald Waltzer
Annen Polka	Wein, Weib und Gesang Walzer	Pizzikato Polka
Jockey Polka	Ouvertüre: Waldmeister	Perpetuum mobile Polka
Rosen aus dem Süden Walzer	Libellen Polka	Kaiserwalzer
Persischer Marsch	Vergnügungszug Polka	Ouvertüre Fledermaus
Verliebte Augen Polka		

TICKETS at 3/6, 10/6, 15/-, 21/- and 25/-

From Royal Albert Hall (KENsington 8212) and all Agents

(Under the auspices of the Anglo-Austrian Music Society) in aid of the
"HELP THE AUSTRIAN CHILDREN FUND"

(Hon. Management: VICTOR HOCHHAUSER)

La Clemenza di Tito, Overture

Zürich December 1960	Tonhalle- Orchester	LP: Concert Hall AM 2218/SMS 2218 LP: Musidisc FC 456

Così fan tutte, Overture

London December 1951	LSO	LP: Decca LXT 2684/LXT 5376
Zürich December 1960	Tonhalle- Orchester	LP: Concert Hall AM 2218/SMS 2218 LP: Musidisc FC 456

Così fan tutte: Excerpts (In uomini; Una donna a 15 anni)

London April 1949	LSO Güden	CD: Preiser 90176 Previously unpublished Decca recordings

Don Giovanni

Vienna June 1955	VPO Vienna Opera Chorus Della Casa, Danco, Güden, Dermota, Corena, Siepi, Böhme	LP: Decca LXT 5103-5106/ SXL 2117-2120 LP: Decca GOS 604-606 CD: Decca 411 4262 Excerpts 45: Decca CEP 613/SEC 5032 LP: Decca LXT 5443 LP: Decca BR 3025/SWL 8003 LP: Decca SDD 382/SDD 460 CD: Decca 440 4882
Chicago November 1964	Chicago Lyric Opera Orchestra & Chorus Stich-Randall, Curtin, Panni, Kraus, Ghiaurov, Kunz, Uppman	LP: Melodram MEL 464

Don Giovanni, Overture

London December 1951	LSO	LP: Decca LXT 2684/LXT 5376 LP: Decca LW 5001 45: Decca CEP 590
Zürich December 1960	Tonhalle- Orchester	LP: Concert Hall AM 2218/SMS 2218 LP: Musidisc FC 456

Don Giovanni: Excerpt (Mi tradi)

London September 1947	Philharmonia Schwarzkopf	78: Columbia LX 1210 45: Columbia SEL 1511 LP: EMI RLS 763

Don Giovanni: Excerpt (Dalla sua pace)

London April 1948	New Symphony Orchestra Dermota	78: Decca K 2125

Don Giovanni: Excerpt (Batti batti)

London April 1948	LSO Güden	CD: Preiser 90176 Previously unpublished Decca recording

Don Giovanni: Excerpt (Vedrai carino)

London April 1948	LSO Güden	78: Decca K 1861 LP: London (USA) LL 1508 CD: Preiser 90176

Die Entführung aus dem Serail

Vienna June 1950	VPO Vienna Opera Chorus Lipp, Loose, W.Ludwig, Klein, Koreh	78: Decca (Switzerland) KX 28341-28353 LP: Decca LXT 2536-2538 LP: Decca ECM 730-731 LP: Decca (France) 411 6741 Excerpts LP: Decca LXT 2635
Vienna February 1966	VPO Vienna Opera Chorus Rothenberger, Popp, Gedda, Frick	LP: EMI 1C 163 00070-00071 LP: Seraphim SIB 6025 CD: EMI CMS 763 2632 Excerpts LP: EMI 1C 063 00844 Complete recording also issued on LP by World Records

Die Entführung aus dem Serail, Overture

London December 1951	LSO	LP: Decca LXT 2684/LXT 5376 LP: Decca LW 5021
Zürich December 1960	Tonhalle- Orchester	LP: Concert Hall AM 2218/SMS 2218 LP: Musidisc FC 456

Die Entführung aus dem Serail: Excerpt (Traurigkeit ward mir zum Lose)

Vienna October 1946	VPO Schwarzkopf	LP: Columbia LX 1249 LP: American Columbia ML 4649 LP: EMI RLS 763/RLS 154 6133 CD: EMI CDH 763 7082

Die Entführung aus dem Serail: Excerpt (Martern aller Arten)

London October 1947	Philharmonia Berger	78: HMV DB 6616 LP: EMI 1C 047 28556 LP: EMI 1C 137 46104-46105

La Finta giardiniera, Overture

Zürich December 1960	Tonhalle- Orchester	LP: Concert Hall AM 2218/SMS 2218 LP: Musidisc FC 456

Idomeneo, Overture

Zürich December 1960	Tonhalle- Orchester	LP: Concert Hall AM 2218/SMS 2218 LP: Musidisc FC 456

Idomeneo: Excerpt (Zeffiretti lusinghieri)

London October 1947	Philharmonia Berger Sung in German	78: HMV DB 6617 LP: EMI 1C 137 46104-46105

Le Nozze di Figaro, Overture

London December 1951	LSO	LP: Decca LXT 2684/LXT 5376
Zürich December 1960	Tonhalle- Orchester	LP: Concert Hall AM 2218/SMS 2218 LP: Musidisc FC 456

Le Nozze di Figaro: Excerpt (Porgi amor)

Vienna June 1950	VPO Reining Sung in German	LP: Decca LXT 2685 CD: Preiser 90083

Le Nozze di Figaro: Excerpt (Dove sono)

London September 1947	Philharmonia Cebotari	78: HMV DA 1875 45: HMV 7ER 5126 LP: Victor LCT 1115 LP: Electrola E 60050 LP: EMI 1C 147 29118-29119 LP: EMI 1C 187 29225-29226 LP: Preiser PR 9860 CD: Preiser 90034
Vienna June 1950	VPO Reining Sung in German	LP: Decca LXT 2685 CD: Preiser 90083

Le Nozze di Figaro: Excerpt (Deh vieni non tardar)

Vienna November 1946	VPO Seefried	Columbia unpublished Without recitative
London September 1947	Philharmonia Seefried	Columbia unpublished
London April 1949	LSO Güden	CD: Preiser 90176 Previously unpublished Decca recording

Le Nozze di Figaro: Excerpt (Non so più)

London October 1947	LSO Güden	78: Decca K 1861 LP: London (USA) LL 1508 CD: Preiser 90176

Il Re pastore: Excerpt (L'amerò, sarò costante)

Vienna November 1946	VPO Schwarzkopf	78: Columbia LX 1096 LP: EMI RLS 763/EX 29 05983 CD: EMI CMS 763 7502

Harold Holt Ltd. in association with
The London Symphony Orchestra Ltd.
present

SEVENTH SERIES OF
BEETHOVEN CONCERTS

LONDON SYMPHONY ORCHESTRA

Leader: Hugh Maguire

Conductor:

JOSEF KRIPS

Soloist:

CLAUDIO ARRAU

Friday, May 17, at 8

Symphony No. 8
Piano Concerto No. 4
INTERVAL
Symphony No. 5

Direction: HAROLD HOLT LTD.
Managing Director: Ian Hunter

HAROLD HOLT LTD. in association with
THE LONDON SYMPHONY ORCHESTRA LTD.
present

SEVENTH SERIES OF BEETHOVEN CONCERTS

LONDON SYMPHONY ORCHESTRA

Leader: Hugh Maguire

Conductor:

JOSEF KRIPS

Soloists:

JENNIFER VYVYAN
NORMA PROCTER
ROWLAND JONES
OWEN BRANNIGAN
ALEXANDRA CHOIR

Conductor: Charles Proctor

Friday, May 31, 1957, at 8

Symphony No. 1

INTERVAL

Symphony No. 9 (Choral)

Direction: HAROLD HOLT LTD.
Managing Director: IAN HUNTER

Der Schauspieldirektor, Overture

London December 1951	LSO	LP: Decca LXT 2684/LXT 5376 LP: Decca LW 5021
Zürich December 1960	Tonhalle- Orchester	LP: Concert Hall AM 2218/SMS 2218 LP: Musidisc FC 456

Die Zauberflöte, Overture

London December 1951	LSO	LP: Decca LXT 2684/LXT 5376 LP: Decca LW 5001 45: Decca CEP 590
Zürich December 1960	Tonhalle- Orchester	LP: Concert Hall AM 2218/SMS 2218 LP: Musidisc FC 456

Die Zauberflöte: Excerpts (Wo willst du, kühner Fremdling, hin?: Der, welcher wandert diese Strassen)

Vienna 1970	VPO Janowitz, Dermota, Beirer, Wächter, Pernerstorfer	CD: Melodram CDM 26522

Die Zauberflöte: Excerpt (Ach, ich fühl's)

London September 1947	Philharmonia Seefried	78: Columbia LX 1145 LP: EMI EX 29 12363 LP version incorrectly names orchestra as VPO

Die Zauberflöte: Excerpt (Dies Bildnis ist bezaubernd schön)

London April 1948	New Symphony Orchestra Dermota	78: Decca K 2125

Die Zauberflöte: Excerpt (In diesen heiligen Hallen)

Vienna 1962	VPO Kreppel	LP: Melodram MEL 665

Mussorgsky

Boris Godunov: Excerpt (Death of Boris)

London	LSO	78: Decca K 2229
April 1949	Arié	LP: Decca LX 3041

Nicolai

Die lustigen Weiber von Windsor, Overture

London	Philharmonia	78: Columbia DX 1484
October 1947		

Offenbach

Les Contes d'Hoffmann: Excerpt (Les oiseaux dans la charmille)

Vienna	VPO	LP: Legendary LR 131
October 1966	Silja	
	Sung in German	

Paumgartner

Rossini in Neapel: Excerpt (Schon die halbe Nacht verfolgt mich eine kleine Melodie)

Vienna	VPO	78: Odeon 04852
January 1937	Tauber	

Ach manch' vergangene Nacht hab' ich mit reizenden Frauen verbracht

Vienna	VPO	LP: EMI 1C 137 178130-178133
January 1937	Tauber	

Puccini

La Bohème: Excerpts (Sì mi chiamano Mimì; Donde lieta uscì)

London October 1947	LSO Güden	Decca unpublished
London April 1949	LSO Güden	78: Decca X 302/K 23023 CD: Preiser 90176

La Bohème: Excerpt (Quando men vo)

London October 1947	LSO Güden	78: Decca M 614 CD: Preiser 90176

Gianni Schicchi: Excerpt (O mio babbino caro)

London October 1947	LSO Güden	78: Decca M 614 CD: Preiser 90176

Schoenberg

Gurrelieder

Vienna June 1969	VSO Singakademie Janowitz, C.Ludwig, Pilz, Sergi, Dickie, Lackner	CD: Hunt CDHP 585

Schubert

Symphony No 6

London April 1948	LSO	78: Decca AK 2119-2122 LP: Decca LXT 2585/ACL 115

Symphony No 8 "Unfinished"

London April 1950	LSO	LP: Decca LX 3012
Vienna 1964	VPO	LP: Concert Hall AM 2341/SMS 2341 <u>Orchestra described on label as</u> <u>Vienna Festival Orchestra</u>
Vienna March 1969	VPO	LP: Decca SXL 6549 LP: Contour CC 7503 LP: London (Japan) K18C 8222

Symphony No 9 "Great"

Amsterdam May 1952	Concertgebouw Orchestra	LP: Decca LXT 2719 LP: Decca ACL 70
London May 1958	LSO	LP: Decca LXT 5471/SXL 2045 LP: Decca SPA 467 LP: Decca (France) 592.047 CD: Decca 425 9572
Vienna 1972	VSO	CD: Orfeo C 234 901

Rosamunde, Overture

London April 1948	LSO	78: Decca K 2071

Schumann

Symphony No 1 "Spring"

London May 1957	LSO	LP: Decca LXT 5347/SXL 2223 LP: Decca BR 3101/SWL 8013 LP: Decca SPA 493 LP: Decca (France) 592.051

Symphony No 4

London November 1952	LSO	LP: Decca LXT 2887
London October 1956	LSO	LP: Decca LXT 5347/SXL 2223 LP: Decca (France) 592.051 CD: Decca 425 9572

Piano Concerto

London March 1953	LSO Kempff	LP: Decca LXT 2806/LW 5337 LP: Decca ECS 802 CD: Decca 433 4042
New York April 1958	RCA Victor Orchestra Rubinstein	LP: RCA RB 16145/SB 2033 LP: RCA (Germany) 26.48064 CD: RCA/BMG 09026 614442

Searle

Symphony No 2 (1958)

London September 1962	LPO	LP: Lyrita SRCS 72

Smetana

Dalibor

Vienna October 1969	VPO Vienna Opera Chorus Rysanek, Spiess, Dallapozza, Wächter Sung in German	CD: Myto 92465

Eduard Strauss

Bahn frei, Polka

Vienna June 1962	VPO	LP: Concert Hall SMS 2880-2885 <u>Orchestra described on label as</u> <u>Vienna Festival Orchestra</u>

Johann Strauss father

Piefke und Puffke, Polka

London April 1950	LSO	78: Decca AK 476 LP: Decca LM 4530

Radetzky March

London October 1947	Philharmonia	78: Columbia DB 2485

Johann Strauss

Accelerationen, Waltz

London April 1948	New Symphony Orchestra	78: Decca K 1936 LP: Decca LK 4021/LW 5012
Vienna September 1957	VPO	LP: Decca LXT 5431/SXL 2047 LP: Decca ADD 133/SDD 133 LP: Contour CC 7522 CD: Decca (Germany) 2894 308682

An der schönen blauen Donau, Waltz

London October 1947	National Symphony Orchestra	78: Decca K 1725 LP: Decca LK 4021/LW 5011
London April 1948	New Symphony Orchestra	LP: London (USA) LL 10
Vienna October 1956	VPO Güden	Decca unpublished This vocal version was announced as a Decca 45 EP CEP 535/SEC 5003 but subsequently withdrawn
Vienna September 1957	VPO	LP: Decca LXT 5431/SXL 2047 LP: Decca ADD 133/SDD 133/BR 3043 LP: Contour CC 7522 CD: Decca (Germany) 2894 308682
Vienna September 1962	VPO	LP: Concert Hall AM 2271/SMSA 2271 LP: Musidisc FC 429 Orchestra described on label as Vienna Festival Orchestra

Annen Polka

London April 1950	LSO	78: Decca M 621 LP: Decca LM 4530

Die Fledermaus, Overture

| London
October 1947 | Philharmonia | 78: Columbia DX 1707 |
| Vienna
June 1962 | VPO | LP: Concert Hall AM 2241/SMSA 2241
LP: Musidisc FC 429
<u>Orchestra described on label as</u>
<u>Vienna Festival Orchestra</u> |

Freikugeln, Polka

| Vienna
June 1962 | VPO | LP: Concert Hall SMS 2880-2885
<u>Orchestra described on label as</u>
<u>Vienna Festival Orchestra</u> |

Frühlingsstimmen, Waltz

| Vienna
October 1946 | VPO
Schwarzkopf | LP: EMI ALP 143 5501
LP: EMI RLS 154 6133
CD: EMI CDM 763 6542/CMS 763 7902
Recording incomplete |
| Vienna
October 1956 | VPO
Güden | 45: Decca CEP 708
LP: Decca ECS 2122 |

Gschichten aus dem Wienerwald, Waltz

| London
October 1947 | Philharmonia | 78: Columbia DX 1503
45: Columbia SCD 2100 |

Kaiserwalzer

London October 1947	National Symphony Orchestra	Decca unpublished Recording incomplete
London April 1948	New Symphony Orchestra	78: Decca K 1874 LP: Decca LK 4021/LW 5011
Vienna September 1957	VPO	LP: Decca LXT 5431/SXL 2047 LP: Decca ADD 133/SDD 133 LP: Contour CC 7522 CD: Decca (Germany) 2894 308682
Vienna June 1962	VPO	LP: Concert Hall AM 2271/SMSA 2271 LP: Musidisc FC 429 <u>Orchestra described on label as</u> <u>Vienna Festival Orchestra</u>

Perpetuum mobile

| London
April 1948 | New Symphony
Orchestra | 78: Decca M 621
LP: Decca LM 4530 |

Rosen aus dem Süden, Waltz

London April 1948	New Symphony Orchestra	78: Decca K 1986 LP: Decca LK 4021/LW 5012
Vienna October 1956	VPO Güden	Decca unpublished This vocal version was announced as a Decca 45 EP CEP 535/SEC 5003 but subsequently withdrawn
Vienna September 1957	VPO	LP: Decca LXT 5431/SXL 2047/BR 3043 LP: Decca ADD 133/SDD 133 LP: Contour CC 7522 CD: Decca (Germany) 2894 308682

I-Tipferl, Polka

Vienna June 1962	VPO	LP: Concert Hall AM 2271/SMSA 2271 LP: Musidisc FC 429 Orchestra described on label as Vienna Festival Orchestra

Tritsch-Tratsch Polka

London April 1950	LSO	78: Decca AK 476 LP: Decca LM 4530

Waldmeister, Overture

Vienna June 1962	VPO	LP: Concert Hall AM 2271/SMSA 2271 LP: Musidisc FC 429 Orchestra described on label as Vienna Festival Orchestra

Wein, Weib und Gesang, Waltz

London April 1950	LSO	LP: Decca LM 4530/LW 5009

Wiener Blut, Waltz

London April 1950	LSO	78: Decca X 415 LP: Decca LM 4530/LW 5009

Der Zigeunerbaron, March

Vienna June 1962	VPO	LP: Concert Hall AM 2271/SMSA 2271 LP: Musidisc FC 429 Orchestra described on label as Vienna Festival Orchestra

Josef Strauss

Dorfschwalben aus Oesterreich, Waltz

Vienna October 1956	VPO Güden	45: Decca CEP 708 LP: Decca ECS 2122

Johann & Josef Strauss

Pizzicato Polka

London October 1947	Philharmonia	78: Columbia DB 2485 LP: American Columbia RL 3036
Vienna September 1957	VPO	LP: Decca LXT 5431/SXL 2047 LP: Decca ADD 133/SDD 133 LP: Contour CC 7522 CD: Decca (Germany) 2894 308682

Richard Strauss

Ariadne auf Naxos: Excerpt (Grossmächtige Prinzessin)

London January 1951	LSO I.Hollweg	LP: Decca LX 3054

Der Rosenkavalier

Moscow October 1971	VPO Vienna Opera Chorus Rysanek, C.Ludwig, De Groote, Kunz, Jungwirth	LP: Melodiya C10 28033 007

Der Rosenkavalier, Suite (arr. Krips)

London May and June 1963	Philharmonia	LP: EMI ALP 2112/ASD 654

Salome: Excerpt (Closing scene)

Vienna June 1956	VPO Borkh	LP: Decca LXT 5250 LP: Decca (France) 411 6691

Till Eulenspiegels lustige Streiche

Vienna 1972	VSO	CD: Orfeo C 234 901B

Stravinsky

L'Oiseau de feu, Suite

London May and June 1963	Philharmonia	LP: EMI ALP 2112/ASD 654 LP: EMI CFP 40328

STAATSOPER

Donnerstag, den 10. Oktober 1963

Im Abonnement XVII. Gruppe. Beschränkter Kartenverkauf
Preise IV

VERDI-GEDENKAUFFÜHRUNG
anläßlich der 150. Wiederkehr des Geburtstages

In italienischer Sprache

Othello

Oper in vier Akten von Giuseppe Verdi

Dirigent: Josef Krips
Inszenierung: Herbert v. Karajan
Bühnenbilder: Wilhelm Reinking
Kostüme: Georges Wakhewitsch
Einstudierung der Chöre: Roberto Benaglio

Othello, Befehlshaber der venezianischen Flotte	Carlos Guichandut
Jago, Fähndrich	Giuseppe Taddei
Cassio, Hauptmann	Piero de Palma
Rodrigo, ein edler Venezianer	Ermanno Lorenzi
Lodovico, Gesandter der Republik Venedig	Nicola Zaccaria
Montano, der frühere Statthalter von Cypern	Siegfried Rudolf Frese
Ein Herold	Harald Pröglhöf
Desdemona, Othellos Gemahlin	Gabriella Tucci
Emilia, Jagos Gattin	Margarita Lilowa

Ort der Handlung: Eine Hafenstadt der Insel Cypern

Technische Einrichtung: Hans Felkel
Beleuchtung: Albin Rotter

Nach dem zweiten Akt eine größere Pause

Anfang 19 Uhr   Ende nach 22 Uhr

Tchaikovsky

Symphony No 5

Vienna September 1958	VPO	LP: Decca LXT 5503/SXL 2109 LP: Decca ADD 142/SDD 142

Symphony No 6 "Pathétique"

Zürich October 1960	Tonhalle- Orchester	LP: Accord 140071 LP: Musidisc FC 432 Originally issued on LP by Concert Hall

Verdi

Aida: Excerpt (Ritorna vincitor)

London September 1947	Philharmonia Welitsch	78: Columbia LB 85 LP: EMI HLM 7006 LP: World Records SH 289 CD: EMI CDH 761 0072/CHS 769 7412

Aida: Excerpt (O patria mia)

London September 1947	Philharmonia Welitsch	Columbia unpublished

Rigoletto: Excerpt (Caro nome)

London October 1947	Philharmonia Berger	Columbia unpublished

Simone Boccanegra: Excerpt (Suona ogni labbro il mio nome)

Vienna March 1969	VPO Ghiaurov, Wächter	CD: Legato SRO 514

La Traviata

Vienna December 1971	VPO Vienna Opera Chorus Cotrubas, Gedda, MacNeil	LP: Estro armonico EA 003

Wagner

Rienzi

Vienna June 1960	ORF Orchestra and Chorus Stich-Randall, C.Ludwig, Svanholm, Schöffler, Pernerstorfer	LP: Melodram MEL 225 CD: Laudis LCD 24016

Rienzi: Excerpt (Erstehe, hohe Roma, neu)

Vienna May 1933	VPO Völker	LP: Teletheater 120.747

Weber

Euryanthe, Overture

London April 1950	LSO	Decca unpublished

Oberon, Overture

London May 1958	LSO	Decca unpublished

Oberon: Excerpt (Ozean, du Ungeheuer)

Vienna June 1956	VPO Borkh	LP: Decca LXT 5250 LP: Decca (France) 411 6691

JOSEF KRIPS

JOSEF KRIPS, yet another of the fine group of Viennese conductors, was born in Vienna and was educated in his native city, where he studied conducting under Weingartner. In 1921 he was engaged at the Vienna Volksoper; from 1925 to 1926 he was first conductor at Dortmund, and from 1926 to 1933 was Generalmusikdirektor at Karlsruhe.

Krips began his connection with the Vienna State Opera in 1933. In 1938, when the Nazis annexed Austria, he was dismissed from his post, and also relieved of his position at the Vienna Academy of Music, where he was Professor of Music.

Fortunately, Krips survived the hardships of the war years. He conducted the first opera performance in Vienna after the war, and many of the Vienna Philharmonic's concerts; and it was due to him more than anyone else that the State Opera won back its position as one of the leading European opera ensembles in the years immediately after the war.

When the Vienna Company came to Covent Garden in 1947, Krips conducted *Don Giovanni, Cosi fan tutte,* and *Figaro*. It is as a Mozart conductor that he has won his greatest successes. He has conducted Mozart opera not only in Vienna and London, but in Paris, Florence, Rome, Amsterdam, and Brussels, and elsewhere in Europe.

Krips' connection with the Salzburg Festival began in 1935 and continued from 1946 until 1950. At Salzburg he conducted performances of *Don Giovanni, Figaro, Cosi fan tutte, Entführung, Clemenza di Tito, Orfeo, Romeo und Julia* (Blacher), and *The Rape of Lucretia*. This last work he also conducted for the English Opera Group during their London season in 1951.

Krips has conducted many orchestral concerts in Europe and America, and has specially close connections with the London Symphony Orchestra.

From the Decca Book of Opera

Otto Klemperer
1885-1973

with valuable assistance from
Michael Gray and Heiko Reysen

Discography compiled by John Hunt

Auber

Fra Diavolo, Overture

Berlin May 1929	Staatskapelle	78: Parlophone (England) E 11201 78: Parlophone (Germany) P 9406 CD: Symposium 1042

Bach

Brandenburg Concerto No 1

Berlin 1924	Staatskapelle	Polydor unpublished Existence of this recording cannot be conclusively confirmed
Paris July 1946	Paris Pro Musica Orchestra	78: Polydor (France) 566209-566211/ 6209-6211 auto 78: Vox (USA) 618 LP: Vox PL 6180 Some issues incorrectly labelled Vienna Pro Musica Orchestra
London October 1960	Philharmonia	LP: Columbia 33CX 1763/SAX 2408 CD: EMI CMS 764 1502
Philadelphia October 1962	Philadelphia Orchestra	CD: AS-Disc AS 533

Brandenburg Concerto No 2

Paris July 1946	Paris Pro Musica Orchestra	78: Polydor (France) 566212-566213/ 6212-6213 auto 78: Vox (USA) 619 LP: Vox PL 6180 Some issues incorrectly labelled Vienna Pro Musica Orchestra
London September and October 1960	Philharmonia	LP: Columbia 33CX 1763/SAX 2408 CD: EMI CMS 764 1502

Brandenburg Concerto No 3

Paris July 1946	Paris Pro Musica Orchestra	78: Polydor (France) 566214-566215/ 6214-6215 auto 78: Vox (USA) 620 LP: Vox PL 6200 Some issues incorrectly labelled Vienna Pro Musica Orchestra
London October 1960	Philharmonia	LP: Columbia 33CX 1764/SAX 2409 CD: EMI CMS 764 1502

Brandenburg Concerto No 4

Paris July 1946	Paris Pro Musica Orchestra	78: Polydor (France) 566216-566217/ 6216-6217 auto 78: Vox (USA) 621 LP: Vox PL 6200 Some issues incorrectly labelled Vienna Pro Musica Orchestra
London October 1960	Philharmonia	LP: Columbia 33CX 1764/SAX 2409 CD: EMI CMS 764 1502

Brandenburg Concerto No 5

Paris July 1946	Paris Pro Musica Orchestra	78: Polydor (France) 566218-566220/ 6218-6220 auto 78: Vox (USA) 622 LP: Vox PL 6220 Some issues incorrectly labelled Vienna Pro Musica Orchestra
Budapest January 1950	Budapest Symphony Orchestra	LP: Hungaroton LPX 12160
London October 1960	Philharmonia	LP: Columbia 33CX 1764/SAX 2409 CD: EMI CMS 764 1502

Brandenburg Concerto No 6

Paris July 1946	Paris Pro Musica Orchestra	78: Polydor (France) 566221-566223/ 6221-6223 auto 78: Vox (USA) 623 LP: Vox PL 6220 Some issues incorrectly labelled Vienna Pro Musica Orchestra
London October 1960	Philharmonia	LP: Columbia 33CX 1763/SAX 2408 CD: EMI CMS 764 1502

Orchestral Suite No 1

London November and December 1954	Philharmonia	LP: Columbia 33CX 1239
London October 1969	New Philharmonia	LP: EMI SLS 808 CD: EMI CMS 764 1502

Orchestral Suite No 2

Budapest June 1949	Budapest Symphony Orchestra	LP: Hungaroton LPX 12379
London November 1954	Philharmonia	LP: Columbia 33CX 1239
London September and October 1969	New Philharmonia	LP: EMI SLS 808 CD: EMI CMS 764 1502

Orchestral Suite No 3

London November and December 1954	Philharmonia	LP: Columbia 33CX 1240
Munich September 1957	Bavarian RO	CD: Orfeo C 201 891A
Berlin May 1964	BPO	LP: Longanesi periodici GCL 41
London September and October 1969	New Philharmonia	LP: EMI SLS 808 CD: EMI CMS 764 1502

Orchestral Suite No 4

Budapest April 1949	Hungarian RO	LP: Hungaroton LPX 12667
London November and December 1954	Philharmonia	LP: Columbia 33CX 1240
London September 1969	New Philharmonia	LP: EMI SLS 808 CD: EMI CMS 764 1502

Harpsichord Concerto in D minor BWV1052

London May 1961	Philharmonia Malcolm	Columbia unpublished

Bist du bei mir (orch. Klemperer)

Los Angeles February 1945	Los Angeles Philharmonic	LP: PAARV PRV 3501
Paris July 1946	Paris Pro Musica Orchestra	78: Polydor (France) 566215/6214 78: Vox (USA) 620 Coupled with Brandenburg No 3

Nun komm' der Heiden Heiland (orch. Klemperer)

Paris July 1946	Paris Pro Musica Orchestra	78: Polydor (France) 566211/6209 78: Vox (USA) 618 Coupled with Brandenburg No 1

Cantata No 202 "Weichet nur, betrübte Schatten"

Amsterdam February 1957	Concertgebouw Orchestra Schwarzkopf	LP: Discocorp RR 537/RR 208 CD: Hunt CD 727 CD: AS-Disc AS 533

Magnificat

Budapest January 1950	Budapest Symphony Orchestra & Chorus Bathy, Sandor, Tiszay, Littasy, Somogyvari	LP: Hungaroton LPX 12160

Mass in B minor

London December 1961	Philharmonia Orchestra & Chorus	Columbia unpublished <u>Choruses only recorded</u>
London March, October and November 1967	New Philharmonia BBC Chorus Giebel, Baker, Gedda, Prey, Crass	LP: EMI SLS 930 CD: EMI CMS 763 3642
London November 1967	New Philharmonia BBC Chorus Giebel, Baker, Gedda, Prey, Crass	CD: Hunt CD 727

Saint Matthew Passion

London November 1960, January, April, May, November and December 1961	Philharmonia Orchestra & Chorus Schwarzkopf, C.Ludwig, Pears, Gedda, Berry, Fischer-Dieskau	LP: Columbia 33CX 1799-1803/ SAX 2446-2450 LP: EMI SLS 827 CD: EMI CMS 763 0582 <u>Excerpts</u> 45: Columbia SEL 1707 LP: Columbia 33CX 1881/SAX 2525 LP: Columbia 33CX 5253/SAX 5253

Bartok

Viola Concerto

Amsterdam January 1951	Concertgebouw Orchestra Primrose	CD: Archiphon ARC 101 CD: Music and Arts CD 752

ROYAL FESTIVAL HALL
General Manager: T. E. Bean

PHILHARMONIA CONCERT SOCIETY LTD.
Artistic Director:
WALTER LEGGE

presents

BEETHOVEN FESTIVAL

PHILHARMONIA
ORCHESTRA
Leader: MANOUG PARIKIAN

KLEMPERER

Tossy Spivakovsky	Claudio Arrau
Aase Nordmo-Loevberg	Christa Ludwig
Waldemar Kmentt	Hans Hotter

Philharmonia Chorus
Chorus Master: WILHELM PITZ

October 11th, 13th, 15th, 17th, 24th, 26th
November 3rd, 4th, 8th, 12th, 15th

Klemperer
Philharmonia Orchestra

BEETHOVEN

Symphony No. 3 in E flat ("Eroica")

33CX1346

Symphony No. 5 in C minor

33C1051

Symphony No. 7 in A

33CX1379

Overtures:
Leonore 1, 2 and 3; Fidelio

33CX1270

COLUMBIA

(Regd. Trade Mark of Columbia Graphophone Co. Ltd.)

33⅓ R.P.M. LONG PLAYING RECORDS

E.M.I. RECORDS LIMITED, 8-11 Great Castle Street, London, W.1

Beethoven

Symphony No 1

Berlin 1924	Staatskapelle	78: Polydor 66231-66234/ 69760-69763 auto LP: DG 2535 811
Turin December 1956	RAI Turin Orchestra	LP: Cetra LAR 37 LP: Cetra (Japan) K22C 324
London October 1957	Philharmonia	LP: Columbia 33CX 1554/SAX 2318 LP: EMI SLS 788/ASD 2569 LP: EMI ED 29 02701/EX 29 03793 CD: EMI CDC 747 1842/CDM 763 3542
Vienna June 1960	Philharmonia	CD: Cetra CDE 1067 CD: Hunt CD 755
Bonn September 1970	New Philharmonia	CD: Hunt CDHP 591

Symphony No 2

London October 1957	Philharmonia	LP: Columbia 33CX 1615/SAX 2331 LP: EMI SLS 788/ASD 2561 LP: EMI ED 29 02521/EX 29 03793 CD: EMI CDC 747 1852/CDM 763 3552
Vienna May 1960	Philharmonia	CD: Cetra CDE 1033 CD: Hunt CD 756

Symphony No 3 "Eroica"

London October and December 1955	Philharmonia	LP: Columbia 33CX 1346 LP: EMI SLS 873 LP: EMI EX 29 04573 CD: EMI CDM 763 8552
Berlin March 1958	Berlin RO	CD: Musica classica 34 001
London October and November 1959	Philharmonia	LP: Columbia 33CX 1710/SAX 2364 LP: EMI SLS 788/ASD 2562 LP: EMI SXLP 30310 LP: EMI ED 29 02711/EX 29 03793 CD: EMI CDC 747 1862/CDM 763 3562
Vienna May 1960	Philharmonia	CD: Cetra CDE 1007 CD: Hunt CD 755 Also issued on CD by Bellaphon
Vienna June 1963	VSO	CD: Orfeo C 233 901A
Bonn September 1970	New Philharmonia	CD: Hunt CDHP 591

Symphony No 4

Amsterdam May 1956	Concertgebouw Orchestra	CD issue announced by Hunt (Arkadia)
London October 1957	Philharmonia	LP: Columbia 33CX 1702/SAX 2354 LP: EMI SLS 788/ASD 2563 LP: EMI ED 29 02701/EX 29 03793 CD: EMI CDC 747 1852/CDM 763 3552
Vienna May 1960	Philharmonia	CD: Cetra CDE 1038 CD: Hunt CD 757/CDGI 7571
Berlin May 1966	BPO	CD: Hunt CD 571 Incorrectly dated May 1964
Munich May 1969	Bavarian RO	CD: Refrain (Japan) DR 920038

Symphony No 5

Vienna April and May 1951	VSO	LP: Vox PL 7070/PL 11870 LP: Vox STPL 513190 LP: Fidelio ATL 4107/TQD 3029 LP: Intercord 125.802/120.922 LP: Columbia (Japan) DXM 167 CD: Allegro 8039
London October and December 1955	Philharmonia	LP: Columbia 33C 1051 LP: EMI SLS 788 LP: EMI EX 29 04573 CD: EMI CDM 763 8682
London October 1959	Philharmonia	LP: Columbia 33CX 1721/SAX 2373 LP: EMI SLS 788/ASD 2564 LP: EMI ED 29 02521/EX 29 03793 CD: EMI CDC 747 1872/CDM 763 3572
Vienna June 1960	Philharmonia	CD: Cetra CDE 1067 CD: Virtuoso 269.7042 CD: Hunt CD 758 CD: Frequenz 041.018
Berlin May 1966	BPO	CD: Hunt CD 571 Incorrectly dated May 1964
Vienna May 1968	VPO	CD: DG 435 3272/435 3212
Munich May 1969	Bavarian RO	CD: Refrain (Japan) DR 910002

Symphony No 6 "Pastoral"

Vienna March 1951	VSO	LP: Vox PL 6960/GBY 6960 LP: Intercord 125.803/120.923 LP: Columbia (Japan) DXM 168 CD: Allegro 8000
Berlin February 1954	Berlin RO	LP: Movimento musica 01.030 Incorrectly labelled BPO
Amsterdam May 1956	Concertgebouw Orchestra	CD: Music and Arts CD 246
London October 1957	Philharmonia	LP: Columbia 33CX 1532/SAX 2260 LP: EMI SLS 788/ASD 2565 LP: EMI ED 29 02531/EX 29 03793 CD: EMI CDC 747 1882/CDM 763 3582
Vienna June 1960	Philharmonia	CD: Cetra CDE 1068 CD: Hunt CD 758

Symphony No 7

London October and December 1955	Philharmonia	LP: Columbia 33CX 1379 LP: EMI SLS 873 LP: EMI EX 29 04573 CD: EMI CDM 763 8682/CDM 769 1832 <u>CDM 769 1832 was the first issue of a stereo version</u>
Amsterdam May 1956	Concertgebouw Orchestra	CD: Archiphon ARC 109
Geneva March 1957	Suisse Romande Orchestra	LP: Movimento musica 08.001 <u>Incorrectly labelled Lausanne March 1955</u>
Vienna June 1960	Philharmonia	CD: Cetra CDE 1008 CD: Hunt CD 756
London October, November and December 1960	Philharmonia	LP: Columbia 33CX 1769/SAX 2315 LP: EMI SLS 788/ASD 2566 LP: EMI ED 29 03281/EX 29 03793 CD: EMI CDC 747 1842/CDM 763 3542
London February 1966	New Philharmonia	CD: Refrain (Japan) DR 920037
London October 1968	New Philharmonia	LP: EMI ASD 2537
Paris October 1968	New Philharmonia	Pathé unpublished

Symphony No 8

Berlin 1924	Staatskapelle	78: Polydor 66264-66266/ 69786-69788 auto
Berlin 1926	Staatskapelle	78: Polydor 66460-66462
Amsterdam May 1956	Concertgebouw Orchestra	CD: AS-Disc AS 115 CD: Music and Arts CD 246
London October 1957	Philharmonia	LP: Columbia 33CX 1554/SAX 2318 LP: EMI SLS 788/ASD 2560 LP: EMI ED 29 03281/EX 29 03793 CD: EMI CDC 747 1872/CDM 763 3572
Vienna June 1960	Philharmonia	CD: Cetra CDE 1033 CD: Hunt CD 756/CDGI 757

Symphony No 9 "Choral"

Amsterdam May 1956	Concertgebouw Orchestra Toonkunstkoor Brouwenstijn, Hermes, Häfliger, Wilbrink	CD: Music and Arts CD 242
London October and November 1957	Philharmonia Orchestra & Chorus Nordmo-Lövberg, C.Ludwig, Kmennt, Hotter	LP: Columbia 33CX 1574-1575/ SAX 2276-2277 LP: EMI SLS 788/SLS 790 LP: EMI SXDW 3051 LP: EMI ED 29 02721/EX 29 03793 CD: EMI CDC 747 1892/CDM 763 3592
Vienna June 1960	Philharmonia Singverein Lipp, Boese, Wunderlich, Crass	CD: Cetra CDE 1051 CD: Hunt CD 759 CD: Stradivarius STR 10003

Missa Solemnis

Vienna March 1951	VSO Akademiechor Steingruber, Schürhoff, Majkut, Wiener	LP: Vox PL 6992/PL 11430 LP: Turnabout THS 65015-65016 LP: Turnabout TV 37072 LP: Intercord 155.803 LP: Columbia (Japan) DXM 164
Cologne June 1955	WDR Orchestra WDR & NDR Choruses Kupper, Wagner, Schock, Greindl	LP: Cetra LO 532 LP: Movimento musica 02.012 CD: Frequenz CMB 2
London September and October 1965	New Philharmonia Orchestra & Chorus Söderström, Höffgen, Kmennt, Talvela	LP: EMI AN 165-166/SAN 165-166 LP: EMI SLS 922 CD: EMI CMS 769 5382

Choral Fantasia

London November 1967	New Philharmonia Alldis Choir Barenboim	LP: EMI SLS 941/SLS 5180 LP: EMI ASD 2608 CD: EMI CMS 763 3602

Ah perfido !, concert aria

Amsterdam April 1951	Concertgebouw Orchestra Brouwenstijn	CD: Music and Arts CD 752

Piano Concerto No 1

London October and November 1967	New Philharmonia Barenboim	LP: EMI SLS 941/SLS 5180 LP: EMI ASD 2616 CD: EMI CMS 763 3602

Piano Concerto No 2

London October and November 1967	New Philharmonia Barenboim	LP: EMI SLS 941/SLS 5180 LP: EMI ASD 2608 CD: EMI CMS 763 3602

Piano Concerto No 3

London October and November 1967	New Philharmonia Barenboim	LP: EMI SLS 941/SLS 5180 LP: EMI ASD 2579 CD: EMI CMS 763 3602

Piano Concerto No 4

Vienna June 1951	VSO Novaes	LP: Vox PL 7090 CD: Vox CDX 25501
Cologne February 1956	WDR Orchestra Fleisher	CD: Hunt CD 733
London October and November 1967	New Philharmonia Barenboim	LP: EMI SLS 941/SLS 5180 LP: EMI ASD 2550 CD: EMI CMS 763 3602

Piano Concerto No 5 "Emperor"

London October and November 1967	New Philharmonia Barenboim	LP: EMI SLS 941/SLS 5180 LP: EMI ASD 2500 CD: EMI CMS 763 3602

Violin Concerto

London January 1966	New Philharmonia Menuhin	LP: EMI ALP 2285/ASD 2285 LP: EMI EG 29 02741 CD: EMI CDC 769 0012/CDM 764 3242

Grosse Fuge

London March 1956	Philharmonia	LP: Columbia 33CX 1438 LP: EMI SLS 873 LP: EMI ED 29 02711/EX 29 03799 CD: EMI CDC 747 1862/CDM 763 3562
London February 1966	New Philharmonia	CD: Refrain (Japan) DR 920037

ROYAL FESTIVAL HALL
General Manager: T. E. BEAN, C.B.E.

PHILHARMONIA CONCERT SOCIETY LTD
Artistic Director: WALTER LEGGE

BEETHOVEN FESTIVAL
1959

PHILHARMONIA ORCHESTRA
Leader: HUGH BEAN

Dr OTTO KLEMPERER

Anthony di Bonaventura

Henryk Szeryng

Joan Sutherland

Ursula Böse

Jon Vickers

~~Gottlob Frick~~
Otto Edelmann

Philharmonia Chorus
Chorus Master: WILHELM PITZ

October 26th

November 1st, 4th, 9th, 16th, 20th, 28th, 30th

ROYAL FESTIVAL HALL
General Manager: T. E. Bean, C.B.E.

PHILHARMONIA CONCERT SOCIETY Ltd
Artistic Director: Walter Legge

BEETHOVEN FESTIVAL
1963

PHILHARMONIA ORCHESTRA
Principal Conductor: Otto Klemperer
Leader: Hugh Bean

OTTO KLEMPERER

CLAUDIO ARRAU   HANS HOTTER
KURT BÖHME   GUNDULA JANOWITZ
PIERRE FOURNIER   WILHELM KEMPFF
DONALD GROBE   NATHAN MILSTEIN
ERNST HAEFLIGER   HANS RICHTER-HAASER
MARGA HÖFFGEN   ELISABETH SÖDERSTRÖM

PHILHARMONIA CHORUS
Chorus Master: Wilhelm Pitz

October 10, 14, 27, 28
November 12, 16, 23
December 1 and 2

Coriolan, Overture

Berlin 1926	Staatskapelle	78: Polydor 66599/57022 78: Decca CA 8091 LP: DG 2535 811 CD: Symposium 1042
London October 1957	Philharmonia	LP: Columbia 33CX 1615/SAX 2331 LP: Columbia 33CX 1930/SAX 2570 LP: EMI SLS 788/ASD' 2564/SXDW 3032 LP: EMI ED 29 02701/EX 29 03793 CD: EMI CDC 747 1902/CDM 763 6112
Vienna June 1960	Philharmonia	CD: Cetra CDE 1008 CD: Virtuoso 269.7042 CD: Hunt CD 759
Vienna June 1963	VSO	CD: Orfeo C 233 901A/C 286 921Z
Munich May 1969	Bavarian RO	CD: Refrain (Japan) DR 920038

Egmont, Overture

Berlin 1926	Staatskapelle	78: Polydor 66600 LP: DG 2535 811
London October 1957	Philharmonia	45: Columbia SEL 1609 LP: Columbia 33CX 1575 LP: Columbia 33CX 1930/SAX 2570 LP: EMI SLS 788/ASD 2563/SXDW 3032 LP: EMI ED 29 02531/EX 29 03793 CD: EMI CDC 747 1882/CDM 763 3582
Vienna May 1960	Philharmonia	CD: Cetra CDE 1008 CD: Virtuoso 269.7042 CD: Hunt CD 757

Egmont, Incidental music: Excerpts (1. Die Trommel gerühret; 2. Freudvoll und leidvoll; 3. Klärchens Tod)

London November 1957	Philharmonia Nilsson (1 and 2)	45: Columbia SEL 1609 (1 and 2) LP: Columbia 33CX 1575 LP: EMI ED 29 02531/EX 29 03793 CD: EMI CDC 747 1882/CDM 763 3582

Fidelio

Budapest November 1948	Budapest Opera Orchestra & Chorus Bathy, Matyas, Rösler, Nagy, Szekely, Maleczky, Koszo Sung in Hungarian	LP: Hungaroton SLPX 12428-12429 Excerpt also published on a record supplied with 1973 book on Klemperer in Budapest
London March 1961	Covent Garden Orchestra & Chorus Jurinac, Morrison, Vickers, Dobson, Frick, Hotter, Robinson	LP: Melodram MEL 407 CD: Melodram CDM 27076
London February 1962	Philharmonia Orchestra & Chorus C.Ludwig, Hallstein, Vickers, Unger, Frick, Berry, Crass	LP: Columbia 33CX 1804-1806/ SAX 2451-2453 LP: EMI SLS 5006 CD: EMI CMS 769 3242 Excerpts LP: Columbia 33CX 1907/SAX 2547 LP: EMI SXLP 30307 Overture LP: Columbia 33CX 1902/SAX 2542 LP: EMI SLS 788/ASD 2562 LP: EMI SXDW 3032/SXLP 30310 LP: EMI ED 29 02721 CD: EMI CDC 747 1902/CDM 763 6112

Fidelio: Excerpts (Abscheulicher!; O namenlose Freude!)

London October 1964	Covent Garden Orchestra Crespin, Pribyl	LP: Rodolphe RP 12445-12446 Conductor of this performance was Norman Del Mar: Klemperer conducted the opera in London in 1961, 1962 and 1969 only

Fidelio, Overture

London November 1954	Philharmonia	LP: Columbia 33CX 1270 LP: EMI SLS 873/EX 29 04573

Die Geschöpfe des Prometheus, Overture

London November 1957	Philharmonia	LP: Columbia 33CX 1615/SAX 2331 LP: Columbia 33CX 1930/SAX 2570 LP: EMI SLS 788/ASD 2561 LP: EMI SXDW 3032/EX 29 13411 CD: EMI CDM 769 1832/CDM 763 3582
Vienna May 1960	Philharmonia	CD: Cetra CDE 1038 CD: Virtuoso 269.7042 CD: Hunt CD 757
London October 1969	New Philharmonia	LP: EMI SXDW 3032/ED 29 04011 CD: EMI CDC 747 1882

ROYAL FESTIVAL HALL
General Manager: T. E. Bean

PHILHARMONIA CONCERT SOCIETY LTD.

Artistic Director:
WALTER LEGGE

presents

PHILHARMONIA
ORCHESTRA
Leader: MANOUG PARIKIAN

OTTO KLEMPERER
GEZA ANDA

BEETHOVEN

Grosse Fugue
Piano Concerto No. 1 in C major, Op. 15
INTERVAL
Symphony No. 7 in A major, Op. 92

Monday, March 25th, 1957
at 8 *p.m.*

Management: IBBS & TILLETT LTD., 124 WIGMORE STREET, W.1

Programme One Shilling

Die Geschöpfe des Prometheus, Adagio and Finale

London October 1969	New Philharmonia	LP: EMI SXDW 3032/ED 29 04011 CD: EMI CDC 747 1882

König Stephan, Overture

London October 1959	Philharmonia	LP: Columbia 33CX 1721/SAX 2373 LP: Columbia 33CX 1930/SAX 2570 LP: EMI SLS 788/SLS 790 LP: EMI SXDW 3032/SXDW 3051 LP: EMI ED 29 04011 CD: EMI CDM 763 6112

Leonore No 1, Overture

London November 1954	Philharmonia	LP: Columbia 33CX 1270 LP: EMI SLS 873/EX 29 04573 CD: EMI CDM 764 1432
London November 1963	Philharmonia	LP: Columbia 33CX 1902/SAX 2542 LP: EMI SLS 788/ASD 2565 LP: EMI SXDW 3032/ED 29 04011 CD: EMI CDC 747 1902/CDM 763 6112

Leonore No 2, Overture

London November 1954	Philharmonia	LP: Columbia 33CX 1270 LP: EMI SLS 873/EX 29 04573 CD: EMI CDM 763 8552
London November 1963	Philharmonia	LP: Columbia 33CX 1902/SAX 2542 LP: EMI SLS 788/ASD 2561 LP: EMI SXDW 3032/ED 29 04011 CD: EMI CDC 747 1902/CDM 763 6112

Leonore No 3, Overture

Berlin 1926	Staatskapelle	78: Polydor 66601-66602/ 57070-57071 LP: DG 2535 811 CD: Koch 311 162
London November 1954	Philharmonia	LP: Columbia 33CX 1270 LP: EMI SLS 873/EX 29 04573 CD: EMI CDM 763 8552
London November 1963	Philharmonia	LP: Columbia 33CX 1902/SAX 2542 LP: EMI SLS 788/SLS 790/ASD 2568 LP: EMI SXDW 3032/SXDW 3051 LP: EMI ED 29 04011 CD: EMI CDC 747 1902/CDM 763 6112
Cologne March 1966	WDR Orchestra	CD: Cetra CDE 1068
Berlin May 1966	BPO	CD: Hunt CD 732

Die Weihe des Hauses, Overture

London July 1956	Philharmonia	LP: Angel (USA) 35329 LP: EMI EX 29 04573
Edinburgh August 1958	Philharmonia	LP: PAARV PRV 3501
London October 1959	Philharmonia	LP: Columbia 33CX 1702/SAX 2354 LP: Columbia 33CX 1930/SAX 2570 LP: EMI SLS 788/ASD 2566 LP: EMI SXDW 3032 LP: EMI ED 29 02531/EX 29 03793 CD: EMI CDC 747 1902/CDM 763 6112
Vienna May 1960	Philharmonia	CD: Cetra CDE 1038

Berlioz

Symphonie fantastique

London April and September 1963	Philharmonia	LP: Columbia 33CX 1898/SAX 2537 LP: EMI SLS 5003/EMX 2030 CD: EMI CDM 764 1432
London January 1966	New Philharmonia	CD: Refrain (Japan) DR 910007

Benvenuto Cellini, Overture

Los Angeles January 1938	Los Angeles Philharmonic	LP: Symposium 1004

Brahms

Symphony No 1

Berlin
February 1928
	Staatskapelle		78: Parlophone (England)
			  E 10807-10812
			78: Parlophone (Germany)
			  P 9615-9620
			78: Odeon O 6890-6895
			LP: EMI 1C 053 28939
			CD: Koch Legacy 3-7053-2

Cologne October 1955	WDR Orchestra		LP: Cetra LO 515 LP: Rococo 2096 CD: Frequenz 041.013 CD: Bella musica BMF 89964/ 31.6005 <u>Rococo edition incorrectly labelled Dresden Staatskapelle/ Knappertsbusch</u>
London December 1955	Philharmonia		Columbia unpublished <u>Recording incomplete</u>
London October 1956 and March 1957	Philharmonia		LP: Columbia 33CX 1504/SAX 2262 LP: EMI SLS 804/ASD 2705 LP: EMI SXLP 30217 CD: EMI CDM 769 6512

Symphony No 2

London October 1956	Philharmonia		LP: Columbia 33CX 1517/SAX 2362 LP: EMI SLS 804/ASD 2706 LP: EMI SXLP 30238 CD: EMI CDM 769 6502

Symphony No 3

London March 1956	Philharmonia	Columbia unpublished <u>Recording incomplete</u>
London March 1957	Philharmonia	LP: Columbia 33CX 1536/SAX 2351 LP: EMI SLS 804/ASD 2707 LP: EMI SXLP 30265 CD: EMI CDM 769 6492

Symphony No 4

London November 1956 and March 1957	Philharmonia	LP: Columbia 33CX 1591/SAX 2350 LP: EMI SLS 804/ASD 2708 LP: EMI SXLP 30214 CD: EMI CDM 769 6492
Munich September 1957	Bavarian RO	CD: Orfeo C 201 891A

Piano Concerto No 2

Cologne April 1954	WDR Orchestra Anda	LP: Movimento musica 01.051 CD: Hunt CD 733
London January 1969	New Philharmonia Ashkenazy	CD: Hunt CD 709

Violin Concerto

Paris June 1960	Orchestre National Oistrakh	LP: Columbia 33CX 1765/SAX 2411 LP: EMI SLS 5004/SXLP 30264 LP: EMI CFP 4398 CD: EMI CDM 769 0342

Haydn Variations

London October 1954	Philharmonia	LP: Columbia 33CX 1241 CD: EMI CDM 764 1462
Amsterdam February 1957	Concertgebouw Orchestra	CD: AS-Disc AS 113 CD: Hunt CD 709 CD: Music and Arts CD 247

Piano Quartet in G (orch. Schoenberg)

Los Angeles May 1938	Los Angeles Philharmonic	CD: Archiphon awaiting publication <u>World premiere performance</u> <u>Excerpts</u> LP: Symposium 1007

Academic Festival Overture

Berlin June 1927	Staatskapelle	78: Electrola EJ 152-153 78: HMV D 1853-1854 LP: EMI 1C 053 28939
London March 1957	Philharmonia	LP: Columbia 33CX 1536/SAX 2351 LP: EMI SLS 804/ASD 2707 LP: EMI SXLP 30255 CD: EMI CDM 769 6512

Tragic Overture

London March 1957	Philharmonia	LP: Columbia 33CX 1517/SAX 2362 LP: EMI SLS 804/SLS 821/ASD 2706 LP: EMI SXLP 30238 CD: EMI CDM 769 6512

Ein deutsches Requiem

Cologne February 1956	WDR Orchestra and Chorus Grümmer, Prey	CD: Hunt CD 716
London January, March, April and May 1961	Philharmonia Orchestra & Chorus Schwarzkopf, Fischer-Dieskau	LP: Columbia 33CX 1781-1782/ SAX 2430-2431 LP: EMI SLS 821 CD: EMI CDC 747 2382
Vienna June 1968	VPO Singverein Lipp, Wächter	CD: Refrain (Japan) DR 920034

Alto Rhapsody

London March 1962	Philharmonia Orchestra & Chorus C.Ludwig	LP: Columbia 33CX 1817/SAX 2487 LP: EMI SLS 821/ASD 2391 LP: EMI SXLP 27 00001 CD: EMI CDM 769 6502

ROYAL FESTIVAL HALL
General Manager: T. E. Bean

PHILHARMONIA CONCERT SOCIETY LTD.

Artistic Director:
WALTER LEGGE

presents

PHILHARMONIA
ORCHESTRA
Leader: MANOUG PARIKIAN

KLEMPERER

BRAHMS PROGRAMME

Variations on Corale St. Antonii, Op. 56a
Symphony No. 3 in F major, Op. 90

INTERVAL

Symphony No. 1 in C minor, Op. 68

Friday, November 16th, 1956

at 8 p.m.

Management: IBBS & TILLETT LTD., 124 WIGMORE STREET, W.1

Programme One Shilling

Preis 40 Pfennig.

Konzerte der Deutschen Nothilfe
Winter 1924/25.

Philharmonie

Freitag, den 17. Oktober 1924, abends 7½ Uhr

Zum hundertsten Geburtstag von Anton Bruckner:

Bruckner-Feier

mit dem

verstärkten Philharmonischen Orchester.

Leitung:

Otto Klemperer

Verband der konzertierenden Künstler Deutschlands, e. V., Berlin W 57, Blumenthalstr. 17.

Bruckner

Symphony No 4 "Romantic"

Vienna March 1951	VSO	LP: Vox PL 6930 LP: Turnabout THS 65019/TV 37073 LP: Columbia (Japan) DXM 158 LP: Intercord 120.925/120.805
Cologne April 1954	WDR Orchestra	LP: Movimento musica 01.052 CD: Hunt CDHP 591
London September 1963	Philharmonia	LP: Columbia 33CX 1928/SAX 2569 LP: EMI SXLP 30167 CD: EMI CDM 769 1272
Munich April 1966	Bavarian RO	CD: Hunt CD 732

Symphony No 5

London March 1967	New Philharmonia	LP: EMI SAX 5288-5289 CD: EMI CDM 763 6122
Vienna June 1968	VPO	CD: Hunt CD 569

Symphony No 6

London January 1961	BBC SO	CD: Hunt CD 720 Incorrectly dated March 1967
Amsterdam June 1961	Concertgebouw Orchestra	LP: Movimento musica 01.056 CD: Music and Arts CD 247
London November 1964	New Philharmonia	LP: Columbia 33CX 1943/SAX 2582 LP: EMI SXLP 30448 CD: EMI CDM 763 3512

Symphony No 7

Munich April 1956	Bavarian RO	CD: Hunt CD 708
Lucerne September 1958	BPO	LP: Movimento musica 01.057 CD: Frequenz CMD 1 CD: Music and Arts CD 551 <u>First movement only</u> CD: Relief CR 1883
London November 1960	Philharmonia	LP: Columbia 33CX 1808-1809/ SAX 2454-2455 LP: EMI ED 29 00411 CD: EMI CDM 769 1262

Symphony No 8

Cologne June 1957	WDR Orchestra	LP: Movimento musica 02.023 CD: Hunt CD 704
London October and November 1970	New Philharmonia	LP: EMI SLS 872 CD: EMI CMS 763 8352

Symphony No 8, Adagio

Berlin 1924	Staatskapelle	78: Polydor 66325-66328/ 69764-69767 auto

Symphony No 9

London February 1970	New Philharmonia	LP: EMI ASD 2719 CD: EMI CDM 763 9162

Te Deum

London January 1961	BBC SO BBC Chorus Harper, Baker, Lewis, Nowakowski	LP: Melodram MEL 214

Chopin

Piano Concerto No 1

Cologne	WDR Orchestra	LP: Cetra LO 507/DOC 37
October 1954	Arrau	CD: Cetra CDE 1004
		CD: Hunt CD 511

Piano Concerto No 2

Vienna	VSO	LP: Vox PL 7100/PL 11380
June 1951	Novaes	CD: Vox CDX 25501

Cherubini

Anacreon, Overture

London	Philharmonia	Columbia unpublished
September 1960		

Corelli

Sonata in D "La follia" (arr. Leonard)

Los Angeles	Los Angeles	CD: Music and Arts CD 720
December 1945	Philharmonic	
	Szigeti	

Debussy

Prélude à l'après-midi d'un faune

Los Angeles	Los Angeles	LP: Symposium 1007
January 1938	Philharmonic	

Nuages et Fêtes (Nocturnes)

Berlin	Staatskapelle	78: Polydor 66464-66465
1926		78: Brunswick 80016-80017
		CD: Symposium 1042

Falla

Nights in the Gardens of Spain

Amsterdam March 1951	Concertgebouw Orchestra Andriessen	CD: Music and Arts CD 752

Dvorak

Symphony No 9 "New World"

London October and November 1963	Philharmonia	LP: Columbia 33CX 1914/SAX 2554 LP: EMI SLS 5003 CD: EMI CDM 763 8692

Franck

Symphony in D minor

London February 1966	New Philharmonia	LP: EMI CX 5276/SAX 5276 LP: EMI SLS 5003 CD: EMI CDM 764 1452

German

Who'll buy my sweet lavender?

Los Angeles June 1937	Los Angeles Philharmonic Bori	LP: Ed Smith EJS 425 LP: MDP Records MDP 033

Gershwin

Rhapsody in Blue: Excerpt

Los Angeles 1937	Los Angeles Philharmonic Iturbi	LP: Symposium 1007 Michael Gray advises that in all probability this performance was conducted by A. Smallens or by Iturbi himself

Prelude No 2 (orch. Brockman)

Los Angeles September 1937	Los Angeles Philharmonic	LP: Citadel CT 7026 LP: Symposium 1007

Gluck

Iphigenie in Aulis, Overture

London September 1960	Philharmonia	LP: Columbia 33CX 1770/SAX 2417 CD: EMI CDM 764 1432

Handel

Messiah

London February, March, July, September, October and November 1964	Philharmonia Orchestra & Chorus Schwarzkopf, G.Hoffman, *Baker, *Boese, *Pears, Gedda, Hines	LP: EMI AN 146-148/SAN 146-148 LP: EMI SLS 915 CD: EMI CMS 763 6212 Excerpts LP: EMI ALP 2288/ASD 2288 *These artists took part in certain recording sessions but not in the issued recording

Concerto grosso op 6 no 7 (transcr. Schoenberg), Excerpts

Los Angeles January 1938	Los Angeles Philharmonic Kolisch Quartet	LP: Symposium 1007 CD: Archiphon awaiting publication

Concerto grosso op 6 no 4

London March and July 1956	Philharmonia	45: Columbia SEL 1594/ESL 6254 LP: Columbia 33C 1053/SBO 2751 LP: EMI CX 5252/SAX 5252 CD: EMI CDM 764 1462

Haydn

Symphony No 88

London October 1964	New Philharmonia	LP: Columbia 33CX 1931/SAX 2571 CD: EMI CMS 763 6672

Symphony No 92 "Oxford"

London September 1971	New Philharmonia	LP: EMI ASD 2818 CD: EMI CMS 763 6672

Symphony No 95

London February 1970	New Philharmonia	LP: EMI ASD 2818 CD: EMI CMS 763 6672

Symphony No 98

London January 1960	Philharmonia	LP: Columbia 33CX 1748/SAX 2395 CD: EMI CMS 763 6672

Symphony No 100 "Military"

London October 1965	New Philharmonia	LP: EMI CX 5266/SAX 5266 LP: EMI ED 29 03571 CD: EMI CMS 763 6672

Symphony No 101 "Clock"

Turin December 1955	RAI Turin Orchestra	LP: Cetra LAR 37 LP: Cetra (Japan) K22C 325
Munich October 1956	Bavarian RO	LP: Melodram MEL 215 LP: Longanesi periodici GCL 62 CD: Refrain (Japan) DR 910002 LP editions incorrectly dated and labelled Berlin RO
London January 1960	Philharmonia	LP: Columbia 33CX 1748/SAX 2395 CD: EMI CMS 763 6672

Symphony No 102

London September and October 1965	New Philharmonia	LP: EMI CX 5266/SAX 5266 CD: EMI CMS 763 6672

Symphony No 104 "London"

London October 1964	New Philharmonia	LP: Columbia 33CX 1931/SAX 2571 LP: EMI ED 29 03571 CD: EMI CMS 763 6672

Hindemith

Nobilissima visione

London October 1954	Philharmonia	LP: Columbia 33CX 1241 CD: EMI CMS 763 8352

Horn Concerto

London October 1954	Philharmonia Brain	Columbia unpublished Recording incomplete

Humperdinck

Hänsel und Gretel, Overture and Dream Pantomime

London September 1960	Philharmonia	LP: Columbia 33CX 1770/SAX 2417 CD: EMI CDM 763 9172 Dream Pantomime only 45: Columbia SCD 2239

Janacek

Sinfonietta

Amsterdam January 1951	Concertgebouw Orchestra	CD: Archiphon ARC 101 CD: Music and Arts CD 752

Klemperer

Symphony No 1

Amsterdam June 1961	Concertgebouw Orchestra	LP: Archiphon ARCH 1 CD: Memories HR 4248-4249

Symphony No 2

London March and October 1968	New Philharmonia	EMI unpublished
London March, October and November 1969	New Philharmonia	LP: EMI ASD 2575/ED 29 03321 CD: EMI CMS 763 1472

Symphony No 3

London February 1970	New Philharmonia	EMI unpublished

Symphony No 4

London March 1969	New Philharmonia	EMI unpublished

Merry Waltz

London October 1961	Philharmonia	LP: Columbia 33CX 1814/SAX 2460 LP: EMI SXLP 30226/ED 29 03321 CD: EMI CDM 763 9172

J'accuse

London March and October 1968	New Philharmonia	EMI unpublished

String Quartet No 7

London February 1970	Philharmonia String Quartet	LP: EMI ASD 2575 CD: EMI CMS 764 1472 <u>Recording made under composer's supervision</u>

Liszt

Piano Concerto No 1

London May 1960 and May 1962	Philharmonia A.Fischer	LP: Columbia 33CX 1842/SAX 2485 CD: EMI CDM 764 1442

Totentanz

Los Angeles February 1945	Los Angeles Philharmonic Segall	LP: PAARV PRV 3501

Mahler

Symphony No 2 "Resurrection"

Vienna March 1951	VSO Singverein Akademiechor Steingruber, Rössel-Majdan	LP: Vox PL 7010/PL 7012/VBX 115 LP: Turnabout THS 65087-65088 LP: Turnabout TV 34249-34250 LP: Columbia (Japan) DXM 160 LP: Intercord 155.804
Amsterdam July 1951	Concertgebouw Orchestra Toonkunstkoor Vincent, Ferrier	LP: Discocorp IGI 374 LP: Decca D264 D2 CD: Decca 425 9702 CD: Verona 27062-27063 Urlicht only CD: Verona 27076
London November 1961 and March 1962	Philharmonia Orchestra & Chorus Schwarzkopf, Rössel-Majdan	LP: Columbia 33CX 1829-1830/ SAX 2473-2474 LP: EMI SLS 806 CD: EMI CDM 769 6822
Munich January 1965	Bavarian Radio Orchestra & Chorus Harper, Baker	CD: Nuova Era 6714 CD: Hunt CD 703
London May 1971	New Philharmonia Orchestra & Chorus Finley, Hodgson	CD: Hunt CDHP 590

ROYAL FESTIVAL HALL

General Manager: T. E. BEAN, C.B.E.

PHILHARMONIA CONCERT SOCIETY

Artistic Director: WALTER LEGGE

PHILHARMONIA ORCHESTRA

LEADER: HUGH BEAN

OTTO KLEMPERER

Weber: Overture, Der Freischütz

Mozart: Clarinet Concerto in A (K.662)

BERNARD WALTON

Interval

Mahler: Das Lied von der Erde

CHRISTA LUDWIG   FRITZ WUNDERLICH

Thursday, April 13, at 8 p.m.

Programme Two Shillings

KLEMPERER

MAHLER   Symphony No. 9

New Philharmonia Orchestra
Led by Desmond Bradley

ROYAL FESTIVAL HALL
General Manager John Denison CBE

Thursday 28 March 1968 at 8

Programme Two Shillings

Symphony No 4

Cologne February 1954	WDR Orchestra Trötschel	LP: Movimento musica 01.054 CD: Frequenz CME 1
Berlin February 1956	Berlin RO Trötschel	LP: Melodram MEL 215 CD: Hunt CD 563
Munich October 1956	Bavarian RO Lindermeier	LP: Longanesi periodici GCL 67 CD: Hunt CDHP 590 GCL 67 incorrectly labelled WDR Orchestra February 1956
London April 1961	Philharmonia Schwarzkopf	LP: Columbia 33CX 1793/SAX 2441 LP: EMI ASD 2799 CD: EMI CDM 769 6672

Symphony No 7

London September 1968	New Philharmonia	LP: EMI SLS 781 LP: EMI CDFP 41 44421 CD: EMI CMS 764 1472

Symphony No 9

London February 1967	New Philharmonia	LP: EMI SAX 5281-5282/SXDW 3021 CD: EMI CMS 763 2772
Paris April 1967	New Philharmonia	Pathé unpublished
Vienna June 1968	VPO	CD: Nuova Era 033.6709 CD: Hunt CD 578
Edinburgh August 1968	New Philharmonia	CD: Hunt CD 563

Das Lied von der Erde

Vienna March 1951	VSO Cavelti, Dermota	LP: Vox PL 7000/PL 11890 LP: Vox GBY 11890/VBX 115 LP: Intercord 125.806/120.926 LP: Columbia (Japan) DXM 150 CD: Tuxedo TUXCD 1036 Tuxedo incorrectly dated 1957
London February and November 1964 and July 1966	Philharmonia/ New Philharmonia C.Ludwig, Wunderlich	LP: EMI AN 179/SAN 179 LP: EMI EL 29 04401 CD: EMI CDC 747 2312

Lieder eines fahrenden Gesellen

Amsterdam November 1948	Concertgebouw Orchestra Schey	CD: Archiphon ARC 101

Kindertotenlieder

Amsterdam July 1951	Concertgebouw Orchestra Ferrier	LP: Decca 417 6341 CD: Decca 425 9952 CD: Verona 27076
Cologne October 1956	WDR Orchestra London	LP: Cetra LO 510 CD: Hunt CD 578

Wo die schönen Trompeten blasen; Das irdische Leben (Des Knaben Wunderhorn)

London February 1964	Philharmonia C.Ludwig	LP: EMI ASD 2391/SXLP 27 00001 CD: EMI CDM 769 4992

Ich bin der Welt abhanden gekommen; Um Mitternacht; Ich atmet' einen linden Duft (Rückert-Lieder)

London February 1964	Philharmonia C.Ludwig	LP: EMI ASD 2391/SXLP 27 00001 CD: EMI CDM 769 4992

Mendelssohn

Symphony No 3 "Scotch"

Vienna June 1951	VSO	LP: Vox PL 7080/PL 11840 LP: Columbia (Japan) DXM 166 <u>3rd and 4th movements not</u> <u>conducted by Klemperer; recording</u> <u>completed by H.Haefner in</u> <u>Klemperer's absence and without</u> <u>his approval</u>
London January 1960	Philharmonia	LP: Columbia 33CX 1736/SAX 2342 LP: EMI ED 29 05791 CD: EMI CDM 763 8532
Munich May 1969	Bavarian RO	CD: Hunt CD 701

Symphony No 4 "Italian"

Vienna April and May 1951	VSO	LP: Vox PL 6980/PL 7860 LP: Fidelio ATL 1043 LP: Columbia (Japan) DXM 161
London February 1960	Philharmonia	LP: Columbia 33CX 1751/SAX 2398 LP: EMI SXLP 30178/ED 29 05791 CD: EMI CDM 763 8532/CDM 764 4482

Violin Concerto

Den Haag June 1954	Residentie Orchestra Martzy	LP: Archiphon 1.5

The Hebrides, Overture

Amsterdam February 1957	Concertgebouw Orchestra	LP: Archiphon 1.4 CD: Memories HR 4248-4249
London February 1960	Philharmonia	LP: Columbia 33CX 1736/SAX 2342
Munich May 1969	Bavarian RO	CD: Hunt CD 701

A Midsummer Night's Dream, Overture and Incidental music

Cologne June 1955	WDR Orchestra and Chorus Möller-Siepermann, H.Ludwig	LP: Movimento musica 01.040 CD: Movimento musica 051.033 CD: Priceless D 14252 Incorrectly dated May 1955
London January and February 1960	Philharmonia Orchestra & Chorus Harper, Baker	LP: Columbia 33CX 1746/SAX 2393 LP: EMI SXLP 30196 CD: EMI CDC 747 2302/CDM 764 1441 Overture LP: EMI SLS 5073 Nocturne & Wedding March 45: Columbia SEL 1708
Munich May 1969	Bavarian Radio Orchestra & Chorus Mathis, Fassbänder	CD: Hunt CD 701

A Midsummer Night's Dream, Overture

Berlin 1926-1927	Staatskapelle	78: Polydor 66602-66603
Amsterdam November 1955	Concertgebouw Orchestra	LP: Archiphon 1.4 CD: Memories HR 4248-4249

Mozart

Symphony No 25

Paris February 1950	Paris Pro Musica Orchestra	78: Polydor (France) 56634-56635/ 6345-6346 auto LP: Vox PL 11820 LP: Columbia (Japan) DXM 172 <u>LP editions incorrectly labelled</u> <u>Vienna Pro Musica Orchestra</u>
Berlin December 1950	Berlin RO	LP: Movimento musica 01.033 LP: Longanesi periodici GCL 30 CD: Frequenz CMC 1 CD: Hunt CD 572
Amsterdam January 1951	Concertgebouw Orchestra	CD: Archiphon ARC 101
London July 1956	Philharmonia	45: Columbia SEL 1594/ESL 6254 LP: Columbia 33CX 1457/SAX 2278 LP: EMI CX 5252/SAX 5252 LP: EMI SLS 5048/EX 29 04823 CD: EMI CMS 763 2722

Symphony No 29

Berlin December 1950	Berlin RO	LP: Movimento musica 01.033 LP: Longanesi periodici GCL 21 LP: Melodram MEL 215 CD: Frequenz CMC 1 CD: Musica classica 34001 CD: Hunt CD 572 <u>Melodram and Musica classica</u> <u>editions incorrectly dated</u> <u>February 1956</u>
London October 1954	Philharmonia	LP: Columbia 33CX 1257
London September 1965	New Philharmonia	LP: EMI CX 5256/SAX 5256 LP: EMI SLS 5048/EX 29 04823 CD: EMI CMS 763 2722

Symphony No 31 "Paris"

London October 1960	Philharmonia	Columbia unpublished <u>Recording incomplete</u>
London October 1963	Philharmonia	LP: Columbia 33CX 1906/SAX 2546 LP: EMI SLS 5048/EX 29 04823 CD: EMI CMS 763 2722

Symphony No 33

London September 1965	New Philharmonia	LP: EMI CX 5256/SAX 5256 LP: EMI SLS 5048/EX 29 04823 CD: EMI CMS 763 2722

Symphony No 34

London October 1963	Philharmonia	LP: Columbia 33CX 1906/SAX 2546 LP: EMI SLS 5048/EX 29 04823 CD: EMI CMS 763 2722

Symphony No 35 "Haffner"

Los Angeles January 1938	Los Angeles Philharmonic	LP: Symposium 1004
London October 1960	Philharmonia	LP: Columbia 33CX 1786/SAX 2436 LP: EMI SLS 5048/EX 29 04823 CD: EMI CMS 763 2722

Symphony No 36 "Linz"

Paris February 1950	Paris Pro Musica Orchestra	78: Polydor (France) 566329-566331/ 6329-6331 auto LP: Vox PL 11820 LP: Turnabout THS 65093 LP: Columbia (Japan) DXM 172 <u>LP editions incorrectly labelled Vienna Pro Musica Orchestra</u>
London July 1956	Philharmonia	LP: Columbia 33CX 1786/SAX 2436 LP: EMI SLS 5048/EX 29 04823 CD: EMI CMS 763 2722

Symphony No 38 "Prague"

Berlin December 1950	Berlin RO	LP: Movimento musica 01.019 LP: Longanesi periodici GCL 21 CD: Frequenz CMC 1 CD: Hunt CD 572
London July 1956	Philharmonia	LP: Columbia 33CX 1486
London March 1962	Philharmonia	LP: Columbia 33CX 1824/SAX 2468 LP: EMI SLS 5048/EX 29 04823 CD: EMI CMS 763 2722
Paris October 1968	New Philharmonia	Pathé unpublished

Symphony No 39

Budapest April 1949	Hungarian Radio Orchestra	LP: Hungaroton LPX 12667
London July 1956	Philharmonia	LP: Columbia 33CX 1486
London March 1962	Philharmonia	LP: Columbia 33CX 1824/SAX 2468 LP: EMI SLS 5048/EX 29 04823 CD: EMI CMS 763 2722

Symphony No 40

London July 1956	Philharmonia	LP: Columbia 33CX 1457/SAX 2278
London March 1962	Philharmonia	LP: Columbia 33CX 1843/SAX 2486 LP: EMI SLS 5003/SLS 5048 LP: EMI EX 29 04823 CD: EMI CDC 747 8522/CMS 763 2722
London November 1970	New Philharmonia	CD: Hunt CD 729 CD: Foyer CF 2037

Symphony No 40, 4th movement rehearsal extract

Stockholm May 1965	Stockholm Philharmonic	CD: BIS CD 424

Symphony No 41 "Jupiter"

London October and November 1954	Philharmonia	LP: Columbia 33CX 1257
London March 1962	Philharmonia	LP: Columbia 33CX 1843/SAX 2486 LP: EMI SLS 5048/EX 29 04823 CD: EMI CDC 747 8522/CMS 763 2722
Vienna May 1968	VPO	CD: Refrain (Japan) DR 910019

Piano Concerto No 20

Lucerne September 1959	Philharmonia Haskil	LP: Discocorp RR 545 LP: CLS Records ARPCL 22046 LP: Columbia (Japan) OS 7079 CD: AS-Disc AS 612

Piano Concerto No 22

Amsterdam July 1956	Concertgebouw Orchestra A.Fischer	LP: Discocorp RR 527 CD: Memories HR 4248-4249

Piano Concerto No 25

London March 1967	New Philharmonia Barenboim	LP: EMI CX 5290/SAX 5290 CD: EMI CDM 763 6202
London November 1970	New Philharmonia Brendel	CD: Hunt CD 729 CD: Foyer CF 2037

Piano Concerto No 27

Montreux September 1956	Gürzenich- Orchester Haskil	LP: Discocorp RR 456 LP: Columbia (Japan) OS 7079 CD: AS-Disc AS 612 CD: Music and Arts CD 716

Violin Concerto No 5

Amsterdam January 1951	Concertgebouw Orchestra Bresser	LP: Archiphon 1.5

The 4 Horn Concerti

London May 1960	Philharmonia Civil	LP: Columbia 33CX 1760/SAX 2406 LP: EMI SXLP 30207/CFP 41 44881 CD: EMI CDZ 767 0122/CDM 767 0322 No 4 only LP: EMI SLS 5073

Adagio and Fugue in C minor

London March 1956	Philharmonia	LP: Columbia 33CX 1438 LP: Columbia 33CX 1948/SAX 2587 LP: LP: EMI SLS 5048/EX 29 04823 CD: EMI CDM 763 6202

Mauerische Trauermusik

London November 1964	New Philharmonia	LP: Columbia 33CX 1948/SAX 2587 LP: EMI SLS 5048/EX 29 04823 CD: EMI CDM 763 6192
Vienna June 1968	VPO	CD: Hunt CD 578

Serenade No 6 "Serenata notturna"

Berlin December 1950	Berlin RO	CD: Hunt CD 572
London March 1956	Philharmonia	LP: Columbia 33CX 1438 CD: EMI CDM 764 1462
London November 1970	New Philharmonia	CD: Hunt CD 729

Serenade No 10 for 13 wind instruments

London November and December 1963	London Wind Quintet & ensemble	LP: EMI CX 5259/SAX 5259/SXDW 3050 CD: EMI CDM 763 3492

ROYAL FESTIVAL HALL
General Manager: T. E. Bean, C.B.E.

PHILHARMONIA CONCERT SOCIETY

ARTISTIC DIRECTOR:
WALTER LEGGE

OTTO KLEMPERER
WILHELM BACKHAUS

MOZART

Symphony No. 39 in E flat, K.543
Piano Concerto in B flat, K.595

Symphony No. 41 in C, K.551 ('The Jupiter')

PHILHARMONIA ORCHESTRA

LEADER: HUGH BEAN

Monday, May 6, 1963, at 8 p.m.

Programme One Shilling and Sixpence

ROYAL FESTIVAL HALL
General Manager: T. E. Bean

PHILHARMONIA CONCERT SOCIETY LTD.

Artistic Director:
WALTER LEGGE

presents

PHILHARMONIA
ORCHESTRA
Leader: MANOUG PARIKIAN

OTTO KLEMPERER

MOZART

Symphony No. 39 in E flat, K.543
Symphony No. 40 in G minor, K.550
INTERVAL
Symphony No. 41 in C, K.551, "Jupiter"

Friday, March 22nd, 1957
at 8 p.m.

Management: IBBS & TILLETT LTD., 124 WIGMORE STREET, W.1

Programme One Shilling

Serenade No 11 for wind

Berlin   Berlin RO   LP: Longanesi periodici GCL 63
September 1952

London   New Philharmonia   LP: EMI SXDW 3050
September 1971   Wind ensemble   CD: EMI CDM 763 3492

Serenade No 12 for wind

London   New Philharmonia   LP: EMI CX 5290/SAX 5290
March 1967   Wind ensemble   LP: EMI SXDW 3050/CFP 41 44481
                                            CD: EMI CDM 763 6202

Vienna   VPO   CD: Refrain (Japan) DR 910019
May 1968

Serenade No 13 "Eine kleine Nachtmusik"

Paris   Paris Pro Musica   78: Polydor (France) 566224-566225/
July 1946   Orchestra   6224-6225 auto
                                            78: Vox (USA) 169
                                            LP: Vox PL 11870
                                            LP: Columbia (Japan) DXM 167
                                            DXM 167 incorrectly labelled VSO

London   Philharmonia   LP: Columbia 33C 1053/SBO 2751
March 1956

London   New Philharmonia   LP: EMI CX 5252/SAX 5252
October and   LP: EMI SLS 5048/EX 29 04923
November 1964   CD: EMI CDM 763 6192

La Clemenza di Tito, Overture

London   New Philharmonia   LP: Columbia 33CX 1948/SAX 2587
October and   LP: EMI SLS 5048/EX 29 04823
November 1964   CD: EMI CDM 763 6192

Così fan tutte

London January and February 1971	New Philharmonia Alldis Choir M.Price, Minton, Popp, Alva, Evans, Sotin	LP: EMI SLS 961 CD: EMI CMS 763 8452 Excerpts LP: EMI 1C 063 02368/1C 037 02368

Così fan tutte, Overture

London October 1964	New Philharmonia	LP: Columbia 33CX 1948/SAX 2587 LP: EMI SLS 5048.EX 29 04823 CD: EMI CDM 763 6192

Don Giovanni

Cologne May 1955	WDR Orchestra and Chorus Zadek, Cunitz, Streich, Simoneau, London, Kusche, Weber	LP: Discocorp RR 478 CD: Frequenz CMA 3 Excerpts LP: Melodram MEL 097
London October 1959	Philharmonia Orchestra & Chorus Schwarzkopf, Sciutti, Sutherland, Alva, Wächter, Taddei, Frick	Columbia unpublished Recording incomplete
London June and July 1966	New Philharmonia Orchestra & Chorus Watson, C.Ludwig, Freni, Gedda, Ghiaurov, Berry, Crass	LP: EMI AN 172-175/SAN 172-175 LP: EMI SLS 923/SLS 143 4623 CD: EMI 763 8412 Excerpts LP: EMI ASD 2508 CD: EMI CDM 769 0552

Don Giovanni: Excerpts

Budapest October 1948	Budapest Opera Orchestra & Chorus Osvath, Orosz, Gyurkovics, Rösler, Losonczy, Szekely, Toth Sung in Hungarian	LP: Hungaroton LPX 12450 LP: Hungaroton LPX 12004-12006 Some excerpts also published on a record supplied with 1973 book on Klemperer in Budapest

Don Giovanni, Overture

London October and November 1964	New Philharmonia	LP: Columbia 33CX 1948/SAX 2587 LP: EMI SLS 5048/EX 29 04823 CD: EMI CDM 763 6192

Die Entführung aus dem Serail

Budapest March 1950	Budapest Opera Orchestra & Chorus Gyurkovics, Gencsy, Rösler, Kishegyi, Szekely Sung in Hungarian	LP: Hungaroton LPX 12636-12637 Overture also issued on a record supplied with 1973 book on Klemperer in Budapest

Die Entführung aus dem Serail, Overture

London September 1960	Philharmonia	LP: Columbia 33CX 1786/SAX 2436 LP: Columbia 33CX 1948/SAX 2587 LP: EMI SLS 5048/EX 29 04823 CD: EMI CDM 763 6192

Idomeneo, Overture

London November 1964	New Philharmonia	Columbia unpublished

Le Nozze di Figaro

London January 1970	New Philharmonia Alldis Choir Söderström, Grist, Berganza, Evans, Bacquier	LP: EMI SLS 955 CD: EMI CMS 763 8492 Excerpts LP: EMI 1C 063 02232/1C 037 02232

Le Nozze di Figaro, Overture

London October and November 1964	New Philharmonia	LP: Columbia 33CX 1948/SAX 2587 LP: EMI SLS 5048/EX 29 04823 CD: EMI CDM 764 4482/CDM 763 6192

Die Zauberflöte

Budapest March 1949	Budapest Opera Orchestra & Chorus Osvath, Nagypal, Pavlanszky, Szekely, Farkas, Sung in Hungarian	LP: Hungaroton LPX 12705-12706 Excerpts LP: Hungaroton LPX 12004-12006
London March and April 1964	Philharmonia Orchestra & Chorus Janowitz, Popp, Pütz, Gedda, Unger, Berry, Frick, Crass	LP: EMI AN 137-139/SAN 137-139 LP: EMI SLS 912 CD: EMI CMS 769 9712 Excerpts LP: EMI ALP 2314/ASD 2314 LP: EMI ESD 100 3261 CD: EMI CDM 763 4512 Overture LP: Columbia 33CX 1948/SAX 2587 LP: EMI EX 29 04823 CD: EMI CDM 763 6192

Die Zauberflöte: Excerpts (O zittre nicht; Der Hölle Rache; Stille, stille)

London January 1962	Covent Garden Orchestra Sutherland, Dobson, Pierce, Veasey, Sinclair	LP: Ed Smith UORC 147 LP: Melodram MEL 660

Offenbach

Les Contes d'Hoffmann: Excerpts

Budapest April 1949	Budapest Opera Orchestra & Chorus Szilvassy, Feher, Fekete, Somogyvari Sung in Hungarian	LP: Hungaroton LPX 12004-12006 Septet also issued on a record supplied with 1973 book on Klemperer in Budapest

La Belle Hélène, Overture

Berlin May 1929	Staatskapelle	78: Parlophone (England) E 10935 78: Parlophone (Germany) P 9469 78: Odeon O 6889 CD: Symposium 1042

Puccini

La Bohème: Excerpts (1. Che gelida manina; 2. Sì, mi chiamano Mimì; 3. O soave fanciulla)

Los Angeles June 1937	Los Angeles Philharmonic Bori (2,3), Bentonelli (1,3)	LP: Ed Smith EJS 292 (1,3) LP: Ed Smith EJS 425 (2,3) LP: Ed Smith EJS 451 (2,3) LP: MDP Records MDP 033 (3) LP: Symposium 1007 (2,3)

Ravel

Alborada del gracioso

Berlin 1926	Staatskapelle	78: Polydor 66463 78: Brunswick 80012 LP: DG 2721 070 CD: Symposium 1042

Rameau

Gavotte with 6 variations (arr. Klemperer)

Vienna May 1968	VPO	CD: Refrain (Japan) DR 910019
London October 1968	New Philharmonia	LP: EMI ASD 2537 CD: EMI CMS 764 1502
Paris October 1968	New Philharmonia	Pathé unpublished

Schoenberg

Verklärte Nacht

Amsterdam July 1955	Concertgebouw Orchestra	LP: Archiphon ARCH 1 CD: Memories HR 4248-4249 CD: Archiphon ARC 101

Schubert

Symphony No 4 "Tragic"

Paris November 1950	Lamoureux Orchestra	LP: Vox PL 7860/GBY 11060 LP: Columbia (Japan) DXM 161
Amsterdam February 1957	Concertgebouw Orchestra	LP: Archiphon 1.4 CD: Memories HR 4248-4249 CD: Frequenz 041.013 CD: Bella musica BMF 89964/ 31.6005
London November 1963	Philharmonia	Columbia unpublished Recording incomplete

Symphony No 5

London May 1963	Philharmonia	LP: Columbia 33CX 1870/SAX 2514 LP: EMI ED 29 04601/EMX 2135 CD: EMI CDM 763 8692

Symphony No 8 "Unfinished"

Berlin 1924	Staatskapelle	78: Polydor 66338-66340/ 69778-69780 auto
Budapest June 1948	Budapest Symphony Orchestra	LP: Hungaroton LPX 12379
Turin December 1956	RAI Turin Orchestra	LP: Cetra LAR 37 LP: Cetra (Japan) K22C 324
London February 1963	Philharmonia	LP: Columbia 33CX 1870/SAX 2514 LP: EMI SLS 5003 LP: EMI ED 29 04601/EMX 2135 CD: EMI CDM 763 8542
Munich April 1966	Bavarian RO	CD: Hunt CD 701
Vienna June 1968	VPO	CD: DG 435 3272/435 3212

Symphony No 9 "Great"

London November 1960	Philharmonia	LP: Columbia 33CX 1754/SAX 2397 LP: EMI ED 29 04261 CD: EMI CDM 763 8542

Schumann

Symphony No 1 "Spring"

London November 1963 and February 1964	Philharmonia	Columbia unpublished
London October 1965	New Philharmonia	LP: EMI CX 5269/SAX 5269 LP: EMI 1C 197 52497-52499 CD: EMI CMS 763 6132

Symphony No 2

London October 1968	New Philharmonia	LP: EMI ASD 2454 LP: EMI 1C 197 52497-52499 CD: EMI CMS 763 6132

Symphony No 3 "Rhenish"

London February 1969	New Philharmonia	LP: EMI ASD 2547 LP: EMI 1C 197 52497-52499 CD: EMI CMS 763 6132

Symphony No 4

London May 1960	Philharmonia	LP: Columbia 33CX 1751/SAX 2398 LP: EMI SXLP 30178 LP: EMI 1C 197 52497-52499 CD: EMI CMS 763 6132
Philadelphia October 1962	Philadelphia	CD: AS-Disc AS 533

Piano Concerto

Vienna June 1951	VSO Novaes	LP: Vox PL 7110/STPL 513420 CD: Vox CDX 25501
London May 1960 and August 1962	Philharmonia A.Fischer	LP: Columbia 33CX 1842/SAX 2485 LP: EMI 1C 197 52497-52499 CD: Priceless C 16442 CD: EMI CDM 764 1452/CDM 764 4482

Faust, Overture

London February 1969	New Philharmonia	LP: EMI ASD 2547 CD: EMI CMS 763 6132

Genoveva, Overture

London October 1968	New Philharmonia	LP: EMI ASD 2454

Manfred, Overture

London October 1965 and February 1966	New Philharmonia	LP: EMI CX 5269/SAX 5269 LP: EMI 1C 197 52497-52499 CD: EMI CDM 763 9172

Shostakovich

Symphony No 9

Turin December 1955	RAI Turin Orchestra	LP: Cetra LAR 37 LP: Replica RPLC 2481

otto klemperer records for EMI

NEW PHILHARMONIA ORCHESTRA

MOZART OVERTURES
La Clemenza di Tito; Le Nozze di Figaro; Don Giovanni; Così fan tutte; Maurerische Trauermusik, K.477
Philharmonia Orchestra: Die Zauberflöte;
Die Entführung aus dem Serail;
Adagio and Fugue in C minor, K.546
Columbia SAX 2587 ⓢ CX1948 Ⓜ

SCHUMANN Symphony No. 1 "Spring";
Manfred Overture
Columbia SAX5269 ⓢ CX5269 Ⓜ

PHILHARMONIA ORCHESTRA
BRAHMS Symphony No. 4 in E minor
Columbia SAX2350 ⓢ CX1591 Ⓜ

MENDELSSOHN A Midsummer Night's Dream, Overture and Incidental Music
with Janet Baker, Heather Harper and Chorus
Columbia SAX2393 ⓢ CX1746 Ⓜ

MENDELSSOHN Hebrides Overture;
Symphony No. 3 in A minor "Scotch"
Columbia SAX2342 ⓢ CX1736 Ⓜ

MENDELSSOHN Symphony No. 4 "Italian";
SCHUMANN Symphony No. 4 in D minor
Columbia SAX2398 ⓢ CX1751 Ⓜ

MOZART Symphonies No. 38 in D "Prague";
No. 39 in E flat, K.543
Columbia SAX2468 ⓢ CX1824 Ⓜ

EMI RECORDS (The Gramophone Co. Ltd.)
EMI House · 20 Manchester Square
London W1

Johann Strauss

Die Fledermaus, Overture

Los Angeles February 1945	Los Angeles Philharmonic	LP: PAARV PRV 3501 LP: Symposium 1007
London October and December 1961	Philharmonia	LP: Columbia 33CX 1814/SAX 2460 LP: EMI SLS 5073/SXLP 30226

Kaiserwalzer

London October 1961	Philharmonia	LP: Columbia 33CX 1814/SAX 2460 LP: EMI SXLP 30226

Wiener Blut, Waltz

London October 1961	Philharmonia	LP: Columbia 33CX 1814/SAX 2460 LP: EMI SXLP 30226 CD: EMI CDM 764 1422

Richard Strauss

Don Juan

Berlin June and October 1929	Staatskapelle	78: Parlophone (England) 11051-11052 78: Parlophone (Germany) P 9495-9496 LP: Past Masters PM 31
Cologne February 1956	WDR Orchestra	CD: Hunt CD 726
London March 1960	Philharmonia	LP: Columbia 33CX 1715/SAX 2367 LP: EMI SXLP 30298/ED 29 06161 CD: EMI CDM 763 3502

Don Quixote

London April 1968	New Philharmonia Du Pré	EMI unpublished Recording incomplete: further sessions conducted by Barenboim but recording remained incomplete

Metamorphosen

London November 1961	Philharmonia	LP: Columbia 33CX 1789/SAX 2437 LP: EMI ED 29 06161 CD: EMI CDM 763 3502

Salome, Dance of the 7 veils

Berlin May 1928	Staatskapelle	78: Electrola EJ 276 78: HMV D 1633 LP: Acanta 98 221776/MA 22177 CD: Koch Legacy 3-7053-2
London March 1960	Philharmonia	LP: Columbia 33CX 1715/SAX 2367 LP: EMI SXLP 30298 CD: EMI CDM 763 3502

Till Eulenspiegels lustige Streiche

Berlin June 1929	Staatskapelle	78: Parlophone (England) 　　E 10925-10925 78: Parlophone (Germany) 　　P 8959-9860 78: Odeon O 7628-7629/ 　　5191-5192 auto CD: Koch Legacy 3-7053-2
Turin December 1955	RAI Turin Orchestra	LP: Cetra LAR 37 LP: Cetra (Japan) K22C 325
Amsterdam February 1957	Concertgebouw Orchestra	CD: Music and Arts CD 551
London March 1960	Philharmonia	LP: Columbia 33CX 1715/SAX 2367 LP: EMI SXLP 30298/ED 29 06161 CD: EMI CDM 764 1462

Tod und Verklärung

London October and November 1961	Philharmonia	LP: Columbia 33CX 1789/SAX 2437 LP: ED 29 06161 CD: EMI CDM 763 3502

Stravinsky

Symphony in 3 movements

London March and May 1962	Philharmonia	LP: Columbia 33CX 1949/SAX 2588 CD: EMI CDM 764 1422

Petrushksa

London March 1967	New Philharmonia	EMI unpublished

Pulcinella, Suite

Turin December 1955	RAI Turin Orchestra	LP: Cetra LAR 37
London February and May 1963 and March 1964	Philharmonia	LP: Columbia 33CX 1949/SAX 2588 CD: EMI CDM 764 1422

ROYAL FESTIVAL HALL
General Manager: T. E. Bean, C.B.E.

PHILHARMONIA CONCERT SOCIETY

ARTISTIC DIRECTOR:
WALTER LEGGE

PHILHARMONIA ORCHESTRA

LEADER: HUGH BEAN

OTTO KLEMPERER
YEHUDI MENUHIN

KLEMPERER	Symphony in Two Movements *(first performance in Britain)*
BRAHMS	Violin Concerto in D
TCHAIKOVSKY	Symphony No. 5 in E minor

Monday, May 7, 1962, at 8 p.m.

Programme One Shilling and Sixpence

Tchaikovsky

Symphony No 4

London January and February 1963	Philharmonia	LP: Columbia 33CX 1851/SAX 2494 LP: EMI EM 29 02823 CD: EMI CMS 763 8382

Symphony No 5

London January 1963	Philharmonia	LP: Columbia 33CX 1854/SAX 2497 LP: EMI EM 29 02823 CD: EMI CMS 763 8382

Symphony No 6 "Pathétique"

London October 1961	Philharmonia	LP: Columbia 33CX 1812/SAX 2458 LP: EMI SLS 5003/EM 29 02823 CD: EMI CMS 763 8382

Thomas

Mignon, Overture

Los Angeles February 1945	Los Angeles Philharmonic	LP: PAARV PRV 3501

Wagner

Der fliegende Holländer

London February and March 1968	New Philharmonia BBC Chorus Silja, Burmeister, Kozub, Adam, Talvela	LP: EMI SLS 934 CD: EMI CMS 763 3442 Excerpts LP: EMI ASD 2724
London March 1968	New Philharmonia BBC Chorus Silja, Burmeister, King, Adam, Talvela	CD: Hunt CD 561

Der fliegende Holländer, Overture

London February 1960	Philharmonia	LP: Columbia 33CX 1697/SAX 2347 LP: EMI SLS 5075/ASD 2695 LP: EMI SXLP 30426 CD: EMI CDC 747 2542/CDM 763 6172

Götterdämmerung, Siegfried's Rhine Journey

London November 1961	Philharmonia	LP: Columbia 33CX 1820/SAX 2464 LP: EMI SLS 5075/ASD 2697 LP: EMI SXLP 30528 CD: EMI CDM 763 6182

Götterdämmerung, Siegfried's Funeral March

London February 1960	Philharmonia	45: Columbia SEL 1677/ESL 6283 LP: Columbia 33CX 1698/SAX 2348 LP: EMI SLS 5075/ASD 2696 LP: EMI SXLP 30525 CD: EMI CDC 747 2552/CDM 763 6182

Lohengrin: Excerpts

Budapest October 1948	Budapest Opera Orchestra & Chorus Rigo, Nemethy, Simandy, Jambor, Losonczy, Remenyi Sung in Hungarian	LP: Hungaroton LPX 12436 LP: Hungaroton LPX 12004-12006 One excerpt also included in a record supplied with 1973 book on Klemperer in Budapest

Lohengrin, Act 1 Prelude

London February and March 1960	Philharmonia	LP: Columbia 33CX 1698/SAX 2348 LP: EMI SLS 5075/ASD 2695 LP: EMI SXLP 30436 CD: EMI CDC 747 2542/CDM 763 6172

Lohengrin, Act 3 Prelude

London February 1960	Philharmonia	LP: Columbia 33CX 1698/SAX 2348 LP: EMI SLS 5075/ASD 2696 LP: EMI SXLP 30526 CD: EMI CDC 747 2542/CDM 763 6172

Die Meistersinger von Nürnberg: Excerpts

Budapest April 1949	Budapest Opera Orchestra & Chorus Osvath, Budanovits, Simandy, Sardi, Losonczy, Szekely, Maleczky Sung in Hungarian	LP: Hungaroton LPX 12340-12341 LP: Hungaroton LPX 12004-12006 Some excerpts also included in a record supplied with 1973 book on Klemperer in Budapest

Die Meistersinger von Nürnberg, Overture

Turin December 1956	RAI Turin Orchestra	LP: Cetra LAR 37 LP: Cetra (Japan) K22C 325
London March 1960	Philharmonia	LP: Columbia 33CX 1698/SAX 2348 LP: EMI SLS 5075/ASD 2696 LP: EMI SXLP 30525 CD: EMI CDC 747 2552/CDM 763 6182
Vienna June 1968	VPO	CD: Hunt CD 578

Die Meistersinger von Nürnberg, Entry of the Masters & Dance of the Apprentices

London March 1960	Philharmonia	45: Columbia SEL 1677/ESL 6283 LP: Columbia 33CX 1698/SAX 2348 LP: EMI SLS 5075/ASD 2696 LP: EMI SXLP 30525 CD: EMI CDC 747 2552/CDM 763 6182

ROYAL FESTIVAL HALL

General Manager: T. E. Bean, C.B.E.

PHILHARMONIA CONCERT SOCIETY

ARTISTIC DIRECTOR:
WALTER LEGGE

PHILHARMONIA ORCHESTRA

Principal Conductor: OTTO KLEMPERER

LEADER: HUGH BEAN

WAGNER:	Overture, Tannhäuser
WAGNER:	Siegfried Idyll
WAGNER:	Vorspiel und Liebestod from 'Tristan und Isolde'
TCHAIKOVSKY:	Symphony No. 6 in B minor, 'Pathétique'

OTTO KLEMPERER

Friday, December 6, 1963, at 8 p.m.

Programme One Shilling and Sixpence

ROYAL FESTIVAL HALL
General Manager: T. E. Bean, C.B.E.

PHILHARMONIA CONCERT SOCIETY

ARTISTIC DIRECTOR:
WALTER LEGGE

OTTO KLEMPERER

FRANZ CRASS

BRUCKNER: Symphony No. 7 in E major

WAGNER: Overture, Die Meistersinger von Nürnberg
WAGNER: Wotan's Farewell and Fire Music (Die Walküre)

PHILHARMONIA ORCHESTRA

Friday, May 3, 1963, at 8 p.m.

Programme One Shilling and Sixpence

Parsifal, Prelude

London November 1961	Philharmonia	LP: Columbia 33CX 1820/SAX 2464 LP: EMI SLS 5075/ASD 2697 LP: EMI SXLP 30528 CD: EMI CDC 747 2552/CDM 763 6182

Das Rheingold, Entry of the Gods into Valhalla

London October 1961	Philharmonia	LP: Columbia 33CX 1820/SAX 2464 LP: EMI SLS 5075/ASD 2697 LP: EMI SXLP 30528 CD: EMI CDC 747 2552/CDM 763 6182

Rienzi, Overture

London March 1960	Philharmonia	LP: Columbia 33CX 1697/SAX 2347 LP: EMI SLS 5075/ASD 2695 LP: EMI SXLP 30436 CD: EMI CDC 747 2542/CDM 763 6172

Siegfried, Forest Murmurs

London October and November 1961	Philharmonia	LP: Columbia 33CX 1820/SAX 2464 LP: EMI SLS 5075/ASD 2697 LP: EMI SXLP 30528 CD: EMI CDC 747 2552/CDM 763 6182

Siegfried Idyll

Berlin 1926-1927	Staatskapelle	78: Polydor 66604-66605/ 57043-57044 78: Brunswick 90135-90136 CD: Symposium 1042 CD: Koch 311 162
London November 1960 and April and October 1961	Philharmonia	LP: Columbia 33CX 1809/SAX 2455 CD: EMI CMS 763 2772
Vienna June 1968	VPO	CD: Hunt CD 708

Tannhäuser, Overture

London February 1960	Philharmonia	LP: Columbia 33CX 1697/SAX 2347 LP: EMI SLS 5075/ASD 2695 LP: EMI SXLP 30436 CD: EMI CDC 747 2542/CDM 763 6172

Tannhäuser, Act 3 Prelude

London March 1960	Philharmonia	LP: Columbia 33CX 1820/SAX 2464 LP: EMI SLS 5075/ASD 2697 LP: EMI SXLP 30528 CD: EMI CDM 763 6172

Tristan und Isolde, Prelude

Berlin June 1927	Staatskapelle	78: Electrola EW 27-28 78: HMV E 476-477
Vienna June 1968	VPO	CD: Nuova Era 033.6709 CD: Hunt CD 578

Tristan und Isolde, Prelude and Liebestod

London March 1960	Philharmonia	LP: Columbia 33CX 1698/SAX 2348 LP: EMI SLS 5075/ASD 2696 LP: EMI SXLP 30525 CD: EMI CDC 747 2542/CDM 763 6172

Tristan und Isolde, Isolde's Liebestod

London March 1962	Philharmonia C.Ludwig	LP: Columbia 33CX 1817/SAX 2462 LP: EMI SXLP 27 00001 CD: EMI CMS 764 0742

Die Walküre, Act 1

London October and November 1969	New Philharmonia Dernesch, Cochran, Sotin	LP: EMI SLS 968 <u>Excerpts</u> LP: EMI 1C 037 02887

Die Walküre, Ride of the Valkyries

London	Philharmonia	45: Columbia SCD 2178
March 1960		LP: Columbia 33CX 1820/SAX 2464
		LP: EMI SLS 5075/ASD 2697
		LP: EMI SXLP 30528
		CD: EMI CDC 747 2552/CDM 763 6182

Die Walküre, Wotan's Farewell and Magic Fire Music

London	New Philharmonia	LP: EMI SLS 968
October 1970	Bailey	LP: EMI 1C 037 02887
		CD: EMI CMS 763 8352

Wesendonk-Lieder

London	Philharmonia	LP: Columbia 33CX 1817/SAX 2462
March 1962	C.Ludwig	LP: EMI ASD 2391/SXLP 27 00001
		CD: EMI CMS 764 0742

Weber

Euryanthe, Overture

Berlin 1926-1927	Staatskapelle	78: Polydor 66629
London September 1960	Philharmonia	LP: Columbia 33CX 1770/SAX 2417 CD: EMI CDM 763 9172

Der Freischütz, Overture

London May 1960	Philharmonia	LP: Columbia 33CX 1770/SAX 2417 CD: EMI CDM 763 9172

Oberon, Overture

London May 1960	Philharmonia	LP: Columbia 33CX 1770/SAX 2417 CD: EMI CDM 763 9172

Weill

Kleine Dreigroschenmusik

Berlin 1931	Staatskapelle	78: Polydor 24172-24173 78: Vox (USA) 451 LP: Past Masters PM 31 CD: Symposium 1042 CD: Koch Legacy 3-7053-2
London October and December 1961	Philharmonia	LP: Columbia 33CX 1814/SAX 2460 LP: EMI SXLP 30226/ED 29 03321 CD: EMI CDM 764 1422

ROYAL FESTIVAL HALL
General Manager: T. E. BEAN, C.B.E.

PHILHARMONIA CONCERT SOCIETY

ARTISTIC DIRECTOR:
WALTER LEGGE

PHILHARMONIA ORCHESTRA

LEADER: HUGH BEAN

MOZART: Pianoforte Concerto in A, K.488

ANNIE FISCHER

BRAHMS: Concerto in A minor for Violin and Violoncello, Op. 102

HENRYK SZERYNG   JANOS STARKER

INTERVAL

BEETHOVEN: Concerto in C for Pianoforte, Violin and Violoncello, Op. 56

ANNIE FISCHER   HENRYK SZERYNG
JANOS STARKER

OTTO KLEMPERER

Friday, November 11, 1960, at 8 p.m.

Programme One Shilling

Erich Kleiber
1890-1956

Discography compiled by John Hunt

Bach

<u>Prelude and Fugue in E flat BWV 552 (arr. Schoenberg)</u>

Berlin   BPO   78: Telefunken E 463-464
1930

Beethoven

Symphony No 2

Berlin 1929	Staatskapelle	78: Polydor 66905-66908/ 　　　516585-516588 auto 78: Brunswick 90140-90143 LP: DG 2548 747 LP: Historia 690 LP: Olympic OL 8120 LP: Eurodisc 28 631 XFK CD: Classical Disk CDC 880451 CD: World Classics WC 44010 <u>Olympic and Eurodisc issues misleadingly suggested that the conductor was Furtwängler</u>
Brussels January 1938	Belgian National Orchestra	78: Telefunken E 2485-2488 LP: Capitol P 8116 LP: Telefunken MA 25008 LP: Telefunken (Japan) MZ 5097. CD: Teldec 9031.764362

Symphony No 3 "Eroica"

Amsterdam May 1950	Concertgebouw Orchestra	78: Decca AX 383-389 LP: Decca LXT 2546/LXT 5215 LP: Decca ECS 792 CD: Decca 433 4062
Vienna April 1955	VPO	LP: Decca LXT 5064 LP: Decca ACL 35/ECS 535 LP: Decca (France) 159.2113 CD: Decca 414 6262/433 3312 <u>LXT 5064 was never published</u>
Stuttgart December 1955	SDR Orchestra	LP: Melodram MEL 209 LP: Discocorp RR 392 LP: Melodiya M10 43483 LP: Longanesi periodici GCL 52

Symphony No 4

Amsterdam April 1950	Concertgebouw	LP: Discocorp IGI 366

Symphony No 5

Amsterdam September 1953	Concertgebouw Orchestra	LP: Decca LXT 2851/LXT 5358 LP: Decca ECM 518/ECS 518 LP: Decca (France) 159.2118 CD: Decca 417 6372
Berlin January 1955	Staatskapelle	LP: Discocorp IGI 330 LP: Melodram MEL 209
Cologne April 1955	WDR Orchestra	LP: Movimento musica 08.001 CD: London (Japan) KICC 2080

Symphony No 6 "Pastoral"

London February 1948	LPO	78: Decca K 1824-1828 LP: Decca LXT 2587 LP: Decca ACL 2
Amsterdam September 1953	Concertgebouw Orchestra	LP: Decca LXT 2872/LXT 5359 LP: Decca ECS 549 LP: Decca (France) 159.2105 CD: Decca 417 6372
Cologne April 1955	WDR Orchestra	LP: Melodram MEL 209 LP: Longanesi periodici GCL 45 CD: Nuova Era NE 2338-2339

Symphony No 7

Amsterdam May 1950	Concertgebouw Orchestra	78: Decca AX 406-410 LP: Decca LXT 2547/LXT 5360 LP: Decca ACL 57/ECS 555 CD: Decca 425 9872

Symphony No 8: 2nd movement only

Berlin 1932	BPO	78: Telefunken SK 1295 LP: Past Masters PM 28

Symphony No 9 "Choral"

Vienna
June 1952
	VPO
	Singverein
	Güden, Wagner,
	Dermota, Weber
		LP: Decca LXT 2725-2726/
		   LXT 5362-5363
		LP: Decca LXT 5645
		LP: Decca LXT 6277-6280/
		   SXL 6277-6280
		LP: Decca ECM 501/ECS 501
		CD: Decca 425 9552

Symphony No 9 "Choral": extract from 4th movement

Stockholm February 1949	Stockholm Philharmonic Orchestra & Chorus Nilsson, Tunell, Bäckelin, S.Björling	CD: Bis BISCD 421

Missa Solemnis

Stockholm March 1948	Stockholm Philharmonic Orchestra & Chorus Nilsson, Tunell, Bäckelin, S.Björling	LP: Discocorp IGI 366

Fidelio

Cologne January 1956	WDR Orchestra and Chorus Nilsson, Wenglor, Hopf, Unger, Frick, Schöffler, Braun	LP: Rococo 1014 LP: Cetra LO 68 CD: Hunt CDLSMH 34048

Coriolan, Overture

Berlin March 1931	BPO	78: Telefunken E 653 LP: Telefunken (Japan) SLC 2322/ K17C 9401

Egmont, Overture

Berlin 1932	BPO	78: Telefunken E 961 LP: Telefunken (Japan) SLC 2322/ K17C 9401

German Dance No 12 in C

Berlin 1932	BPO	78: Telefunken SK 1295 LP: Past Masters PM 28

4 Viennese Waltzes

Berlin 1923-1924	Staatskapelle	78: Vox 01879

Berg

Wozzeck, 3 fragments

Cologne November 1953	WDR Orchestra Kupper	LP: Cetra DOC 3
Munich May 1955	Bavarian RO and Chorus Kupper	CD: Stradivarius STR 10064

Berlioz

Le carnaval romain, Overture

Berlin 1928	Staatskapelle	78: Polydor 66647 78: Decca CA 8197 78: Fonit 91072

Benvenuto Cellini, Overture

Berlin 1930	BPO	78: Telefunken E 532-533 LP: Telefunken (Japan) SLC 2323/ K17C 9402

La Damnation de Faust, Marche hongroise

Berlin 1930	BPO	78: Telefunken E 533/SK 1215 LP: Past Masters PM 28 LP: Telefunken (Japan) SLC 2323/ K17C 9402

Symphonie fantastique, 2nd movement (Un bal)

Berlin 1931	BPO	78: Telefunken E 808

Bizet

Carmen, Suite

Prague 1936	Czech Philharmonic Orchestra	78: Telefunken E 2041-2042/ TE 503-504 LP: Telefunken (Japan) SLC 2323/ K17C 9402

Staats-Oper
Unter den Linden

Berlin, Montag, den 13. Januar 1930

Anfang **19½** (7½ Uhr)

Jahres-Abonnements-Vorstellung Nr. 13
Teil-Ab.: Abteil. D Mo. Nr. 5

Anfang **19½** (7½ Uhr)

Neu einstudiert:
Die Entführung aus dem Serail

Oper in drei Akten von Wolfgang Amadeus Mozart
Musikalische Leitung: General-Musikdirektor Erich Kleiber
In Szene gesetzt von Karl Holy

Selim Bassa	Felix Fleischer-Janczak
Constanze, Geliebte des Belmonte	Gitta Alpar
Blonde, Mädchen der Constanze	Irene Eisinger
Belmonte	Helge Roßwaenge
Osmin, Aufseher über das Landhaus des Bassa	Emanuel List
Pedrillo, Bedienter des Belmonte und Aufseher über die Gärten des Bassa	Carl Jöken
Claas, ein Schiffer	Emil Lücke
Anführer der Leibwache	Georg Katz, Bernhard Sperber
Leute aus dem Volke	Charlotte Lindemann, Hertha Ahrendt, Otto Wünsche, Robert Steininger

Ein Stummer. Weiber. Gefolge. Wachen

Die Szene ist auf dem Landgute des Bassa

Gesamtausstattung: P. Aravantinos
Bühnentechnische Leitung: Rudolf Klein

Große Pause nach dem zweiten Akt

Dienstag, den 21. Juni 1932

Zum 1. Male:

Anfang 20 (8) Uhr

WIENER BLUT

Operette in drei Akten von Johann Strauß
Dirigent: Generalmusikdirektor Erich Kleiber
Gesamtausstattung: Benno v. Arent

Inszenierung: Dr. Kurt Singer a. G.
Mitwirkende: Vera Schwarz, Luise Ullrich, Margarete Slezak, Marcel Wittrisch, Oskar Karlweis, Waldemar Henke, Leopold Hainisch

Ersatz-, Gut-, Umtauschscheine, Ferienkarten und Zusatzabonnement ungültig

Staats-Theater
Opernhaus

Berlin, Montag, den 14. Dezember 1925

14. Karten-Reservesatz
(Außer Abonnement.)

Uraufführung:

Georg Büchners

Wozzeck

Oper in drei Akten (15 Szenen) von **Alban Berg**
Musikalische Leitung: General-Musikdirektor Erich Kleiber.
In Szene gesetzt von Franz Ludwig Hörth

Wozzeck	Leo Schützendorf
Tambourmajor	Fritz Soot
Andres	Gerhard Witting
Hauptmann	Waldemar Henke
Doktor	Martin Abendroth
1. Handwerksbursch	Ernst Osterkamp
2. Handwerksbursch	Alfred Borchardt
Der Narr	Marcel Noë
Marie	Sigrid Johanson
Margret	Jessyka Koettrik
Mariens Knabe	Ruth Iris Witting
Soldat	Leonhard Kern

Soldaten und Burschen, Mägde und Dirnen, Kinder.

Gesamtausstattung: P. Aravantinos.

Technische Einrichtung: Georg Linnebach

Nach dem 2. Akt findet eine längere Pause statt

Kein Vorspiel

Den Besuchern der heutigen Vorstellung wird das neu erschienene Heft der „Blätter der Staatsoper" unentgeltlich verabfolgt.

Bittner

Das höllische Gold: Excerpt (Wohin? Ins Haus)

Berlin	Berlin RO	LP: BASF 22.177-6
December 1932	Klose, Erhard	

Brahms

Violin Concerto, 2nd and 3rd movements

New York	NBC Orchestra	Radio Recorders Hollywood
1945	Heifetz	This was an acetate disc

Dallapiccola

2 pezzi per orchestra

Munich	Bavarian RO	LP: La musica LM 86
May 1955		CD: Stradivarius STR 10064

Dvorak

Symphony No 9 "New World"

Berlin 1929	BPO	78: Polydor 66909-66913 78: Brunswick 90150-90154 LP: Top Classic TC 9056 CD: Musica classica 2003-2004
Berlin November 1954	Staatskapelle	LP: Discocorp RR 398 LP: Longanesi periodici GCL 8/ GCL 9104

Cello Concerto

Cologne March 1955	WDR Orchestra Janigro	LP: Discocorp IGI 308 LP: Movimento musica 01.049 CD: Movimento musica 011.006

Carnival Overture

London February 1948	LPO	78: Decca K 1989

Scherzo capriccioso

Berlin March 1931	BPO	78: Telefunken E 655

The Wild Dove, Wedding Dance

Berlin 1932	BPO	78: Telefunken E 1052

Slavonic Dance op 46 no 1

Berlin 1927	Staatskapelle	78: Polydor 66653 78: Brunswick 90087

Slavonic Dance op 46 no 6

Berlin 1928	Staatskapelle	78: Parlophone E 11018 78: Odeon 6763

Falla

<u>Jota (arr. Kochanski)</u>

New York 1945	NBC Orchestra Heifetz	Radio Recorders Hollywood <u>This was an acetate disc</u>

Gluck

<u>Iphigenia in Aulis, Overture</u>

Berlin May 1931	BPO	78: Telefunken E 844

Handel

<u>Alcina, Ballet music</u>

Berlin 1932	BPO	78: Telefunken SK 1270 LP: Rococo 2048 CD: Musica classica 2003-2004

<u>Berenice, Overture</u>

London May 1949	LPO	78: Decca AX 448
Berlin January 1955	Staatskapelle	LP: Discocorp IGI 330

Hartmann

<u>Symphony No 6</u>

Munich May 1955	Bavarian RO	CD: Stradivarius STR 10064

Haydn

Andante Cantabile (String Quartet op 3 no 5)

Berlin 1932	BPO	78: Telefunken B 1340

3 German Dances (arr. Deutsch)

Berlin 1932	BPO	78: Telefunken B 1340

Herbert

Cuban Serenade; Spanish Serenade

New York 1945	NBC Orchestra	Radio Recorders Hollywood This was an acetate disc

Heuberger

Der Opernball, Overture

Berlin 1929	Staatskapelle	78: HMV C 1799
Berlin 1932	BPO	78: Telefunken SK 1195 LP: Past Masters PM 28 CD: Archiphon ARC 102 CD: Biddulph WHL 002

Janacek

Lachian Dance No 1

Berlin 1931	BPO	78: Telefunken E 1052 LP: Past Masters PM 28

Lanner

Die Schönbrunner, Waltz

Berlin 1932	BPO	78: Telefunken E 990

Liszt

Les Préludes

Prague 1936	Czech Philharmonic Orchestra	78: Telefunken E 2022-2023 LP: Telefunken (Japan) SLC 2323/ K17C 9402

Tarantella (Venezia e Napoli)

Berlin 1932	BPO	78: Telefunken E 1154 LP: Past Masters PM 28

Mendelssohn

A Midsummer Night's Dream, Scherzo and Wedding March

Berlin 1928	BPO	78: Polydor 66731 LP: DG 2740 259

A Midsummer Night's Dream, Nocturne

Berlin 1928	BPO	78: Polydor 66850 LP: DG 2721 070

Meyerbeer

Das Feldlager in Schlesien, Overture

Berlin 1933	BPO	78: Telefunken SK 1271

Mozart

Symphony No 33

Cologne November 1953	WDR Orchestra	LP: Discocorp RR 398 LP: Longanesi periodici GCL 30

Symphony No 33: 2nd and 3rd movements

Berlin 1923-1924	Staatskapelle	78: Vox 01533

Symphony No 36 "Linz"

Stuttgart December 1955	SDR Orchestra	LP: Discocorp RR 521 LP: Movimento musica 01.019 <u>Movimento musica incorrectly</u> <u>labelled WDR Orchestra</u>

Symphony No 38 "Prague"

Vienna February 1929	VPO	78: HMV C 1686-1688/ C 7234-7236 auto CD: Musica classica 2003-2004 CD: Preiser 90115

Symphony No 39

Berlin 1928	Staatskapelle	78: HMV D 1448-1450 78: Victor 9438-9440 LP: Rococo 2048 CD: Musica classica 2003-2004 CD: Koch Legacy 3-7011-2
Cologne January 1956	WDR Orchestra	LP: Amadeo AVRS 5010 LP: Decca ACL 226 LP: Discocorp IGI 308 CD: Stradivarius STR 10004 CD: Amadeo 423 4132 CD: Nuova Era 2338-2339

Symphony No 40

London May 1949	LPO	78: Decca AX 448-450 LP: Decca LX 3022/ACL 66/ECS 518 LP: Turnabout THS 65093 CD: Decca 425 9872

Eine kleine Nachtmusik

Berlin 1934	BPO	78: Telefunken E 1669-1670 LP: Capitol P 8038 LP: Telefunken (Jaoan) SLC 2322/ K17C 9401 CD: Musica classica 2003-2004

Serenade No 11

Berlin 1923-1924	Staatskapelle Wind Octet	78: Vox 06210-06212

Oboe Concerto

Cologne January 1956	WDR Orchestra Faber	CD: London (Japan) KICC 2080

Die Entführung aus dem Serail, Overture

Berlin 1923-1924	Staatskapelle	78: Vox 08129

Idomeneo, Overture

Berlin 1928	BPO	78: Polydor 66729/95296 78: Brunswick 90106 LP: DG 2548 747/2700 708/2740 259

Le Nozze di Figaro

Vienna May 1955	VPO Vienna Opera Chorus Della Casa, Güden, Danco, Siepi, Poell	LP: Decca LXT 5088-5091/ SXL 2087-2090 LP: Decca GOS 585-587 CD: Decca 417 3152 Excerpts LP: Decca LXT 5277/LXT 5459 LP: Decca LW 5253/SXL 2035 LP: Decca BR 3026/SDD 237/SDD 288 CD: Decca 440 4882

Le Nozze di Figaro, Overture

Berlin 1923-1924	BPO	78: Vox 08129

German Dance K509 no 6

Berlin	BPO	78: Polydor 66730
1928		78: Brunswick 90107
		78: Decca CA 8171
		LP: DG 2740 259

German Dance K571 no 4

Berlin	BPO	78: Polydor 66730
1928		78: Brunswick 90107
		78: Decca CA 8171
		LP: DG 2740 259
		LP: Rococo 2048

German Dance K571 no 6

Berlin	BPO	78: Polydor 66729
1928		78: Brunswick 90106
		LP: DG 2740 259
		LP: Rococo 2048

German Dance K600 no 1

Cologne	WDR Orchestra	LP: Orbis 23517
January 1956		LP: Amadeo AVRS 5010
		LP: Decca ACL 226
		CD: Amadeo 423 4132

German Dance K600 no 2

Berlin	Staatskapelle	78: Polydor 66532
1927		LP: DG 2548 747

German Dance K600 no 3

Berlin	BPO	78: Polydor 66729
1928		78: Brunswick 90106
		LP: DG LPEM 19078
		LP: DG 2740 259
		LP: Rococo 2048

German Dance K600 no 4

Berlin	BPO	78: Polydor 66730
1928		78: Brunswick 90107
		78: Decca CA 8171
		LP: DG 2740 259

German Dance K600 no 5 "Der Kanarienvogel"

Berlin 1927	Staatskapelle	78: Polydor 66532 LP: DG 2548 747
Cologne January 1956	WDR Orchestra	LP: Orbis 23517 LP: Amadeo AVRS 5010 LP: Decca ACL 226 CD: Amadeo 423 4132

German Dance K602 no 3 "Die Leyerer"

Berlin 1927	Staatskapelle	78: Polydor 66532 LP: DG 2548 747
Cologne January 1956	WDR Orchestra	LP: Orbis 23517 LP: Amadeo AVRS 5010 LP: Decca ACL 226 CD: Amadeo 423 4132

German Dance K605 no 2

Berlin 1928	BPO	78: Polydor 66730 78: Brunswick 90107 78: Decca CA 8171 LP: DG 2740 259

German Dance K605 no 3 "Die Schlittenfahrt"

Berlin 1927	Staatskapelle	78: Polydor 66532 LP: DG 2548 747
Cologne January 1956	WDR Orchestra	LP: Orbis 23517 LP: Amadeo AVRS 5010 LP: Decca ACL 226 CD: Amadeo 423 4132

A 1933 filmed performance of this particular dance, with Kleiber conducting the BPO, was included in a videotape entitled "Great Conductors"

MUNICIPALIDAD DE LA CIUDAD DE BUENOS AIRES

Teatro COLON

1949

DOMINGO 23 DE OCTUBRE, a las 15

5a. y Ultima Función del Abono Especial Vespertino

La Flauta Mágica

Opera en tres actos y 14 cuadros. Libro de Schikeneder. Música de Mozart.

R E P A R T O :

Sarastro	LUDWIG WEBER
Tamino	ANTON DERMOTA
Orador	ANGEL MATTIELLO
Reina de la noche	BLANCA ROSA BAIGORRI
Pamina, su hija	NILDA HOFMANN
Damas de la reina { Primera dama	Maria del Carmen Ecignard
Segundo dama	MARIA CHERRY
Tercera dama	ZAIRA NEGRONI
Papageno	RENATO CESARI
Papagena	OLGA CHELAVINE
Monostatos	ROBERTO MAGGIOLO
Primer genio	Delia Barciocco
Segundo genio	Ilse Kuhn
Tercer genio	NOEMI SOUZA
Sacerdote	Gilberto Burgueño
Hombres en arnés	DUILIO DE MATTHAEIS, CARLOS FELLER, Renato Sassola, Gilberto Burgueño

Director de orquesta:

ERICH KLEIBER

Director de escena: Otto Erhardt   Director del coro: Rafael Terragnolo

Decorados y figurines de Héctor Basaldúa   Trajes realizados por Juan Mancini

Se ruega al público se halle ubicado en sus localidades al iniciarse la función.

PRECIO DE LAS LOCALIDADES

Con Impuesto

Galeas bajos y balcón c/6 entradas	$ 187.—	Tertulia 1º fila	$ 25.—
" altos y balgnaire	" 176.—	" 2º fila	" 22.—
" cazuela	" 110.—	" 3º fila	" 19.—
" galería	" 77.—	Galería	" 13.—
Plateo y plateo balcón	" 33.—	Delantera de paraíso	" 9.—
Cazuela 1º fila	" 25.—	Entrada a palcos	" 22.—
2º fila	" 25.—	" a cazuela y tertulia	" 5.—
3º fila	" 22.—	" a paraíso	" 2.—

Freitag, den 30. November 1934

2. Sinfonie-Konzert

der Staatskapelle

Leitung: **Erich Kleiber**

Gottfried Heinr. Stölzel (1690–1749):
Concerto a due chori
 Allegro – Adagio – Allegro

Alban Berg:
Sinfonische Stücke aus der Oper „Lulu"
(Uraufführung)
 Rondo (Andante)
 Ostinato (Allegro)
 Lied der Lulu (Commodo)
 Variationen (Moderato)
 Adagio

Sopran-Solo: **Lillie Claus**

Pause

L. van Beethoven: Sinfonie Nr. VIII (F-Dur) op. 93
 Allegro vivace e con brio
 Allegretto scherzando
 Tempo di menuetto
 Allegro vivace

Ende gegen 22 Uhr

Nach den ersten Einleitungstakten beider Sätze geschlossen · Der Berechtigung des empfangenen Musikstückes kann niemals mehr Einlaß erlangen

Staatstheater:

Mittwoch, 12. Dezember 1934

Cenaui

Oper in 4 Bildern von Giuseppe Verdi
Neuere Bearbeitung für die deutsche Bühne von Julius Kapp

Klara Rembs · Marcel Wittrisch · Herbert Janssen · Wilhelm Bohnen
Musikalische Leitung: Leo Blech · Inszenierung: Carl Hagemann
Bühnenbild: Carl Voß · Kostüme: Carl Walser

Spielplan der Staats-Theater		
Staats-Oper		**Schauspielhaus**
Nov. Do.		
30.	Ein Maskenball (20)	Der Große Kurfürst (19½)
1.		Das Glas Wasser (20)
2.		Der Große Kurfürst (20)
3.	... Tristan und Isolde (19)	Don Juan, Deutsches Goethes, Schillers Goethes... (19)
	... (Beginn bis 17.30, Nachmittag)	

Nicolai

Die lustigen Weiber von Windsor, Overture

Berlin 1927	Staatskapelle	78: Polydor 66556
Berlin 1934	BPO	78: Telefunken E 1713 78: Telefunken (Japan) SLC 2322/ K17C 9401

Reznicek

Donna Diana, Overture

Berlin 1932	BPO	78: Telefunken SK 1215/SK 1205 LP: Past Masters PM 28 LP: Telefunken (Japan) SLC 2322/ K17C 9401 CD: Archiphon ARC 102

Rimsky-Korsakov

Le coq d'or, Bridal procession

New York 1945	NBC Orchestra	Radio Recorders Hollywood This was an acetate disc

Rossini

William Tell, Overture

Berlin 1927	Staatskapelle	78: Polydor 66596-66597

Saint-Saens

Danse macabre

Berlin 1930	Staatskapelle	78: Telefunken E 461

Schubert

Symphony No 3

New York March 1946	NBC Orchestra	LP: Discocorp IGI 307

Symphony No 3, 2nd and 3rd movements

Berlin 1928	Staatskapelle	78: Parlophone E 11248 78: Odeon 6820

Symphony No 5

New York December 1947	NBC Orchestra	LP: Discocorp IGI 307
Hamburg January 1953	NDR Orchestra	CD: Nuova Era 2338-2339

Symphony No 8 "Unfinished"

Berlin 1928	BPO	78: Polydor 66717-66719
Berlin January 1935	BPO	78: Telefunken E 1777-1779 LP: Telefunken MA 25008 CD: Musica classica 2003-2004 CD: Teldec 9031.764362

Symphony No 9 "Great"

Cologne November 1953	WDR Orchestra	LP: Amadeo AVRS 5012 LP: Decca ACL 237 LP: Movimento musica 01.050 CD: Amadeo 423 4142
Hamburg April 1954	NDR Orchestra	LP: Rococo 2068

Rosamunde, Overture and Andante (Ballet in B minor)

Berlin 1928	Staatskapelle	78: Telefunken EJ 359-360 LP: Rococo 2048

Rosamunde, Entr'acte in B flat and Ballet in G

Berlin 1928	Staatskapelle	78: Polydor 66598
Hamburg April 1954	NDR Orchestra	LP: Discocorp RR 521

Smetana

The Moldau (Ma Vlast)

Berlin	Staatskapelle	78: Polydor 66652-66653
1929		78: Brunswick 90086-90087
		LP: DG 2721 070

The Bartered Bride, Overture

Berlin	BPO	78: Telefunken E 1017
1932		

Johann Strauss

Accelerationen, Waltz

Berlin 1932	BPO	78: Telefunken E 1156 LP: Capitol P 8061 LP: Telefunken (Japan) SLC 2321/ K17C 9400 CD: Archiphon ARC 102

An der schönen blauen Donau, Waltz

Berlin 1923	Staatskapelle	78: Vox 01896-01897 CD: Archiphon ARC 102
Berlin 1932	BPO	78: Telefunken E 963 LP: Telefunken (Japan) SLC 2321/ K17C 9400

Du und Du, Waltz

Vienna February 1929	VPO	78: HMV C 1676 78: Victor 11-8361 LP: Turnabout THS 65066 CD: DG 435 3352 CD: Preiser 90115 CD: Archiphon ARC 102 CD: Biddulph WHL 002

Die Fledermaus, Overture

Berlin 1927	Staatskapelle	78: Polydor 66552 LP: Past Masters PM 28 LP: Telefunken (Japan) SLC 2321/ K17C 9400
Berlin June 1933	BPO	78: Telefunken E 1536 CD: Biddulph WHL 002

Gschichten aus dem Wienerwald, Waltz

Berlin 1923-1924	Staatskapelle	78: Vox 08234-08235
New York December 1947	NBC Orchestra	LP: Discocorp IGI 307

Kaiserwalzer

Berlin 1932	BPO	78: Telefunken E 964 LP: Mercury MG 20002 LP: Telefunken (Japan) SLC 2321/ K17C 9400 CD: Archiphon ARC 102 CD: Biddulph WHL 002

Künstlerleben, Waltz

Vienna   VPO   78: HMV C 1697
February 1929   78: Victor 12950
                                  LP: EMI 1C 147 30226-30227
                                  CD: Preiser 90115
                                  CD: Archiphon ARC 102
                                  CD: Biddulph WHL 002

1001 Nacht, Waltz

Berlin   BPO   78: Telefunken E 1233
1932   78: Capitol EDL 8065
                                  LP: Capitol P 8061
                                  LP: Telefunken (Japan) SLC 2321/
                                      K17C 9400

Wein, Weib und Gesang, Waltz

Berlin   BPO   78: Telefunken E 1206
1932   78: Telefunken (Japan) SLC 2321/
                                      K17C 9400
                                  CD: Archiphon ARC 102

Der Zigeunerbaron, Overture

Berlin   Staatskapelle 78: Vox 08015
1923-1924

Berlin   BPO   78: Telefunken E 1492
June 1933   LP: Telefunken (Japan) SLC 2321/
                                      K17C 9400
                                  CD: Preiser 90090
                                  CD: Archiphon ARC 102
                                  CD: Biddulph WHL 002

New York   NBC Orchestra LP: Discocorp IGI 307
December 1947

London   LPO   78: Decca K 1954
February 1948

Rehearsal extract from an unspecified Johann Strauss work with Kleiber and BPO, recorded in 1930, was issued privately on Telefunken 78 P 129

Josef Strauss

Dorfschwalben aus Oesterreich, Waltz

Vienna February 1929	VPO	78: HMV C 1685 78: Victor C 15 CD: EMI CDH 764 2992/CHS 764 2942 CD: Preiser 90115
Berlin June 1933	BPO	78: Telefunken E 1422 78: Mercury 16031 LP: Mercury MG 15004 LP: Telefunken (Japan) SLC 2321/ K17C 9400 CD: Biddulph WHL 002

Sphärenklänge, Waltz

London February 1948	LPO	78: Decca K 1924

Richard Strauss

Daphne

Buenos Aires September 1948	Teatro Colon Orchestra Bampton, Svanholm, Dermota, Weber	LP: Discocorp IGI 295

Der Rosenkavalier

Buenos Aires October 1947	Teatro Colon Orchestra & Chorus Bampton, Chelavine, Cavelti, List, Destal	LP: Discocorp IGI 355
Vienna June 1954	VPO Vienna Opera Chorus Reining, Güden, Jurinac, Weber, Poell	LP: Decca LXT 2954-2957 LP: Decca 4BB 115-118 CD: Decca 425 9502

Der Rosenkavalier: Excerpts (Mir ist die Ehre widerfahren; Da lieg' ich)

Munich July 1952	Bavarian State Orchestra Berger, Grümmer, Böhme	LP: Orfeo S 120 8421

Der Rosenkavalier, Waltz sequence

Berlin 1931	BPO	78: Telefunken E 853
Berlin September 1934	BPO	78: Telefunken E 1688 78: Telefunken (Japan) SLC 2322/ K17C 9401 CD: Biddulph WHL 002

Don Juan

Berlin 1925-1926	Staatskapelle	78: Vox 08245-08246

Till Eulenspiegels lustige Streiche

Berlin March 1931	BPO	78: Telefunken E 651-652 CD: Musica classica 2003-2004

Stravinsky

L'oiseau de feu, Suite

Berlin 1928	Staatskapelle	78: Parlophone 10954-11017-11018 78: Odeon 6816-6762-6763

Fireworks

Berlin 1932	BPO	78: Telefunken SK 1205 LP: Past Masters PM 28

Suppé

Light Cavalry, Overture

Berlin 1933	BPO	78: Telefunken F 1322 78: Capitol 89-80088 LP: Capitol P 8108 LP: Telefunken (Japan) SLC 2322/ K17C 9401

Tchaikovsky

Symphony No 4

Paris July 1949	Paris Conservatoire Orchestra	78: Decca AK 2272-2276 LP: Decca LXT 2511

Symphony No 6 "Pathétique"

Paris October 1953	Paris Conservatoire Orchestra	LP: Decca LXT 2888/LXT 5370
Cologne March 1955	WDR Orchestra	LP: Discocorp IGI 308 LP: Melodram MEL 213 CD: Nuova Era NE 2338-2339

Capriccio italien

Berlin 1933	BPO	78: Telefunken E 1406

GESELLSCHAFT DER MUSIKFREUNDE IN WIEN

Außerordentliches Chorkonzert

Dirigent:

ERICH KLEIBER

Mittwoch, den 23. November 1955, 19:30
Donnerstag, den 24. November 1955, 19:30

STAATS-OPER

Berlin, Freitag, den 14. April 1933

Anfang **18½** (6½ Uhr)

194. Abonnements-Vorstellung

Gut- u. Umtauschscheine ungültig

Anfang **18½** (6½ Uhr)

Parsifal

Ein Bühnenweihfestspiel in drei Aufzügen von Richard Wagner
Musikalische Leitung: General-Musikdirektor Erich Kleiber
In Szene gesetzt von Franz Ludwig Hörth

Amfortas	Rudolf Bockelmann
Titurel	Martin Abendroth
Gurnemanz	Alexander Kipnis
Parsifal	Fritz Wolff
Klingsor	Eugen Fuchs
Kundry	Rose Pauly
Erster } Gralsritter	Waldemar Henke
Zweiter }	Leonhard Kern
Erster	Susanne Fischer
Zweiter } Knappe	Margery Booth
Dritter }	Gustav Rödin
Vierter }	Karl Laufkötter

Klingsors Zaubermädchen: Käte Heidersbach, Elfriede Marherr, Susanne Fischer, Delia Reinhardt, Margherita Perras, Margery Booth und Chöre

Altsolo: Margarete Klose

Die Brüderschaft der Gralsritter, Jünglinge und Knappen

Chöre: Professor Hugo Rüdel

Gesamt-Ausstattung: P. Aravantinos

Bühnentechnische Einrichtung: Rudolf Klein

Verdi

Requiem

Vienna November 1955	VSO Singverein Rovere, Madeira, Lambert, Neri	CD: Melodram CDM 28044

Aida, Prelude

Berlin 1923-1924	Staatskapelle	78: Vox 01532

Rigoletto, Prelude

Berlin 1923-1924	Staatskapelle	78: Vox 01532

I Vespri siciliani

Florence May 1951	Maggio musicale Orchestra & Chorus Callas, Kokolios, Christoff, Mascherini	LP: Penzance Records 6 LP: FWR Records 645 LP: Cetra LO 5 LP: Melodram MEL 420 CD: Melodram MEL 36020 CD: Legendary LR 1008

Wagner

Der fliegende Holländer, Overture

Berlin   Staatskapelle   78: Vox 08296-08297
1925-1926

Götterdämmerung, Siegfried's Funeral March

Berlin   BPO   78: Telefunken E 612
1931   LP: Telefunken (Japan) SLC 2323/
                                                                   K17C 9402

Die Meistersinger von Nürnberg, Prelude

Berlin   Staatskapelle   78: Vox 08034
1923-1924

Tannhäuser, Overture

Berlin   Staatskapelle   78: Vox 8434-8435
1925-1926

Tristan und Isolde

Munich   Bavarian State   LP: Melodram MEL 014
July 1952   Orchestra & Chorus
                  Braun, Klose,
                  Treptoe, Frantz,
                  Grossman

Tristan und Isolde: Excerpts

Buenos Aires   Teatro Colon   LP: Rococo 5380
August 1948   Orchestra & Chorus   CD: Melodram MEL 25007
                  Flagstad, Ursuleac,
                  Svanholm, Hotter,
                  Weber

Weber

Symphony No 1

Cologne	WDR Orchestra	LP: Orbis 23517
January 1956		LP: Amadeo AVRS 5010
		LP: Decca ACL 226
		CD: Amadeo 423 4132
		CD: London (Japan) KICC 2080

Aufforderung zum Tanz (orch. Berlioz)

Berlin	BPO	78: Telefunken E 988
1932		LP: Telefunken (Japan) SLC 2323/ K17C 9402
		CD: Archiphon ARC 102
		CD: Biddulph WHL 002

Der Freischütz

Cologne	WDR Orchestra	LP: Discocorp IGI 300
March 1955	and Chorus	LP: Estro armonico EA 014
	Grümmer, Streich,	LP: Cetra LO 42
	Hopf, Pröbstl,	CD: Hunt CDLSMH 34033
	Poell	Excerpts
		LP: Gioielli della lirica GML 74

Der Freischütz, Overture and Entr'acte

Berlin	Staatskapelle	78: Vox 08190-08198
1923-1924		

ERICH KLEIBER

KLEIBER WAS without doubt one of the greatest operatic conductors of his day. Beloved by his public and by all orchestras who have worked with him, he has become a legend. Because of his wonderful stick technique, which takes account of each and every musician under his charge, his opera readings often achieve the transparency and clarity of chamber music.

He was born in Vienna in 1890, and studied philosophy and the history of art at the University of Prague, whilst at the same time attending conducting classes at the Conservatory. At the age of twenty-two he became a conductor of the Darmstadt Court Opera (1912–18); from 1919 to 1921 he was at Wuppertal, and from 1922 to 1923 at Mannheim; then in 1923 he was appointed Generalmusikdirektor of the Berlin State Opera, a position he held until he left in 1933.

His directorship of the Berlin Opera was one of the most brilliant periods in the theatre's history, with the world premières of *Wozzeck* and Milhaud's *Christophe Colomb* and the introduction of such operas as *Jenufa* and *Schwanda* to the repertory.

Between 1937 and 1949 Kleiber conducted nearly every year at the Teatro Colon, Buenos Aires, where he had made his home, and had become an Argentine citizen. There his performances of Gluck, Mozart, Wagner, and Strauss came as a revelation to South American audiences, whose staple operatic diet lay more in the direction of Italian opera.

Kleiber made his Covent Garden début in 1938, conducting *Rosenkavalier* and *Der fliegende Holländer*, but his real popularity in this country dates from the autumn of 1950, when he began a series of regular appearances at Covent Garden which lasted until 1953. These included wonderful performances of *Rosenkavalier*, *Elektra*, *The Queen of Spades*, *Tristan*, and, of course, *Wozzeck*.

In Italy Kleiber conducted *I Vespri Siciliani* at the Florence Festival in 1951 and Wagnerian performances in Rome in 1952 and 1953.

In 1950 he returned to Germany to conduct some performances at the Berlin State Opera—and subsequently conducted in Dresden. He was appointed Generalmusikdirektor (his old position) at the State Opera in Berlin in 1954, ready for the reopening of the theatre in September 1955; but he resigned a few months later as a protest against political interference, just as he had done in the time of Hitler.

From the Decca Book of Opera

Credits

Valuable help with information for the
preparation of this volume came from :-

Yoshihiro Asada, Osaka
Paul Bowen, Thames Ditton
Simon Clark, Bedford
Clifford Elkin, Glasgow
Michael Gray, Alexandria Virginia
Ken Jagger, London
Roderick Krüsemann, Amsterdam
David Long, Maidenhead
Bruce Morrison, Gillingham
Jim Parsons, Birmingham
John Raymon, London
Heiko Reysen, Munich
Yutaka Sasaki, Tokyo
Seiichi Semba, Ehime
Akira Tanaka, Tokyo
Werner Unger, Kehl-am-Rhein
Malcolm Walker, Harrow
Björn Westberg, Saltsjö-Boo
Nicola Zaccaria, Athens

Drawing of John Hunt by Philip Boardman

Music and Books published by Travis & Emery Music Bookshop:
Mellers, Wilfrid: Caliban Reborn - Renewal in Twentieth Century Music
Mellers, Wilfrid: François Couperin and the French Classical Tradition
Mellers, Wilfrid: Harmonious Meeting
Mellers, Wilfrid: Le Jardin Retrouvé, The Music of Frederic Mompou
Mellers, Wilfrid: Music and Society, England and the European Tradition
Mellers, Wilfrid: Music in a New Found Land: ... ... American Music
Mellers, Wilfrid: Romanticism and the Twentieth Century (from 1800)
Mellers, Wilfrid: The Masks of Orpheus: ...... the Story of European Music.
Mellers, Wilfrid: The Sonata Principle (from c. 1750)
Mellers, Wilfrid: Vaughan Williams and the Vision of Albion
Panchianio, Cattuffio: Rutzvanscad Il Giovine
Pearce, Charles: Sims Reeves, Fifty Years of Music in England.
Playford, John: An Introduction to the Skill of Musick.
Purcell, Henry et al: Harmonia Sacra ... The First Book, (1726)
Purcell, Henry et al: Harmonia Sacra ... Book II (1726)
Quantz, Johann: Versuch einer Anweisung die Flöte traversiere zu spielen.
Rameau, Jean-Philippe: Code de Musique Pratique, ou Methodes.
Rastall, Richard: The Notation of Western Music.
Rimbault, Edward: The Pianoforte, Its Origins, Progress, and Construction.
Rousseau, Jean Jacques: Dictionnaire de Musique
Rubinstein, Anton : Guide to the proper use of the Pianoforte Pedals.
Sainsbury, John S.: Dictionary of Musicians. Vol. 1. (1825). 2 vols.
Simpson, Christopher: A Compendium of Practical Musick in Five Parts
Spohr, Louis: Autobiography
Spohr, Louis: Grand Violin School
Tans'ur, William: A New Musical Grammar; or The Harmonical Spectator
Terry, Charles Sanford: Four-Part Chorals of J.S. Bach. (German & English)
Terry, Charles Sanford: Joh. Seb. Bach, Cantata Texts, Sacred and Secular.
Terry, Charles Sanford: The Origins of the Family of Bach Musicians.
Tosi, Pierfrancesco: Opinioni de' Cantori Antichi, e Moderni
Van der Straeten, Edmund: History of the Violoncello, The Viol da Gamba ...
Van der Straeten, Edmund: History of the Violin, Its Ancestors... (2 vols.)
Walther, J. G.: Musicalisches Lexikon ober Musicalische Bibliothec

Travis & Emery Music Bookshop
17 Cecil Court, London, WC2N 4EZ, United Kingdom.
Tel. (+44) 20 7240 2129

© Travis & Emery 2009

Music and Books published by Travis & Emery Music Bookshop:

Anon.: Hymnarium Sarisburiense, cum Rubricis et Notis Musicis.
Agricola, Johann Friedrich from Tosi: Anleitung zur Singkunst.
Bach, C.P.E.: edited W. Emery: Nekrolog or Obituary Notice of J.S. Bach.
Bateson, Naomi Judith: Alcock of Salisbury
Bathe, William: A Briefe Introduction to the Skill of Song
Bax, Arnold: Symphony #5, Arranged for Piano Four Hands by Walter Emery
Burney, Charles: The Present State of Music in France and Italy
Burney, Charles: The Present State of Music in Germany, The Netherlands ...
Burney, Charles: An Account of the Musical Performances ... Handel
Burney, Karl: Nachricht von Georg Friedrich Handel's Lebensumstanden.
Cobbett, W.W.: Cobbett's Cyclopedic Survey of Chamber Music. (2 vols.)
Corrette, Michel: Le Maitre de Clavecin
Crimp, Bryan: Dear Mr. Rosenthal ... Dear Mr. Gaisberg ...
Crimp, Bryan: Solo: The Biography of Solomon
d'Indy, Vincent: Beethoven: Biographie Critique
d'Indy, Vincent: Beethoven: A Critical Biography
d'Indy, Vincent: César Franck (in French)
Frescobaldi, Girolamo: D'Arie Musicali per Cantarsi. Primo & Secondo Libro.
Geminiani, Francesco: The Art of Playing the Violin.
Handel; Purcell; Boyce; Geene et al: Calliope or English Harmony: Volume First.
Hawkins, John: A General History of the Science and Practice of Music (5 vols.)
Herbert-Caesari, Edgar: The Science and Sensations of Vocal Tone
Herbert-Caesari, Edgar: Vocal Truth
Hopkins and Rimboult: The Organ. Its History and Construction.
Hunt, John: Adam to Webern: the recordings of von Karajan
Isaacs, Lewis: Hänsel and Gretel. A Guide to Humperdinck's Opera.
Isaacs, Lewis: Königskinder (Royal Children) A Guide to Humperdinck's Opera.
Lacassagne, M. l'Abbé Joseph : Traité Général des élémens du Chant.
Lascelles (née Catley), Anne: The Life of Miss Anne Catley.
Mainwaring, John: Memoirs of the Life of the Late George Frederic Handel
Malcolm, Alexander: A Treaty of Music: Speculative, Practical and Historical
Marx, Adolph Bernhard: Die Kunst des Gesanges, Theoretisch-Practisch
May, Florence: The Life of Brahms
Mellers, Wilfrid: Angels of the Night: Popular Female Singers of Our Time
Mellers, Wilfrid: Bach and the Dance of God
Mellers, Wilfrid: Beethoven and the Voice of God

Travis & Emery Music Bookshop
17 Cecil Court, London, WC2N 4EZ, United Kingdom.
Tel. (+44) 20 7240 2129

1999: 978-1-901395-97-6: The Furtwaengler Sound Sixth Edition: Discography and Concert Listing.
1999: 978-1-901395-98-3: The Great Dictators: 3 Discographies: Evgeny Mravinsky, Artur Rodzinski, Sergiu Celibidache.
1999: 978-1-901395-99-0: Sviatoslav Richter: Pianist of the Century: Discography.
2000: 978-1-901395-04-4: Philharmonic Autocrat 1: Discography of: Herbert Von Karajan [Third Edition].
2000: 978-1-901395-05-1: Wiener Philharmoniker 1 - Vienna Philharmonic and Vienna State Opera Orchestras: Discography Part 1 1905-1954.
2000: 978-1-901395-06-8: Wiener Philharmoniker 2 - Vienna Philharmonic and Vienna State Opera Orchestras: Discography Part 2 1954-1989.
2001: 978-1-901395-07-5: Gramophone Stalwarts: 3 Separate Discographies: Bruno Walter, Erich Leinsdorf, Georg Solti.
2001: 978-1-901395-08-2: Singers of the Third Reich: 5 Discographies: Helge Roswaenge, Tiana Lemnitz, Franz Voelker, Maria Mueller, Max Lorenz.
2001: 978-1-901395-09-9: Philharmonic Autocrat 2: Concert Register of Herbert Von Karajan Second Edition.
2002: 978-1-901395-10-5: Sächsische Staatskapelle Dresden: Complete Discography.
2002: 978-1-901395-11-2: Carlo Maria Giulini: Discography and Concert Register.
2002: 978-1-901395-12-9: Pianists For The Connoisseur: 6 Discographies: Arturo Benedetti Michelangeli, Alfred Cortot, Alexis Weissenberg, Clifford Curzon, Solomon, Elly Ney.
2003: 978-1-901395-14-3: Singers on the Yellow Label: 7 Discographies: Maria Stader, Elfriede Troetschel, Annelies Kupper, Wolfgang Windgassen, Ernst Haefliger, Josef Greindl, Kim Borg.
2003: 978-1-901395-15-0: A Gallic Trio: 3 Discographies: Charles Muench, Paul Paray, Pierre Monteux.
2004: 978-1-901395-16-7: Antal Dorati 1906-1988: Discography and Concert Register.
2004: 978-1-901395-17-4: Columbia 33CX Label Discography.
2004: 978-1-901395-18-1: Great Violinists: 3 Discographies: David Oistrakh, Wolfgang Schneiderhan, Arthur Grumiaux.
2006: 978-1-901395-19-8: Leopold Stokowski: Second Edition of the Discography.
2006: 978-1-901395-20-4: Wagner Im Festspielhaus: Discography of the Bayreuth Festival.
2006: 978-1-901395-21-1: Her Master's Voice: Concert Register and Discography of Dame Elisabeth Schwarzkopf [Third Edition].
2007: 978-1-901395-22-8: Hans Knappertsbusch: Kna: Concert Register and Discography of Hans Knappertsbusch, 1888-1965. Second Edition.
2008: 978-1-901395-23-5: Philips Minigroove: Second Extended Version of the European Discography.
2009: 978-1-901395--24-2: American Classics: The Discographies of Leonard Bernstein and Eugene Ormandy.

Discography by Stephen J. Pettitt, edited by John Hunt:
1987: 978-1-906857-16-5: Philharmonia Orchestra: Complete Discography 1945-1987

Available from: Travis & Emery at 17 Cecil Court, London, UK. (+44) 20 7 240 2129. email on sales@travis-and-emery.com .

© Travis & Emery 2009

Discographies by Travis & Emery:
Discographies by John Hunt.

1987: 978-1-906857-14-1: From Adam to Webern: the Recordings of von Karajan.
1991: 978-0-951026-83-0: 3 Italian Conductors and 7 Viennese Sopranos: 10 Discographies: Arturo Toscanini, Guido Cantelli, Carlo Maria Giulini, Elisabeth Schwarzkopf, Irmgard Seefried, Elisabeth Gruemmer, Sena Jurinac, Hilde Gueden, Lisa Della Casa, Rita Streich.
1992: 978-0-951026-85-4: Mid-Century Conductors and More Viennese Singers: 10 Discographies: Karl Boehm, Victor De Sabata, Hans Knappertsbusch, Tullio Serafin, Clemens Krauss, Anton Dermota, Leonie Rysanek, Eberhard Waechter, Maria Reining, Erich Kunz.
1993: 978-0-951026-87-8: More 20th Century Conductors: 7 Discographies: Eugen Jochum, Ferenc Fricsay, Carl Schuricht, Felix Weingartner, Josef Krips, Otto Klemperer, Erich Kleiber.
1994: 978-0-951026-88-5: Giants of the Keyboard: 6 Discographies: Wilhelm Kempff, Walter Gieseking, Edwin Fischer, Clara Haskil, Wilhelm Backhaus, Artur Schnabel.
1994: 978-0-951026-89-2: Six Wagnerian Sopranos: 6 Discographies: Frieda Leider, Kirsten Flagstad, Astrid Varnay, Martha Moedl, Birgit Nilsson, Gwyneth Jones.
1995: 978-0-952582-70-0: Musical Knights: 6 Discographies: Henry Wood, Thomas Beecham, Adrian Boult, John Barbirolli, Reginald Goodall, Malcolm Sargent.
1995: 978-0-952582-71-7: A Notable Quartet: 4 Discographies: Gundula Janowitz, Christa Ludwig, Nicolai Gedda, Dietrich Fischer-Dieskau.
1996: 978-0-952582-72-4: The Post-War German Tradition: 5 Discographies: Rudolf Kempe, Joseph Keilberth, Wolfgang Sawallisch, Rafael Kubelik, Andre Cluytens.
1996: 978-0-952582-73-1: Teachers and Pupils: 7 Discographies: Elisabeth Schwarzkopf, Maria Ivoguen, Maria Cebotari, Meta Seinemeyer, Ljuba Welitsch, Rita Streich, Erna Berger.
1996: 978-0-952582-77-9: Tenors in a Lyric Tradition: 3 Discographies: Peter Anders, Walther Ludwig, Fritz Wunderlich.
1997: 978-0-952582-78-6: The Lyric Baritone: 5 Discographies: Hans Reinmar, Gerhard Huesch, Josef Metternich, Hermann Uhde, Eberhard Waechter.
1997: 978-0-952582-79-3: Hungarians in Exile: 3 Discographies: Fritz Reiner, Antal Dorati, George Szell.
1997: 978-1-901395-00-6: The Art of the Diva: 3 Discographies: Claudia Muzio, Maria Callas, Magda Olivero.
1997: 978-1-901395-01-3: Metropolitan Sopranos: 4 Discographies: Rosa Ponselle, Eleanor Steber, Zinka Milanov, Leontyne Price.
1997: 978-1-901395-02-0: Back From The Shadows: 4 Discographies: Willem Mengelberg, Dimitri Mitropoulos, Hermann Abendroth, Eduard Van Beinum.
1997: 978-1-901395-03-7: More Musical Knights: 4 Discographies: Hamilton Harty, Charles Mackerras, Simon Rattle, John Pritchard.
1998: 978-1-901395-94-5: Conductors On The Yellow Label: 8 Discographies: Fritz Lehmann, Ferdinand Leitner, Ferenc Fricsay, Eugen Jochum, Leopold Ludwig, Artur Rother, Franz Konwitschny, Igor Markevitch.
1998: 978-1-901395-95-2: More Giants of the Keyboard: 5 Discographies: Claudio Arrau, Gyorgy Cziffra, Vladimir Horowitz, Dinu Lipatti, Artur Rubinstein.
1998: 978-1-901395-96-9: Mezzo and Contraltos: 5 Discographies: Janet Baker, Margarete Klose, Kathleen Ferrier, Giulietta Simionato, Elisabeth Hoengen.

www.ingramcontent.com/pod-product-compliance
Lightning Source LLC
Chambersburg PA
CBHW070937230426
43666CB00011B/2469